School Libraries 3.0

School Libraries 3.0

Principles and Practices for the Digital Age

Rebecca P. Butler

ROWMAN & LITTLEFIELD
Lanham • Boulder • New York • London

Executive Editor: Charles Harmon
Associate Editor: Robert Hayunga
Production Editor: Lara Graham
Cover Designer: Matthew Pirro

Credits and acknowledgments of sources for material or information used with permission appear on the appropriate page within the text.

Published by Rowman & Littlefield
A wholly owned subsidiary of The Rowman & Littlefield Publishing Group, Inc.
4501 Forbes Boulevard, Suite 200, Lanham, Maryland 20706
www.rowman.com

Unit A, Whitacre Mews, 26-34 Stannary Street, London SE11 4AB

British Library Cataloguing in Publication Information Available

Library of Congress Cataloging-in-Publication Data

Butler, Rebecca P.
  School libraries 3.0 : principles and practices for the digital age / Rebecca P. Butler.
    pages cm
  Includes bibliographical references and index.
  ISBN 978-0-8108-9312-2 (cloth : alk. paper) – ISBN 978-0-8108-8580-6 (pbk. : alk. paper) – ISBN 978-0-8108-8581-3 (ebook) 1. School libraries–United States–Administration. 2. School librarians–United States. I. Title.
  Z675.S3B87 2015
  025.1'978–dc23   2015003740

∞™ The paper used in this publication meets the minimum requirements of American National Standard for Information Sciences—Permanence of Paper for Printed Library Materials, ANSI/NISO Z39.48-1992.

Printed in the United States of America

To my family—
your support is what keeps me going

Contents

Editorial Advisory Board

List of Figures and Textboxes

FIGURES

TEXTBOXES

Preface

I wrote *School Libraries 3.0: Principles and Practices for the Digital Age* for two distinct purposes and audiences.

First, I have designed it as a textbook for college and university students taking a school library administration course. I have taught such a course at least once a year for the past 20 years. In addition, I have taught a similar course for technology specialists for several years as well. I have taken what I consider the most important things found in these two courses and incorporated them into this textbook. I have intentionally interwoven technology throughout the book and have not treated it as a stand-alone chapter because today's school librarian—and certainly the school librarian of tomorrow—is working in an environment of web resources, multimedia, mixed methods, and varying programs and services. One cannot separate out print versus nonprint or digital versus analog. Indeed, the world of the school librarian is ever-expanding. As terms, responsibilities, and formats advance, we must embrace the changes and advance with them.

Second, I wrote this book for working school librarians seeking to upgrade, update, or enhance their understanding of the school library, its environment, its mission, and its audiences.

THE TITLE

The title of this book, *School Libraries 3.0: Principles and Practices for the Digital Age*, is meant as a representation of the evolving school library field, not only the present, but also the future. Much as Web 2.0 "is the move toward a more social, collaborative, interactive and responsive web" and "marks a change in us as a society as well as the Internet as a technology" in that "we aren't just using the Internet as a tool—we are becoming a part of it" (Nations 2014, 1), so, too, is this text intended to reach from today's world into that yet coming.

THE ORGANIZATION

The chapters in *School Libraries 3.0* look to the future as well as address those things that work currently.

Chapter 1, "The School Library and the School Librarian," covers a brief history of our field; views the school library, librarian, and our clientele through today's lens of digital access to information; and then turns to school library and technology professional organizations (international, national, state, regional, and local) that support our chosen occupations. Next, a number of professional journals of importance to us in our field are discussed, as well as those Internet tools through which we network with other professionals such as ourselves. Finally, this chapter, as do all other chapters in this book, offers discussion questions and activities to support the chapter information.

Chapter 2, "Standards and Guidelines," focuses on national, state, and professional organization standards and guidelines—those adhered to by colleges and universities that train school librarians, and those followed by school librarians—as we help our K–12 students learn about literature, technology, research, materials' ethics, and more.

The third chapter, "Policies and Procedures," first addresses the parts of a school library policy and procedures manual. It then moves into the tools and criteria that a school librarian uses when he or she selects and evaluates materials for acquisition and placement in the school library physical and virtual facilities. Next, chapter 3 concentrates on materials acquisition, maintenance of media and equipment, and weeding the library collection. Technology plans are also covered, since the school library in today's world almost always handles a wide variety of technology.

Chapter 4, "Follow the Money," is the chapter where library budgets are explained and demonstrated, gifts addressed, and grants and grant writing tackled. While all are important issues for the school librarian, the skill of grant writing can bring in supplemental library materials and equipment, as well as specialized media that might not normally be available to a particular library. Indeed, every librarian needs to know how to apply for and write a grant.

Chapter 5, "Facilities," has, tangentially, a money theme running through it as well, in that without money, the library facility would not be able to expand or provide an up-to-date physical facility and furnishings to students and faculty. This chapter speaks to the ideal school library, as well as school library design and development subjects.

The sixth chapter, "The School Librarian, Relationships and Personnel," covers school librarians and their relationships with administration, faculty, and students, as well as with those personnel who more commonly may work with the school librarian in a supportive role: library assistants or aides; technology, literacy, and additional teacher-coaches; and student, parent, and community library volunteers. In chapter 6, detailed descriptions of individual responsibilities of library personnel are included.

Chapter 7, "Services," is most concerned with the services that the school library and librarian deliver to users. For example, there are district-level services; community services (when the library does not have something a user needs, it is possible that there is a community source that may be able to help); digital services—for example, those things available on the Internet for school library users, whether provided by the library itself (library web page, data bases, etc.) or something that is available generally on the World Wide Web; data-based decision making; and response to intervention—a relatively new concept in the library, one where the librarian can help at-risk students through materials, needed lesson plans on various subjects, and so on. Scheduling of classes in the library, whether flexible, fixed, or mixed, are also foci of chapter 7.

Related to library services are the concepts of "Programming and Collaboration," which is the title of chapter 8. This chapter looks at student and faculty needs and wants, curriculum integration, and library skills instruction, including offering a sample lesson plan. Chapter 8 also attends to the "flipped library" as a type of library instruction that some school librarians are beginning to adopt.

The ninth chapter of this book, "Ethics, Intellectual Freedom, and Copyright," reflects on the school librarian and how he or she models and works with the various ethical and legal issues that can occur in the library and school community. Concerns with library ethics in general, banned materials and how to deal with challenges, copyright infringements and how to work within the law to use media, access to information concerns, and acceptable use policies are dealt with in this chapter. An intellectual freedom lesson plan is also offered as part of chapter 9.

Because school librarians may find themselves as the "only one" in a particular school (or sometimes even in a particular district) and because there is normally only one school library in a school, advocacy—presenting what the library professional and the library do and why—is another extremely important issue. Thus, chapter 10, "Advocacy," contains information on why a school librarian needs to advocate for him- or herself and the library as well as how to do so. Among the subjects discussed in this chapter are research as advocacy, advocating via publicity, and advocating within the local community.

Chapter 11, "The 'Extra' Things," covers just that; in this chapter are included subjects not often studied, discussed, or addressed in school library administration classes. Examples of those things as covered in this chapter are natural and man-made disasters and how these can be dealt with from the library point of view; the issue of time and how to manage it (like everyone else in the school, the librarian finds that there is more to do than there are hours in the day); and how school librarians can take care of themselves in light of their career responsibilities, problems, and questions.

The last chapter in this book, chapter 12, is entitled "Evaluation and the Future." As such, subjects found in this chapter include school library assessments and rubrics, curriculum mapping as an evaluation tool, facilities' evaluation, and assessing the various levels of library personnel. This chapter additionally considers school libraries of the future and how to embrace change.

Lastly, appendixes A through E provide the reader with annotated bibliographies of selected school library policies and procedures manuals, professional organization websites, national and state standards and guidelines, instruction and collaboration tools, and grant resources.

As technologies rapidly evolve in the 21st century, so too will the school library and the responsibilities of the school librarian. Thus, school librarians need to be aware of trends and advancements in their field and be willing to change and grow professionally as needed. I hope that this book is able to help you, the reader, in this regard, as you work in this exciting, wonderful career.

REFERENCE

Nations, Daniel. 2014. "What Is Web 2.0?" http://webtrends.about.com/od/web20/a/what-is-web20.htm

Acknowledgments

I would like to thank all the master's and doctoral students at Northern Illinois University and East Tennessee State University who have taken my school library administration courses over the past 20 years; your questions, comments, and discussions have greatly influenced the writing of this book. I also wish to acknowledge my graduate assistants at both universities, who have supported my research and teaching as I worked at finding and creating materials to support the school library students. Additionally, I want to thank the following school librarians, former and current students, colleagues, and others who sent me names, photos, floor plan examples, and lessons when I requested samples: Leslie Berg, Emily Butler, Sarah L. Cooley, Judith and Stephen Condren, Lisa Daugherty, Barbara Fiehn, Renee Hale, Kristy Gaynor, Cheri GoGo, Jill Johnson, Michelle Johnson, Amy Kauth, Megan Knops, Mary Marks, Mark S. Melka, Sara Meyer, and Bethann Preis. Lastly, I am grateful to my husband, Tom, and son, Benjamin, who willingly read book drafts and made suggestions, and my parents who have encouraged me throughout the process. Thank you all so much for your help and support!

1

The School Library and the School Librarian

School librarian, school library media specialist, LRC (learning resource center) director, teacher librarian or library teacher, library information specialist, whatever name we are called, we are those individuals who manage the school library, or the media center, the learning center, the . . . Well, you get the idea! While all of the previous terms have been used in the past (and may still be being used in some schools), in respect to the 2010 decision of the American Association of School Librarians, this book will use the terms *school librarian* and *school library* (Bray and Hollandsworth 2011; Pentlin 2010). Accordingly, in this chapter we take a preparatory look at the history of the field of school librarianship as well as its professional organizations, periodicals, and online communications. Here, too, we begin the observation of what the school librarian does in today's world.

A VERY BRIEF HISTORY OF THE FIELD

Books, articles, chapters, and dissertations have been written, solely or in part, about the history of school libraries in the United States (Bowie 1986; Butler 1999; Marks, n.d.; Mathews 1998). In this chapter section, we take a very brief look at the history of our field.

As early as the 1740s, it is recorded that Benjamin Franklin recommended schools contain a library, but it would be almost a century later before the United States would see a second mention of school libraries, when the governor of New York at that time, DeWitt Clinton, advocated for the same, resulting in passage of a New York law allowing school districts to set aside some of their monies for this purpose (Morris 2010). This legislation launched a momentum for school libraries that began gaining national recognition, and by 1840, the states of Ohio, Massachusetts,

Michigan, Connecticut, and Rhode Island had also passed legislation in support of school libraries (Marks, n.d.). Thus, the concept of school libraries in the United States began to grow.

As more and more states began appreciating the importance of school libraries and acting toward the establishment of such, young national education and library organizations, as well as interested individuals, began to develop standards by which these libraries might be held. Early standards included the national Certain reports of 1916, 1925, and 1932, which focused on specific grades—for example, high school and elementary libraries—as well as state reports, such as the 1927 Koos Report and the Martha Wilson Score Card of 1928. Many of these early standards focused on the number of books, chairs, and tables per student in the library facility (Bowie 1986; King 1929), while later national and state standards (American Association of School Librarians, American Library Association, and Association for Educational Communications and Technology 1975; American Association of School Librarians and Association for Educational Communications and Technology 1998; American Library Association and Association for Educational Communications and Technology 1998; American Library Association and National Education Association 1969; Library and Media Services Section, n.d.) also included such things as the organizing of library resources, budget, staff, early audiovisual equipment and materials, and collaborating with teachers.

Perhaps one way to look at some of these formative years is through the stories of a few early school librarians. One such person is Mildred Batchelder, who in 1935 was appointed as the first school library specialist at the American Library Association (ALA) and who remained in evolving positions at ALA for the next 30 years. (The Batchelder Award "established [by the Association for Library Service to Children] in her honor in 1966, is a citation awarded to an American publisher for a children's book considered to be the most outstanding of those books originally published in a foreign language in a foreign country, and subsequently translated into English and published in the United States" [Association for Library Service to Children 2013b, 1].) In the late 1920s, Batchelder took the position of school librarian at Haven School, Evanston, Illinois (Bader 2011; Batchelder 1990). At that time, the library served as a school library during the day and a public library at night and on weekends (the door to the school would be locked at night and the outside door opened). She said that in those early days, she was sometimes paid in gasoline coupons, which she would then have to trade to someone else, because she did not drive. She also added that when she was first hired, the public (night) librarian did all book selection and ordering, which was not to Batchelder's liking! Another school librarian, who worked in the 1940s and early 1950s in Wisconsin, told the story of how she was informed by school administrators that if she got married while working in the district, she would be let go in favor of a single (female) librarian who had no one to support her (Davis 1991). And a 1960s–1970s–era librarian talked at length about classroom cloakrooms being converted into audiovisual rooms to store 16 mm films and projectors as well filmstrips and their projectors (Newman 1992).

Certainly, one of the most important things to change the vision of the school library came from the launching of Sputnik in 1957 by the former Soviet Union. As a result of this start to what would become the space race, the United States Congress passed the National Defense Education Act (NDEA) of 1958. The idea behind this act was to ensure that American school children be better prepared in science, math, and foreign languages by the provision of federal funds to strengthen these areas within the school (Flattau et al. 2006). Another benefit of the NDEA was that technology in the schools became a more viable concern. The evolution of school libraries as warehouses of books and other print materials into resource centers complete with audiovisual materials (from the 1950s through the 1970s, this term was used rather than the term *technology* that we use today) had truly begun.

While Sputnik remains a watershed moment for school libraries in the United States, the 1960s–1980s were a time of educational ferment—a time when selecting and using library materials in a variety of formats became a reality for the school librarian and his or her clientele. Since the 1980s, the technology race has sped along so rapidly that what is cutting edge one day appears to be on the edge of obsolescence the next. Thus, school libraries, like the rest of the K–12 school, continue to scramble to keep up with the swift advancements in education technology.

WHAT IS THE SCHOOL LIBRARY TODAY?

What is the school library of today? Effectively, it is that facility in the school where resources and services designed to support the curriculum, students, and faculty are provided. It is (or, as this book will argue, it should be) run by a professionally trained school librarian. Library resources/materials vary and include books and magazines, DVDs, games, Internet access, and more. Indeed, the school library of today offers resources in many formats: print and nonprint, digital and analog, hardware and software. In addition to library resources, through the work of the school librarian, the school library also offers services. Services can include literacy initiatives; collaborations with teachers; teaching research and other library competencies to students; author visits; book fairs; technology training for faculty; web management; provision of educational and recreational materials to students; providing a comfortable and secure environment for students and faculty to use for research and study; and so on. A recent New Jersey study (Peterson 2013) found that the school library

> was seen as a pedagogical center. It provided the instructional support for teachers [and] for students to engage with information in all of its forms to build knowledge . . . to develop the whole arena of digital citizenship . . . was portrayed very much as this learning center, this place that the whole school owned, where teachers could experiment, where teachers and school librarians could take risks and play with ideas and play with technology that supported inquiry. (Peterson 2013, 1)

Indeed, the school library, as we shall see throughout this book, can be a wonderful place!

WHO IS THE SCHOOL LIBRARIAN TODAY?

The school librarian of today is a many-skilled leader and information specialist in his or her school. Because information is obtained both in print and digital (and analog) forms, today's school librarian needs to be both a print and technology expert. This means that he or she is comfortable, whether working in an online database or teaching how to use a print encyclopedia. Consequently, the school librarian wears many hats. Among them may be information provider; library teacher; curriculum developer; technology coordinator; personnel supervisor; cataloger; storyteller; webmaster; library manager; materials' selector; library supply coordinator; instructional designer; disciplinarian; collaborator (with fellow teachers and librarians); copyright, intellectual freedom, and privacy expert; book shelver; hardware evaluator; software reading program administrator; teacher trainer; personnel supervisor; and program planner. The school librarian might also find him- or herself as a library advocate, technology troubleshooter, literacy specialist, entertainment coordinator, grant writer, and so much more! Then there are those duties that the school librarian may be assigned, even though these responsibilities are not normally in the library professional's job description: hall monitor, bus duty, high school annual adviser, and so on. The school librarian, indeed, is a busy person whose responsibilities evolve throughout a typical workday.

WHO ARE OUR CLIENTELE?

The clientele of the school library and school librarian is primarily made up of those groups that most commonly inhabit the school: students, faculty, administration, other school personnel, sometimes parents (in that they may be working with and/ or helping their children) and perhaps the community in which the school resides. (While it is less likely that the community at large is a school library user, it does happen in cases where there is no close or accessible public library available.)

THE LIBRARY PROFESSIONAL AND ORGANIZATIONS

There are many professional organizations to which a school library professional might choose to belong. In addition to general education organizations, such as the National Education Association, there are a number of library, school library, and related (specializing in something of interest to school librarians) organizations from which to select. This section looks at some of these professional organizations.

International and National Organizations

The main library organization to which any librarian might belong is the American Library Association. This organization is "the oldest and largest library association in the world, with members in academic, public, school, government, and special libraries" (American Library Association 2013b, 1). The ALA hosts both a summer conference and a midwinter conference annually. While both are excellent venues to network with many kinds of librarians from around the world, the midwinter conference stresses meetings of ALA's various committees and other suborganizations, while the summer conference covers key issues of importance for all librarians. For example, the summer 2013 conference included "digital content and e-books, technology in libraries, innovation, books and hundreds of authors, leadership, library advocacy, community engagement, and library marketing" (American Library Association 2013a, 1). This summer conference is an amazing place, just for the vendor exhibits, which if one takes the time to at least glance at the various displays can take at least a day to walk through. It is also a great networking venue and has a wide variety of presentations, meetings, author signings, dinners, and programs to attend. In addition, with members in 115-plus countries, the ALA is not only a powerful organization in its own right, but it also serves as the umbrella organization for any number of more specialized library organizations. The one of most importance to school librarians is the American Association of School Librarians.

The mission of the American Association of School Librarians (AASL) is "to advocate excellence, facilitate change, and develop leaders in the school library field" (American Association of School Librarians 2013a, 1). AASL is the premier national organization for school librarians. Every other year, the AASL hosts a national conference with general and concurrent sessions, an exhibition/vendor area, educational tours, author events, workshops, and more. This is an excellent conference for the school librarian to attend in that he or she can network with peers from across the country (and in some cases from other countries), and all programming focuses specifically on the school library. Attending this conference is strongly recommended for all school librarians and other interested parties.

"The mission of the International Association of School Librarianship (IASL) is to provide an international forum for those people interested in promoting effective school library media programs as viable instruments in the educational process" (International Association of School Librarianship 2007, 1). While American school librarians tend to join AASL, school librarians in other countries, as well as school librarians in American schools overseas and higher education faculty involved in international school library issues, find the IASL is an excellent organization of which to be a member. Their annual conference is held in and hosted by school library people of a different country every year. Attending this conference is a good way to network with people like you from around the world.

Another national organization of interest to some school librarians is the Association for Library Service to Children (ALSC). This group, "a division of the American Library Association (ALA), is the world's largest organization dedicated to the support and enhancement of library service to children [including] creative programming and best practices to continuing education and professional connections" (Association for Library Services to Children 2013a, 1).

For those school librarians with a definite technology bent, the Association for Educational Communications and Technology (AECT) would be another good choice. (I would recommend this organization in addition to ALA and AASL.) AECT "is a professional association of thousands of educators and others whose activities are directed toward improving instruction through technology" (Association for Educational Communications and Technology 2013c, 1). In addition to the parent organization, AECT also has a division entitled School Media and Technology, which concentrates on "educational technology and its application to the learning process in the K–12 school environment" (Association for Educational Communications and Technology 2013b, 1).

School librarians are also often interested in international or national organizations that center on a specific area within their field. Examples of such organizations include the International Literacy Association (ILA), the International Visual Literacy Association (IVLA), and the National Telemedia Council (NTC). These three examples are discussed next.

The International Literacy Association (ILA) is "a global advocacy organization. . . . We publish cutting-edge research on literacy, and we translate this research into practical resources for educators, students, and leaders involved in spreading literacy all across the world" (International Literacy Association 2015, 1).

The International Visual Literacy Association (IVLA) "is an eclectic organization of professionals working toward a fuller understanding of the way we derive meaning from what we see and the way we interact with our visual environment" (International Visual Literacy Association 2012, 1). IVLA members are a diverse lot and include higher education professionals, corporate personnel, educational technologists, artists, librarians, and many more.

A countrywide organization that emphasizes a subject interest for some school librarians is the National Telemedia Council (NTC). This professional organization, like IVLA and IRA, includes a diverse membership that can include school librarians. NTC looks to advocates for media literacy, which "empowers people to be both critical thinkers and creative producers of an increasingly wide range of messages using image, language, and sound. It is the skillful application of literacy skills to media and technology messages" (National Association for Media Literacy Education 2013, 1).

Remember that there are professional organizations that focus on a particular subject of interest to individual school librarians. Pick and choose the ones that suit you best.

States also have professional organizations for school librarians.

State Organizations

There is usually at least one organization per state that is important to school librarians. Many of these are affiliates of national or international professional organizations. Let's take the state of Illinois as an example. Illinois has an organization specifically for school librarians, the Illinois School Library Media Association; a statewide organization that focuses on K–12 computer education (an important focus in many Illinois school libraries), Illinois Computing Educators; and the state version of the national group AECT covered earlier. Let's look at these examples.

The Illinois School Library Media Association (ISLMA) delivers "leadership and support for the development, promotion, and improvement of the school library media profession and programs in Illinois" (Illinois School Library Media Association 2012, 1). ISLMA is an affiliate organization of AASL, the national school library association described earlier. School librarians in all 50 states and the District of Columbia can join similar organizations for their state, an adjacent state, or region (American Association of School Librarians 2013b).

Through professional development, advocacy, leadership, outreach, funding, and collaborating among members, another statewide organization, Illinois Computing Educators (ICE), works "to lead the educational community in enhancing learning through technology (Illinois Computing Educators, "About," n.d., 1). ICE is an affiliate of another organization that some school librarians belong to, the International Society for Technology in Education.

A third statewide organization of interest to school librarians in Illinois is the Illinois Association for Educational Communications and Technology. This organization, an affiliate of AECT (mentioned earlier under international and national organizations), "is dedicated to the improvement of teaching and learning through the effective use of media, technology, and telecommunications [and] is a place to find the best practices in instructional technology" (Illinois Association for Educational Communications and Technology 2013, 1). Twenty-four states maintain affiliates with AECT (Association for Educational Communications and Technology 2013a).

Check for your state organizations easily by surfing the web for the national organization and adding the terms *state* and *affiliates*.

Regional and Local Organizations

In addition to international, national, and statewide professional associations for, or of interest to, school librarians, there also exist regional and local organizations. Again, let's use Illinois as an example. Illinois Computing Educators is a statewide organization to which some school librarians in the state belong. In turn, ICE has a number of chapters, which correspond to different regions within the state. Among them are NICE (representing the northern Chicago suburbs), SpICE (covering Springfield, Illinois, and the surrounding area), and ICE-SI (corresponding to southern Illinois) (Illinois Computing Educators, "Chapters," n.d.). Most of the other

49 states and the District of Columbia also have regional and/or local professional school library and technology organizations.

THE LIBRARY PROFESSIONAL AND JOURNALS

All of the organizations just described publish journals and/or newsletters. In addition, there are many professional periodicals for school librarians that are not officially associated with a specialized organization. Let's look at a few of these professional journals. Be aware that most of these journals can be accessed completely in print and/or completely or partially via the Internet and that many are used as selection and purchasing tools.

American Libraries is the main journal of the American Library Association. All ALA members automatically are subscribed to this journal, which features articles, editorials, and ads for the plethora of libraries and librarians that make up the ALA membership.

Knowledge Quest is the professional journal of the American Association of School Librarians. *Knowledge Quest* is automatically sent to all members of AASL. In this case, school libraries and librarians and their interests, needs, and concerns are showcased in the articles and editorials. Each issue of *Knowledge Quest* is assigned a theme. Recent themes (2013) include Imaging the Future, Rising to the Challenge, and Mentoring through Partnerships (American Association of School Librarians 2013d).

As a teacher of current and future school librarians, one of the professional periodicals that I usually recommend to them is *School Library Journal* (*SLJ*). Billed online as "the largest reviewer of children's and young adult material, from books to digital content" (*School Library Journal* 2013, 1), the reviews provided by this journal, alone, make it an exceptional selection source for all school librarians. Reviewers published in *SLJ* are fellow librarians or others with a strong interest in children's and adolescent literature (print and e-books, digital and analog, fiction and nonfiction). Reviews tell the reader the pros and cons of the item being reviewed and can be trusted to reflect the beliefs of the reviewer and his or her take as to what school librarians are looking for in a particular resource. In addition to the reviews, *SLJ* also features articles, editorials, columns, job listings, author interviews, and more. Topics featured in *SLJ* can comprise in any one issue: technology, video games, trends in picture books, curriculum issues, graphic novels, awards and contests, conferences, social media, literacy, apps, the digital divide, and so much more (*School Library Journal* 2013). When searching for professional reading, you may wish to add this journal to your list.

VOYA (*Voice of Youth Advocates*) is an excellent choice for middle school and high school librarians. Full of articles on current themes of interest to adolescents, as well as columns and book and media reviews (fiction and nonfiction) by practicing school and public librarians, this periodical is not only informative but an outstanding selection tool.

Horn Book Magazine contains articles, reviews, editorials, and advertisements concerned with children and young adult literature. It reviews books in each issue, as well as publishes articles on authors, juvenile literature, and more. This selection/ review source has been published since 1924 (Horn Book 2013).

An additional purchasing tool is *Media and Methods Magazine*, which advertises itself as "the leading technology and education magazine used for purchasing deci- sions in K–12 schools" (*Media and Methods Magazine*, n.d., 1). This periodical is used as a selection tool by technology specialists, administrators, school librarians, and others. It also contains articles covering a variety of multimedia topics.

Another specialized journal for the school librarian is *Teacher Librarian*. Accord- ing to its website, the *Teacher Librarian* focuses "on the essential role of the school librarian, or 'teacher-librarian,' as an educator and a partner and collaborator with classroom teachers, school administrators, and others" (E. L. Kurdyla Publishing LLC 2013, 1). The emphasis of this journal relates to the first point listed under the Teaching and Learning heading in AASL's *Empowering Learners: Guidelines for School Library Media Programs* (2009, 20), "Building Collaborative Partnerships."

School Library Monthly, formerly named *School Library Media Activities Monthly*, features informative articles for school librarians, provides daily and monthly re- sources and activities that school librarians can use with their students, often offers library-related lesson plans and so much more. This is a popular journal, especially with many elementary school librarians.

Still another journal for school librarians, *Library Media Connection* bills itself as "more than a publication . . . a community of practitioners passionate about learning and literacy. We provide our readers with the tools and resources they need to create the 21st century school library" (*Library Media Connection*, n.d., 1).

If you use the Big6 (designed for middle and high school students) or the Super3 (designed for younger students) as models when you teach information literacy/research skills, then you may wish to access the Big6 at http://big6.com/pages/about/big6-skills- overview.php for news, sample lessons, workshop information, and so forth, on these two approaches to teaching information and technology proficiencies (Big6 2013).

There are more print and online sources of journals and related websites for school librarians. The preceding list is a sampling of those that might be used to support us in our professional lives.

THE LIBRARY PROFESSIONAL AND INTERNET COLLABORATION

In our ever-growing technological world, full of social networking and other web-based communication means, it is important to take a look at some of the ways that school librarians connect with each other in the digital environment. With this in mind, a selection of online communications tools for library professionals is addressed. (As with the professional journals presented earlier, some of these communication tools are part of the larger umbrella of a particular school library organization. Those with such designations are identified.)

Listservs

TechTerms.com defines a listserv as "a small program that automatically sends messages to multiple e-mail addresses on a mailing list. When someone subscribes to a mailing list, the listserv will automatically add the address and distribute future email messages to that address along with all the others on the list. When someone unsubscribes, the listserv simply removes the address" (TechTerms.com 2013, 1). Listservs/discussion groups have been available to school librarians since the 1990s, and some feel that these older communication tools are showing their age. That said, the idea of discussing various themes, strands, and issues with similar professionals from across the state, country, or even world is appealing to some (Lambert 2009), especially since a school librarian may be the only person exactly like him- or herself within a particular school (or even district in some cases). Listserv strengths are that they are easy and fast ways to communicate with lots of similar people, including experts, who you might not otherwise be able to meet. Weaknesses of listservs include (1) many listservs are quite broad (although some do have archives that arrange by themes, dates, etc.) (CITES, n.d.; LM_Net, n.d.); (2) some people use them instead of doing research, leading to the listserv becoming less of a place to share ideas; (3) some become so specialized that they attract few users; (4) listservs can be used for the wrong reasons (such as to flame a fellow participant); and (5) the plethora of email that can result from one listserv may clog up an email inbox (Lambert 2009). Another negative is when a user forgets that he or she is responding to a whole group of people (remember that a listserv can range from 10 users to thousands of others), rather than to the one individual who sent the communication. When a message is sent out that should not have been shared with the whole group, this can result in group apologies and the equivalent of an online red face for the sender.

(Please note: When electing to join a large listserv, such as LM_Net [the listserv of AASL], set up an email account specifically to receive all of the listserv's emails. Unless you ask that communications be sent to you in bunches, large listservs can result in up to hundreds of emails per day, closing down many email accounts.)

Now, let's take a look at a few listservs of interest to school librarians. Probably the listserv with the widest school librarian membership on earth is LM_Net. "LM_NET is the original listserv for the world-wide school library community. LM_NET provides an excellent way to network with other library professionals, connect to new ideas in library practice, seek advice, and ask library related questions" (LM_Net Home, n.d., 1). For the library professional looking to network with numerous school librarians from many places around the globe, LM_Net is certainly a good spot to start. This listserv can be joined in the classic sense, where the member receives every email posted to it, in a digest form, and/or accessed through its archives, which can be sorted by date or threads (theme) depending on what information a particular member needs. (Here are a few examples of themes from the 2010 LM_Net Archives:

"College and/or Career Readiness," "Scaredy Squirrel Goes to the Library Orientation Video," and "Wiki Help—What Tool Allows Individual Page Permissions?" [LM_Net by Thread 2010, 1].) LM_Net is a very supportive listserv for school librarians, with basically one possible negative—the amount of communication sent to its mailing list per day can be overpowering for some.

Many state school library organizations also have listservs. These include OKLMS Listserv (Oklahoma), ISLMANET (Illinois), and CCBC-Net (New Mexico) (Illinois School Library Media Association 2011; New Mexico State Library 2012; Oklahoma State Department of Education 2013). These listservs function in much the same way as LM_Net, except that those participating are usually members of the state organization or interested in the particular state from which the listserv operates.

Next we turn to two other types of online communication tools, the blog and the wiki.

Blogs and Wikis

What is a blog? According to WordPress.org, a blog

> is an abbreviated version of "weblog," which is a term used to describe web sites that maintain an ongoing chronicle of information. A blog features diary-type commentary and links to articles on other Web sites, usually presented as a list of entries in reverse chronological order. Blogs range from the personal to the political, and can focus on one narrow subject or a whole range of subjects. (WordPress.org, n.d., 1)

More and more school librarians are blogging in the 21st century. Such blogs are created by individual school librarians—for instance, "The Blue Skunk Blog" (Johnson 2015); by library organizations, such as the Association for Library Service to Children (2013c); or by other interested individuals and groups, a case in point being LibraryLaw.com (2008).

A wiki, on the other hand, is basically a web page that can be edited. It works well for collaborative efforts, such as group projects, and can also link to other web pages (Common Craft 2013; Educause 2005). Individuals, professional organizations, and other people/groups working or interested in school libraries may create, use, and/or amend wikis. Sometimes wikis are employed as a place to share and modify exemplary or popular library activities and tips (Cobb Library Media Wiki 2011; Union School Library 2012). At other times, a professional organization might use a wiki as a site to share information on "book and media awards . . . programming resources . . . events and communication . . . learning . . . [and] best practices for virtual committees" (Association for Library Service to Children 2013d, 1) or to create a national working "bibliography of resources for school librarians, principals, parents, charter school organizers, library paraprofessionals, government officials, and college instructors" (American Association of School Librarians 2013c, 1).

Concepts of blogs and wikis have been around since the late 1990s; how about social media?

Social Media

While it has been posited that social networking actually began in the 1970s (Digital Trends Staff 2014), it was not until the early 2000s that the notion of social media really exploded on the scene. Since that time, school librarians, as well as millions (and in some cases billions) of others, have adopted social networking tools (Smith 2015) in their personal lives and—in their professional ones. LinkedIn, Facebook, Twitter, Shelfari, Goodreads, and more—all are examples of social media tools that can be and are used as Internet collaboration tools. Although LinkedIn categorizes itself as a professional network (LinkedIn 2013) and Twitter calls itself "a real-time information network," albeit one allowing 140 characters (Twitter 2013, 1), Facebook (WhatIs.com 2013), and many more are seen mainly as social entities. Then there are the subject-oriented networks, like Shelfari and Goodreads, which spotlight online socializing about books (Goodreads 2013; Shelfari 2013). Nonetheless, all of these are sometimes used for professional communications connected to school libraries. School librarians and their clientele (students and faculty) may, for instance, choose to hold a library or classroom book club within Shelfari or Goodreads, if their institution permits the students to access these social networks. Similarly, a school librarian may create a Facebook page for his or her library or tweet about new resources.

An alternative to the myriad of established social media is to generate your own, using a Ning, which assists "consumers and brands [to] create and engage with passionate social communities across all digital mediums" (Ning 2013, 1). With a Ning, a school librarian or other interested parties might fashion a specific online community, such as was done with TeacherLibrarianNing. This particular Ning is identified as being "for those of us who connect, teach, share, and lead in new information landscapes" (Valenza 2015, 1).

Thus, from listservs to Nings, communication between and among school librarians and those they serve appears to be at an all-time high. Be on the lookout—new tools are probably being created as you read this chapter!

KEY CONCEPTS FROM THIS CHAPTER

- Although what we are called and where we work can be ascertained by a variety of names, most commonly we identify ourselves as school librarians working in school libraries.
- In the 1740s, Benjamin Franklin recommended that American schools contain libraries.
- By 1840, several states had passed legislation in support of school libraries.
- Early school standards and guidelines focused more on the number of items in a school library than on quality.

- Sputnik (1957) and the NDEA (1958) were major influences on the evolution of school libraries from warehouses of books to multimedia centers.
- School libraries of today
  - contain or provide access to resources in a variety of formats: print, hardware and software, and Internet based;
  - are instructional centers;
  - offer services and programming for the entire school.
- School librarians have multiple skills and can work in print, digital, and technology-based environments.
- School libraries serve students, faculty, administration, and sometimes parents and other community members.
- School library professional organizations
  - can be international, national, statewide, regional, or local;
  - make available networking opportunities, professional journals, and conferences;
  - introduce school librarians to new materials and equipment;
  - support school librarians through information provision.
- The American Association of School Librarians is the major national organization for school librarians.
- Professional journals
  - may be associated with a professional organization;
  - contain articles on subjects of interest to school librarians;
  - include editorials, advertisements, columns, and more;
  - inform their readership of trends;
  - are often good review sources—thus supporting school librarians in library materials, equipment, and other selection needs.
- There are many collaboration tools for school librarians available on the Internet. School librarians can network with others like themselves through listservs, blogs and wikis, and a variety of social media.

Coming in chapter 2: "Standards and Guidelines."

DISCUSSION QUESTIONS

1. Why was Sputnik an influence on school libraries in the mid-20th century?
2. If you could join either a national or a statewide school library professional organization (but not both), which would you join and why?
3. What is your favorite professional journal for school librarians? Describe the reasons for your choice.
4. State the differences between a listserv, blog, and Ning. State the similarities.

ACTIVITIES

1. Search for school library history. Use print sources as well as electronic. What do you find? Consider how school libraries have evolved and list the subject areas that caused this evolution.
2. Go online and search for professional (international, national, statewide, and regional) school library organizations. Which ones focus solely on the school librarian as compared to others, such as the American Library Association, which serves as an umbrella organization for many types of librarians? After studying several, choose two that you would like to join.
3. Find a current professional school library magazine/journal. This can be in paper format or online. Examples include *Knowledge Quest*, *School Library Journal*, and *VOYA*. Read the articles; look through the advertisements; and so on. Write a review of it, including the following: (a) journal's bibliographic data; (b) type of information the journal covers; (c) whether journal is practical, research oriented, or both; (d) journal features (articles, departments, columns, advertisements, etc.); (e) whether you would recommend or not to other school librarians and why; and (f) anything else you consider of importance.
4. Join a professional listserv/blog/social networking or other internet collaboration tool. (You may join more than one, if you wish.) For example, listservs/discussion groups include LM-Net, ISLMA-Net, aaslforum@ala.org, and el-mss@ala.org. "Lurk" until you feel comfortable; then begin responding to and asking questions. Consider the Internet collaborating tool you are using in light of your introduction to and use of it by analyzing your learning experience. You may use the following questions for direction in your analysis. (These questions are meant to be somewhat broad.) (a) What did you learn? (b) What did you already know? (c) What was most important? (d) What was least important? (e) Is there anything you wish had been included that wasn't? (f) Would you use this in your professional life? (g) Would you recommend it to others?

REFERENCES

American Association of School Librarians. 2009. *Empowering Learners: Guidelines for School Library Media Programs.* Chicago, Ill.: American Association of School Librarians.

———. 2013a. "AASL Governing Documents: Mission and Goals: Mission." http://www.ala .org/aasl/about/governing-docs.

———. 2013b. "Affiliate Assembly Regions." http://www.ala.org/aasl/aboutaasl/affils/regions.

———. 2013c. "Essential Links: Resources for School Library Program Development: Main Page." http://aasl.ala.org/essentiallinks/index.php?title=Main_Page.

———. 2013d. "*Knowledge Quest.*" http://www.ala.org/aasl/kq.

American Association of School Librarians, ALA, and Association for Educational Communications and Technology. 1975. *Media Programs: District and School.* Chicago, Ill.: American

Library Association, and Washington, D.C.: Association for Educational Communications and Technology.

American Association of School Librarians and Association for Educational Communications and Technology. 1988. *Information Power: Guidelines for School Library Media Programs.* Chicago, Ill.: American Library Association, and Washington, D.C.: Association for Educational Communications and Technology.

———. 1998. *Information Power: Building Partnerships for Learning.* Chicago, Ill.: American Library Association.

American Library Association. 2013a. "Chicago Annual Conference and Exhibition: Highlights." http://ala13.ala.org/highlights.

———. 2013b. "Frequently Answered Questions." http://www.ala.org/Template.cfm?Section =alafaq.

American Library Association and National Education Association. 1969. *Standards for School Media Programs.* Chicago, Ill.: American Library Association, and Washington, D.C.: National Education Association.

Association for Educational Communications and Technology. 2013a. "AECT State Affiliates." http://aect.site-ym.com/?page=aect_state_affiliate.

———. 2013b. "Divisions: School Media and Technology." http://www.aect.org/newsite/.

———. 2013c. "What Is AECT?" http://www.aect.org/newsite/.

Association for Library Service to Children. 2013a. "About." https://www.facebook.com/ Associationforlibraryservicetochildren/info.

———. 2013b. "About the (Mildred L.) Batchelder Award." http://www.ala.org/alsc/awards grants/bookmedia/batchelderaward/batchelderabout.

———. 2013c. "ALSC Social Networks." http://www.ala.org/alsc/compubs/alsc20.

———. 2013d. "Main Page: Welcome to the Association for Library Service to Children (ALSC) Wiki." http://wikis.ala.org/alsc/index.php/Main_Page.

Bader, Barbara. 2011. "Mildred Batchelder: The Power of Thinking Big." http://www.hbook .com/2011/08/using-books/library/mildred-batchelder-the-power-of-thinking-big/.

Batchelder, Mildred L. 1990. Taped interview with Rebecca P. Butler.

Big6. 2013. "Information and Technology Skills for Student Success: Big6 Skills Overview." http://big6.com/pages/about/big6-skills-overview.php.

Bowie, Melvin M. 1986. *Historic Documents of School Libraries.* Salt Lake City, Utah: Hi Willow Research & Publishing.

Bray, Marty and Hollandsworth, Randy. 2011. "School Library Media Specialists: What's in a Name? A Lot It Seems . . ." *TechTrends* 55 (4): 19–20.

Butler, Rebecca P. 1999. "Contending Voices: Intellectual Freedom in American Public School Libraries, 1827–1940." *School Libraries Worldwide* 5 (1): 30–39.

CITES. n.d. "Archives of ISLMANET-L@LISTSERV.ILLINOIS.EDU." https://listserv .illinois.edu/archives/islmanet-l.html.

Cobb Library Media Wiki. 2011. "Cobb Library Media Wiki Home Page." https://cobbk12-org.campuspack.net/Groups/CI_Library_Media_Education_-_Spinks/Cobb_Library_ Media_Wiki.

Common Craft. 2013. "Wikis in Plain English." http://www.commoncraft.com/video/wikis.

Davis, Sally. 1991. Taped interview with Rebecca P. Butler.

Digital Trends Staff. 2014. "The History of Social Networking." http://www.digitaltrends .com/features/the-history-of-social-networking/.

Educause. 2005. "7 Things You Should Know about . . . Wikis." *Educause Learning Initiative.* (July).Flattau, Pamela Ebert, Bracken, Jerome, Van Atta, Richard, Bandeh-Ahmadi, Ayeh, de la Cruz, Rodolfo, and Sullivan, Kay. 2006. *The National Defense Education Act of 1958: Selected Outcomes.* Washington, D.C.: Science and Technology Policy Institute.

E. L. Kurdyla Publishing LLC. 2013. *"Teacher Librarian: The Journal for School Library Professionals."* http://www.kurdylapublishing.com/2011/11/teacher-librarian-the-journal-for-school-library-professionals/.

Goodreads. 2013. Home page. http://www.goodreads.com/.

Horn Book. 2013. *Horn Book Magazine.* http://www.hbook.com/horn-book-magazine-2/.

Illinois Association for Educational Communications and Technology. 2013. Home page. http://www.wiu.edu/users/iaect/INDEX.htm.

Illinois Computing Educators. n.d. "About ICE: ICE's Mission." http://www.iceberg.org/about_us.

———. n.d. "Chapters." http://www.iceberg.org/chapters.

Illinois School Library Media Association. 2011. "ISLMA ISLMANET-L." http://www.islma.org/listserv.htm.

———. 2012. "ISLMA Mission and Goals: Mission Statement." http://www.islma.org/about_islma.htm.

International Association of School Librarianship. 2007. "The Mission of IASL." http://www.iasl-online.org/about/.

International Literacy Association. 2015. "About the International Literacy Association." http://www.reading.org/General/AboutIRA.aspx.

International Visual Literacy Association. 2012. "What Is the IVLA?" http://www.ivla.org/drupal2/content/what-ivla.

Johnson, Doug. 2015. "The Blue Skunk Blog." http://doug-johnson.squarespace.com/.

King, William A. 1929. *The Elementary School Library.* New York, N.Y.: Charles Scribner's Sons.

Lambert, Greg. 2009. "Where Do Listservs Fit in a Social Media World?" *AALL Spectrum* (June): 8–9, 13.

Library and Media Services Section. n.d. *Standards for Educational Media Programs in Illinois.* Springfield, Ill.: Office of the Superintendent of Public Instruction Michael J. Bakalis, Superintendent.

LibraryLaw.com. 2008. *LibraryLaw Blog.* http://blog.librarylaw.com/librarylaw/school_libraries/.

LinkedIn. 2013. "About Us." http://www.linkedin.com/about-us.

LMC: Library Media Connection. n.d. "LMC Main Page." http://www.librarymediaconnection.com/lmc/.

LM_Net. n.d. "List Archives." http://lmnet-archive.iis.syr.edu/.

LM_Net by Thread. 2010. http://lmnet-archive.iis.syr.edu/LM_NET/2010/Sep_2010/threads.html.

LM_Net Home. n.d. "About." http://lmnet.wordpress.com/about/.

Marks, Mary. n.d. "In Our Voices, Through Our Eyes: An Oral History of the Illinois School Library Media Association." Unpublished dissertation. DeKalb, Ill.: Northern Illinois University.

Mathews, V.H. 1998. "The Way We Were and How It Was: 1945–1970." *The Emerging School Library Media Center: Historical Issues and Perspectives*, edited by Kathy Howard Latrobe. Englewood, Colo.: Libraries Unlimited.

Media & Methods Magazine. n.d. "Home." http://www.media-methods.com/index.php.

Morris, F.J. 2010. "School Library: A Historical Perspective." *Administering the School Library Media Center.* 5th ed. Santa Barbara, Calif.: Libraries Unlimited.

National Association for Media Literacy Education. 2013. "Media Literacy Defined." http:// namle.net/publications/media-literacy-definitions/.

Newman, Irene. 1992. Interview with Rebecca P. Butler.

New Mexico State Library. 2012. "Electronic Discussion Lists for Librarians." http://www .nmstatelibrary.org/services-for-nm-libraries/programs-services/librarians-toolkit/listservs-for-librarians.

Ning. 2013. "What Is Ning? About Ning." http://www.ning.com/about-us/.

Oklahoma State Department of Education. 2013. "Library Media: School Library Programs." http://ok.gov/sde/library-media.

Pentlin, Floyd. 2010. "Who're You Gonna Call? The 'School Librarian.'" http://www.aasl.ala .org/aaslblog/?p=913.

Peterson, Karyn M. 2013. "CISSL Study Helps Define Role of Successful NJ School Libraries." http://www.slj.com/2013/05/librarians/cissl-study-helps-define-role-of-successful-nj-school-libraries/.

School Library Journal. 2013. Facebook page. https://www.facebook.com/SchoolLibraryJournal.

Shelfari. 2013. Home page. http://www.shelfari.com/.

Smith, Craig. 2015. "How Many People Use 275 of the Top Social Media, Apps and Services? (February 2015)." http://expandedramblings.com/index.php/resource-how-many-people-use-the-top-social-media/.

TechTerms.com. 2013. "Listserv." http://www.techterms.com/definition/listserv.

Twitter. 2013. "About Twitter." https://twitter.com/about.

Union School Library. 2012. "Union School Library Media Center." http://rutherfordunion schoollibrary.wikispaces.com/Union+School+Library+Media+Center.

Valenza, Joyce. 2015. "GlobalTL: A Community for Teacher-Librarians and Other Educators." http://teacherlibrarian.ning.com/.

WhatIs.com. 2013. "Definition: Facebook." http://whatis.techtarget.com/definition/Facebook.

WordPress.org. n.d. "Introduction to Blogging." http://codex.wordpress.org/Introduction_to_ Blogging.

2

Standards and Guidelines

In chapter 1, we looked briefly at some of the early standards for school libraries (the Certain reports of the first three decades of the 20th century, the American Library Association/American Association of School Librarians and the Association for Educational Communications and Technology's *Information Power* publications in the later part of the 20th century, and several state standards and guidelines). Since 1916, many national and state organizations in the United States have created standards and guidelines for school libraries and school librarians.

Standards aim for consistency, should leave little room for doubt, and are best understood when clearly and simply stated. Because policies and procedures (see chapter 3) are sometimes redundant, standards help clarify the aims of a particular group. In 2001, the National Research Council defined educational standards thusly: "Standards serve as a basis of educational reform across the nation as educators and policy makers respond to the call for a clear definition of desired outcomes of schooling and a way to measure student success in terms of these outcomes" (University Library 2013, 1). Likewise, a guideline, according to the *Merriam-Webster Dictionary* (2013), is "a rule or instruction that shows or tells how something should be done" (1). In the second decade of the 21st century, there are many sets of standards and guidelines for school librarians to use as they work with K–12 students. Additionally, there are a number of sets that higher education faculty may follow when teaching people to be school librarians. In this chapter, we look at some of the most prominent of these.

NATIONAL STANDARDS AND GUIDELINES

Many national school library and technology professional organizations have established standards and guidelines for school librarians to use when working in the

K–12 educational environment. Two of the more well known of these are addressed next. In addition, this section will look briefly at those standards followed by many institutions of higher learning who train individuals to become school librarians.

SCHOOL LIBRARY PROFESSIONAL ASSOCIATION STANDARDS

The American Association of School Librarians (AASL) is, by far, the premier national school library professional organization in the United States. AASL states that their learning standards "offer a vision for teaching and learning to both guide and beckon the school library profession as education leaders. The learning standards shape the library program and serve as a tool for school librarians to use to shape the learning of students in the school" (American Association of School Librarians 2013b, 1).

AASL's Standards for the 21st-Century Learner (2007) can be accessed online at http://www.ala.org/aasl/standards-guidelines/learning-standards. There are four main standards with a number of skills, dispositions in action, responsibilities, and self-assessment strategies identified for each one. These standards are identified on page 3 of the Standards for the 21st-Century Learner pamphlet in this manner:

> Learners use skills, resources, and tools to: (1) Inquire, think critically, and gain knowledge. (2) Draw conclusions, make informed decisions, apply knowledge to new situations, and create new knowledge. (3) Share knowledge and participate ethically and productively as members of our democratic society. (4) Pursue personal and aesthetic growth.

Through these standards, the school librarian is directed to

> build a learner who can thrive in a complex information environment . . . [via teaching, modeling and providing for that learner] . . . ethical behavior in the use of information . . . technology skills . . . equitable access . . . multiple literacies . . . thinking [and] knowledge sharing skills . . . [in a] . . . warm, stimulating, and safe environment" (American Association for School Librarians 2007, 2–3).

Additionally, AASL has provided a number of books and websites to support school librarians as they follow the standards and guidelines. A listing of these items is available at http://www.ala.org/aasl/standards-guidelines#standards. Two of these books bear mentioning here. The book *Standards for the 21st-Century Learner in Action* (2009b) "provides support for SLMSs and other educators in teaching the essential learning skills" (American Association of School Librarians 2009b, 10). This is done by presenting benchmarks, through examples and lessons, to be achieved by identified grade levels, K–12. The second book, *Empowering Learners: Guidelines for School Library Media Programs*, supplies guidelines for learning in school libraries, and "advances school library media programs to meet the needs of the changing school library environment" (American Association of School Librarians 2009a, 5). In addition to AASL, there are other national professional organizations with standards and/or guidelines for and/or followed by school librarians. Consequently we look at a set of technology standards.

TECHNOLOGY STANDARDS USED BY SCHOOL LIBRARIANS

The International Society for Technology in Education (ISTE) published the "ISTE.S: Advanced Digital Age Learning" standards for students in 2007. These "are the standards for evaluating the skills and knowledge students need to learn effectively and live productively in an increasingly global and digital world" (International Society for Technology in Education 2012, 1). While these standards were established generally for education, school librarians—through their use of and provision to students of digital and other technologies—also may choose to follow these in the school venue. There are six main standards that address students in terms of technology use, digital media, and ethics: "1. Creativity and Innovation; 2. Communication and Collaboration. 3. Research and Information Fluency. 4. Critical Thinking, Problem Solving, and Decision Making; 5. Digital Citizenship; and 6. Technology Operations and Concepts" (International Society for Technology in Education 2007, 1–2).

STANDARDS AND GUIDELINES FOR THE EDUCATION OF SCHOOL LIBRARIANS

Some school library and/or technology education professional organizations team with federally authorized agencies to provide standards and guidelines that colleges and universities, which are training individuals to be school librarians, might follow. The higher education institutions generally go through a rigorous process to become certified by the organizations and agencies. Possibly the most prominent of these, for school library training, in the United States is the 2010 ALA/AASL Standards for the Initial Preparation of School Librarians. (This set of standards can be found at http://www.ala.org/aasl/education/ncate in pdf form.) These standards were developed from a pairing of the American Library Association/American Association of School Librarians (ALA/AASL) with the National Council for the Accreditation of Teacher Education (NCATE). (Please note that NCATE is currently transitioning, along with the Teacher Education Accreditation Council [TEAC] into the Council for the Accreditation of Educator Preparation [CAEP]. All higher education institutions preparing teachers will come up for their next accreditation under CAEP [Church 2011; Council for the Accreditation of Educator Preparation 2010].)

The 2010 ALA/AASL Standards for the Initial Preparation of School Librarians include five standards (short and long descriptions), along with the elements, rubrics, support research, and references to aid in the use of each of the standards. The short standard descriptions are as follows: "Standard 1: Teaching for Learning; Standard 2: Literacy and Reading; Standard 3: Information and Knowledge; Standard 4: Advocacy and Leadership; Standard 5: Program Management and Administration"; these standards " apply to all master's programs that prepare candidates to develop and manage library and information services in a PreK–12 setting, regardless of degree name or professional title" (American Library Association and the American Association of School Librarians 2010, 1, 6, 10, 14, 17). Next we turn to an example of standards for technology education.

The AECT Standards for Professional Education Programs (2012 version) were, as the title alludes, created in 2012 by the Association for Educational Communications and Technology (AECT) in order to establish benchmarks for those in higher education who train people to be technology professionals. Because most school librarians in the 21st century also work with technology, this particular set of standards similarly impacts those working in school libraries today. The five standards are

> AECT Standard 1 (Content Knowledge): Candidates demonstrate the knowledge necessary to create, use, assess, and manage theoretical and practical applications of educational technologies and processes. AECT Standard 2 (Content Pedagogy): Candidates develop as reflective practitioners able to demonstrate effective implementation of educational technologies and processes based on contemporary content and pedagogy. AECT Standard 3 (Learning Environments): Candidates facilitate learning by creating, using, evaluating, and managing effective learning environments. AECT Standard 4 (Professional Knowledge and Skills): Candidates design, develop, implement, and evaluate technology-rich learning environments within a supportive community of practice. AECT Standard 5 (Research): Candidates explore, evaluate, synthesize, and apply methods of inquiry to enhance learning and improve performance. (Association for Educational Communications and Technology 2012, 1–2)

In addition to national standards for the K–12 school library environment and for the training of school librarians and technology personnel, there are standards identified by state.

STATE STANDARDS AND GUIDELINES

Standards and guidelines are not endemic to national groups. States and statewide professional organizations may also establish specifications for K–12 student learning and/or the training of school librarians. Many times such state standards and guidelines, whether developed by a state department of education or by a statewide school library professional group, align intentionally or inadvertently with national standards, such as AASL's Standards for the 21st-Century Learner or ISTE.S: Advanced Digital Age Learning standards (Colorado Department of Education 2013; Illinois School Library Media Association 2010; Illinois State Standards 2002; Indiana Department of Education 2010; Oregon School Library Standards, n.d.). In addition, such standards and guidelines often provide information such as goals and principles, rubrics, student impact/benefits, and directions on how to implement said recommended criteria (Illinois School Library Media Association 2010; Texas State Library and Archives Commission 2011). Indeed, there are a variety of school library and technology standards and guidelines for school librarians to follow—and write into their lesson plans—at the national and state levels. But wait—there are more!

COMMON CORE STATE STANDARDS

The Common Core State Standards (CCSS) are "a state-led effort that established a single set of clear educational standards for kindergarten through 12th grade in English language arts and mathematics that states voluntarily adopt" (Common Core State Standards Initiative 2012, 1). First published in 2010 by the National Governors Association Center for Best Practices and the Council of Chief State School Officers "in collaboration with educational organizations, teachers, researchers, higher learning experts and business leaders from across the country" (National PTA, n.d., 1), these standards were the result of collaboration by 48 U.S. states along with two U.S. territories and the District of Columbia. While there is a national aspect to this set of standards, in fact, "curricula vary from state to state and district to district" ("10 Myths about the Common Core State Standards" 2013–2014, 43). The idea behind these standards is that of a consistent quality education with "clear expectations for what each student must know to leave school prepared for college and career. . . . The CCSS . . . do not tell teachers how to achieve the goal, but they will allow teachers to share best practices from state to state" (National PTA, n.d., 1). Additionally, new assessments are being developed that can compare student learning from state to state (Common Core State Standards Initiative 2012).

How do the CCSS impact what school librarians do? For one, "the CCSS emphasize collaboration between students but also provide opportunities for educators across curricular areas to brainstorm, team teach, or work together in other ways" (Master's in ESL 2013, 1). School librarians are, by their nature, working with the entire school. Thus, we can collaborate with our fellow teachers in terms of CCSS support. Second, school librarians support reading and literacy and provide collections to support both curricular and pleasure reading. "Who better than librarians to collaborate with teachers to identify literature and text for students to read in the content areas?" (Kramer 2013, 1). Third, 21st century school libraries usually contain a variety of technology. Following the CCSS may involve students and faculty accessing and using technology for their standardized test-taking. Once again, school librarians could be instrumental in providing computer lab access, and so on. Fourth, because the CCSS are interdisciplinary, school librarians can provide information, materials, and instruction to bond various subject areas, curricular themes, and courses to each other. This supports teachers and students as well as the school's mission.

School librarians can offer Common Core support to their faculty in the form of

- online and print catalogs for companies which produce materials identified to be used with the Common Core (e.g., Albert Whitman, HarperCollins, etc.);
- free Common Core materials (via the web; e.g., Cory Doctorow's *Little Brother*, etc.) (Common Core Standards Initiative 2012)
- professional periodicals with Common Core information and reviewed materials (e.g., *Booklist*);
- online library guides on Common Core subjects;
- more knowledge about the Common Core through the Internet, professional journals, and white papers (Cravey 2013; Achieve and American Association of School Librarians 2013).

Please be aware here that the AASL provides a series of tables aligning the Standards for the 21st-Century Learner with the Common Core State Standards. These are available at http://www.ala.org/aasl/standards-guidelines/crosswalk (American Association of School Librarians 2013a). This alignment endorses us, as school librarians, in our work with the CCSS, students, and faculty. This is particularly important since there are no CCSS specifically for school libraries, and because the school library champions the many aspects of the entire school (curriculum, information access and use, pleasure requests).

Lastly, not all educators agree with the CCSS concept. Some argue the emphasis on standardized testing results in have and have-nots among the nation's children in terms of literacy, and that having such standards may result in the exclusion from the school and curriculum of any media not related to the CCSS (Krashen 2013).

STEM AND NEXT GENERATION SCIENCE STANDARDS

Because of "the critical role that STEM education plays in enabling the U.S. to remain the economic and technological leader of the global marketplace of the 21st century" (STEM Education Coalition, n.d., 1), STEM (science, technology, engineering, mathematics) is emphasized in many American public schools today. The Next Generation Science Standards (NGSS), "a collaborative, state-led process [of] . . . new K–12 science standards . . . that are rich in content and practice . . . across disciplines and grades to provide all students an internationally benchmarked science education" (Next Generation Science Standards 2014b, 1), can help support STEM education in American schools. "States can use the NGSS, as they are using the CCSS (Common Core State Standards) in English language arts and mathematics, to align curriculum, instruction, assessment, and professional preparation and development" (Next Generation Science Standards 2014a, 1). As with the CCSS, there appear to be no specific standards for school libraries within the NGSS; however, much as with the CCSS, school librarians can help support the subjects of science, mathematics, and technology, as well as students and teachers through collaboration, through STEM- and NGSS-focused library services and programming, and in providing materials to support such foci.

Undoubtedly, more educational, school library, and technology standards are on the horizon. Be prepared to consider these as they come along and work with them as you work with your students, collaborate with your fellow teachers, and promote the programming, services, and collection of the library.

KEY CONCEPTS FROM THIS CHAPTER

- Standards aim for consistency.
- There are two main types of standards for school librarians—those to apply when working in the K–12 environment and those that focus on school librarian training.
- The Standards for the 21st-Century Learner, created by the American Association of School Librarians, are the leading national standards for school librarians.
- School librarians may also use technology standards in their work.
- States and many statewide professional organizations also institute standards that school librarians follow.
- Many state standards are comparable to national standards.
- The Common Core State Standards have been adopted by most states.
- The CCSS promote consistency and allow for standardized testing.
- There are no CCSS for school libraries; school librarians must collaborate with their fellow faculty, given these standards.
- Not all educators are partial to the CCSS.
- There may be more educational, school library, and technology standards being developed at any time. Be prepared to support them through the materials and services, policies and procedures, and so on of the school library.

Coming in chapter 3: "Policies and Procedures."

DISCUSSION QUESTIONS

1. Discuss how a school librarian might use a set of national technology standards, such as ISTE.S: Advanced Digital Age Learning, to support school library programming.
2. Some states have a set of school library standards or guidelines created by the state board of education (or a similar state group) in addition to a set of standards or guidelines generated by the state professional school library association (e.g., Illinois State Standards: Library Information Specialist and *Linking for Learning*, the Illinois state library guidelines, published by the Illinois School Library Media

Association). When there are two (or more) sets of state criteria, by which set should you, as the school librarian, abide? Argue for and against each.

3. Discuss why the Common Core are called state standards, when they appear to be part of a national movement?

ACTIVITIES

1. Read AASL's Standards for the 21st-Century Learner (http://www.ala.org/aasl/standards-guidelines/learning-standards). These standards have been established to create a framework for the school library of the 21st century. Issues stressed include collaboration, multiple literacies (reading, technology, visual, and more), effective practices, equitable access to multiple materials, ethics, inquiry/learning, assessments, and leadership. Consider what you have read and answer the following questions:
   • How can/will these standards influence the school library of the present? Future?
   • How can we, as school librarians, be better leaders in the school environment, our communities, and so on?
   • Why is collaboration so important?
2. Find and read a set of your state's school library standards/guidelines or those of a state of interest to you. Why do you believe your state/state school library organization felt the need to create state guidelines when national ones exist?
3. Read "Common Core Standards" (Fontichiaro, 2011; http://www.schoollibrarymonthly.com/curriculum/Fontichiaro2011-v28n1p49.html). According to Martens of the Iowa Department of Education, there are five key areas in which librarians can support the implementation of Common Core Standards:
   • Creating sound persuasive arguments with evidence
   • Reading comprehension strategies
   • Effectively using primary and secondary sources
   • Reading and analyzing complex texts
   • Reading and comprehending informational text in all content areas

   Pick one of these five and describe how you would implement it in a school library of your choice.

REFERENCES

"10 Myths about the Common Core State Standards." 2013–2014. *American Educator* 37 (4): 43.

Achieve and American Association of School Librarians. 2013. *Implementing the Common Core State Standards: The Role of the School Librarian.* Chicago, Ill.: American Association of School Librarians.

American Association of School Librarians. 2007. "Standards for the 21st-Century Learner." http://www.ala.org/aasl/standards-guidelines/learning-standards.

———. 2009a. *Empowering Learners: Guidelines for School Library Media Programs*. Chicago, Ill.: American Association of School Librarians.

———. 2009b. *Standards for the 21st-Century Learner in Action*. Chicago, Ill.: American Association of School Librarians.

———. 2013a. "AASL Learning Standards and Common Core State Standards Crosswalk." http://www.ala.org/aasl/standards-guidelines/crosswalk.

———. 2013b. "Learning Standards and Program Guidelines." http://www.ala.org/aasl/standards-guidelines#standards.

American Library Association and the American Association of School Librarians. 2010. "2010 ALA/AASL Standards for the Initial Preparation of School Librarians." http://www.ala.org/aasl/education/ncate.

Association for Educational Communications and Technology. 2012. "Documents: AECT Standards for Professional Education Programs (2012 version)." http://aect.site-ym.com/?documents.

Church, Audrey. 2011. "Keeping Current: Standards for Preparing 21st-Century School Librarians." *School Library Monthly* 27 (6): 54–56.

Colorado Department of Education. 2013. "Colorado School Libraries." http://www.cde.state.co.us/cdelib/librarydevelopment/schoollibraries/index.

Common Core State Standards Initiative. 2012. "Learn More about the Common Standards." http://www.corestandards.org/resources/frequently-asked-questions.

Council for the Accreditation of Educator Preparation. 2010. "Transition Q & A." http://caepnet.org/about/transition/.

Cravey, Nancy. 2013. "Finding Inspiration in the Common Core." *Knowledge Quest* 42 (1): 18–22.

Fontichiaro, Kristin, comp. 2011. "Common Core Standards." http://www.schoollibrary-monthly.com/curriculum/Fontichiaro2011-v28n1p49.html.

Illinois School Library Media Association. 2010. *Linking for Learning: The Illinois School Library Media Program Guidelines*. 3rd ed. Canton, Ill.: Illinois School Library Media Association.

Illinois State Standards. 2002. "Library Information Specialist [27.450]." 2nd ed. Springfield, Ill.: Illinois State Board of Education.

Indiana Department of Education. 2010. "Indiana Content Standards for Educators: School Librarian." *www.doe.in.gov/sites/default/files/licensing/school-librarian.pdf*.

International Society for Technology in Education. 2007. "ISTE.S: Advanced Digital Age Learning." http://www.iste.org/standards/standards-for-students (ISTE Standards•S [PDF]).

———. 2012. "Standards: Digital Age Learning." http://www.iste.org/standards/standards-for-students.

Kramer, Pamela K. 2013. "Common Core and School Librarians: An Interview with Joyce Karon." http://www.schoollibrarymonthly.com/articles/Kramer2011-v28n1p8.html.

Krashen, Stephen. 2013. "Access to Books and Time to Read versus the Common Core State Standards and Tests." *English Journal* 103 (2): 21–29.

Master's in ESL. 2013. "Using the Common Core Standards in ESL Teaching: Part I: Standards-Based Educational Reform." http://www.mastersinesl.org/teaching-esl/using-the-common-core-standards-in-esl-teaching/.

Merriam-Webster Dictionary. 2013. "Guideline." http://www.merriam-webster.com/dictionary/guideline.

National PTA. n.d. "Common Core State Standards—Frequently Asked Questions." http://www.pta.org/advocacy/content.cfm?ItemNumber=3683#What%20was%20the%20process%20for%20developing%20and%20writing%20the%20Standards?

Next Generation Science Standards. 2014a. "About the Standards: Frequently Asked Questions." http://www.nextgenscience.org/frequently-asked-questions#4.1.

———. 2014b. "Explore the NGSS." http://www.nextgenscience.org/.

Oregon School Library Standards. n.d. "Oregon School Library Standards with Indicators and Alignments." https://docs.google.com/spreadsheet/ccc?key=0AmhJKmiVkK-QdF9FRlZkNXhLNWRxOFdQQkJ0NUthSGc#gid=4.

STEM Education Coalition. n.d. "About." http://www.stemedcoalition.org/contact-us-2/.

Texas State Library and Archives Commission. 2011. "School Library Programs: Standards and Guidelines for Texas." https://www.tsl.state.tx.us/ld/schoollibs/sls/stand1.html.

University Library. 2013. "Education Standards." http://www.library.illinois.edu/sshel/education/educstandards.html#general.

3

Policies and Procedures

The *Merriam-Webster Online Dictionary* defines a policy as "a high-level overall plan embracing the general goals and acceptable procedures especially of a governmental body" (*Merriam-Webster Online* 2013b, 1). A procedure, on the other hand, is termed, "a particular way of accomplishing something or of acting" (*Merriam-Webster Online* 2013c, 1). Policies and procedures are important aspects for the school librarian, because he or she works with a wide range of people, resources, services, programming, and more. As such, it is important to be organized, know what the rules are, and how to apply them at all times. This chapter focuses on school library policies and procedures and the handbook or manual in which they usually reside.

THE SCHOOL LIBRARY POLICIES AND PROCEDURES MANUAL

Having the support of a current school library policies and procedures manual (or handbook) can make a world of difference when the school librarian experiences a book challenge, a copyright infringement issue involving school faculty or students, a setback with library computer maintenance, or another problem with the library materials, programming, and so on. This is because a good manual sets out the policies and procedures for running all aspects of the school library. Therefore, if the only library manual you can find was done on a mimeograph ("a duplicator for making many copies that utilizes a stencil through which ink is pressed" [*Merriam-Webster Online* 2013a, 1]), is ratty and worn, or cannot be found at all, it is time to develop a new one—and keep it where you can access it easily and quickly. Luckily, examples of school library policies and procedures manuals and how to create them exist on the Internet, as well as in textbooks and some professional magazines (Alabama

Department of Education 2008; Indian Prairie Community Unit School District 204, 2006; Library Media Services 2005; Pappas 2005). So why is such a manual or handbook important? Let's take a look.

What Is in It?

While school library policies and procedures manuals can vary widely, depending on who writes them and the school library/school district in question, there are some basic pieces that are found in most: (1) an introduction and/or mission statement; (2) goals and objectives for the school library program; and (3) a collection development policy containing sections on materials' selection and evaluation, acquisition, gifts, maintenance, weeding, intellectual freedom, copyright, and Internet access/ acceptable use/responsible use policy.

Introduction and/or Mission Statement

Usually, one of the first things in such a manual is the introduction and/or mission statement. The introduction often covers why the manual was created and how it will be used, who wrote it, how policy and procedures were developed, the intended audience, how often it will be updated, and the mission statement or library philosophy. The mission statement (in place of or as part of the introduction) additionally contains the purpose of the library (example: to contribute to student learning in all formats), the responsibilities of the school librarian in terms of the school library audience, and the reasoning behind the presence of the school library as an entity within the school (Bradshaw Primary, n.d.; Indian Prairie Community Unit School District 204, n.d.; Quail Valley Middle School, n.d.).

Goals and Objectives

Another area of most school library policies and procedures manuals is that of dealing with goals and objectives. This section looks at what the library is trying to accomplish and the rationale for library successes, its programs of most importance, and what will be used to assess library achievements. Here is a sample goal statement: "Our goal is that the programs and services we offer will encourage students to become life-long readers, learners, and library patrons" (Quail Valley Middle School, n.d., 1).

Now let's move on to one of the largest pieces of most school library policy and procedures manuals—the collection development section.

Collection Development

"A collection development policy is a written statement of your library's intentions for building its collection. . . . Every library, no matter how small, should have a collection development policy. Such a policy is really an expanded version of the mission or purpose of the library" (Arizona State Library, Archives and Public Records 2013, 1). The school library collection development policy is the set of rules that states the how and why of collection building, including how to select and evaluate library resources in all formats, themes, and whether fiction or not for a wide-ranging and diverse clientele; what is involved in acquisition, maintenance, and weeding of equipment and materials; copyright policy; the library position on intellectual freedom, including procedures for handling complaints; and other criteria needed to support the collection, influenced by student curriculum and faculty (and sometimes entertainment) needs. The preceding means that general collection development policies may mention who the library serves; what programming and service essentials are required in that particular library; selection priorities and limitations; possible funding sources; how to deal with materials' duplications, networks, interlibrary loan, and public (community/surrounding area) resources; and how learning materials will be disseminated to those who need such media.

Following is a discussion of selection and evaluation, acquisition, maintenance, and weeding and their corresponding divisions in the collection development policy. (Acceptable use policies [AUPs] are located in chapter 9, "Library and Ethics." Intellectual freedom and property [specifically copyright] parts of the collection development policy are also covered in chapter 9, and for gift policy information, see chapter 4, "Follow the Money.")

Selection and Evaluation of Library Materials

An extremely important responsibility of the school librarian involves selecting and evaluating media: (1) print (books, magazines, poetry, and more); (2) software (movies in many formats, DVDs, computer programs, etc.); (3) hardware (computers, projectors, tablets, handhelds, e-readers, and so on); and (4) digital/Internet sources (e.g., web pages, Nings, and other social media used for educational purposes; instructional video games; video-conferencing tools; periodical and newspaper subscription databases; digital resource subscription communities; and open [i.e., free] education resources, including federal government sites, such as the NASA website and sites with Creative Commons licenses) (Discovery Education 2014; NASA 2014; Opensource.com, n.d.).

Next, we look at selection and evaluation tools and criteria.

In an ideal world, the school librarian would have the time, ability to use, and access to all media he or she was considering adding to the school library collection. The reality is that in most instances, said librarian must rely on selection tools and specific selection criteria to inform him or her as to what should be acquired.

Selection Tools

Selection tools can be found in print or on the web, in professional journals, or in commercial catalogs. One important selection tool is the review. The reason for a review is to inform and evaluate a particular medium for the user. Given school librarians, a review could be about anything that they might wish to obtain for their collection: books, journals, plays, sheet music, audio recordings, DVDs, computer software, educational games, movies, podcasts, web pages, even Nings (platforms for creating a social network). Reviews are especially helpful when the school librarian is unable to physically access an item that he or she is considering for the library collection. In such a case, the review may be that on which the librarian bases his or her decision. Given how significant a review might be, the author of the review and its content are very important indeed.

So, what goes in a good review? A strong book review might have the informational data for the book (author, title, illustrator [for example, a picture book], publisher, ISBN, and cost); the grades/ages for which the book is written; a brief summary; the book's theme and relevance; number of pages; comparison with similar books; literary quality/strengths and weaknesses of the item; attractiveness to possible audiences; recommendation by the reviewer; and the name and work title of the reviewer (e.g., May Smith, Garner Hayes Elementary School Library) (Abel 1979; *Library Media Connection* 2015; *School Library Journal* 2015; Thomson 1991; *VOYA* 2015).

Next, let's look at what might go into a movie review. Such a review could include the informational data (title, format, length [e.g., 1 hour, 40 minutes in length], number of discs/DVDs [whatever the format is], producer, distributer, and ISBN); the grades/ages for which the video was created; a brief summary; the video's theme and relevance; comparison with similar videos; literary quality/strengths and weaknesses of the item; attractiveness to possible audiences; recommendation by the reviewer; and the name and work title of the reviewer (Abel 1979; *Library Media Connection* 2015; *School Library Journal* 2015; *VOYA* 2015).

Please note that several things in any review (such as title, audience attractiveness, etc.) will be similar, no matter the format of the item being reviewed. Once you are reading reviews with any regularity, you will also notice that most are one paragraph in length. Because school librarians wear the many hats discussed in chapter 1, they do not have a lot of time and usually appreciate the succinctness of most media reviews. Other things to consider about reviews: ideally read more than one—reviews are subjective, based on a reviewer's knowledge, experience, and opinion. Therefore, it is best to get more than one view before you consider purchasing an item. In addition, try to read reviews written by school or public librarians. These two groups are most likely to have opinions with which you may agree.

Reviews can be found in many places: in professional journals, such as *School Library Journal* and *VOYA*; in newspapers and school and public library annotated reading lists; in books such as (using young adult books as an example) *Best Books for Young Adults*, *Essential Guide to Spanish Reading for Children and Young Adults*, and *A Core Collection for Young Adults* (Carter 2000; America Reads Spanish 2009; *School Library Journal* 2015; *VOYA* 2015; Welch 2011). Please remember that many of these review locations, or similar ones, are found online (*School Library*

Journal 2013), in print, or both. It is even possible to obtain professional review "snippets" (or in some cases full text professional reviews) for particular items, posted on a commercial bookstore or vendor's website (Amazon 2013; Bound to Stay Bound 2011).

There are also other ways to find out about media you may be interested in obtaining for your library collection. For example, you can choose to peruse publishers' catalogs (print and on the web). Such catalogs usually have a photograph of the item in question as well as a cleverly written advertisement in a format similar to a written review. You may also choose to look at advertisements for media published in print and on the Internet in professional and other journals, newspapers, newsletters, and more. When using such advertisements and commercial catalogs, please remind yourself that publishing companies are trying to sell to you. Thus, all information provided is presented in a positive/salable form.

Another way to learn about new media is word of mouth. If you trust the speaker or it is someone with agency (i.e., a school librarian, technology specialist, or faculty member who knows what is needed to support a particular class), then you may be in luck. Using lists from professional organizations (such as ALA/ALSC's Caldecott Award list [Association for Library Service to Children 2013]) or from an interested individual's personal website (Ford 2013), is an alternative approach to consider when thinking to add to your library collection. If you are an elementary librarian, for instance, the Caldecott list might be something you would want to peruse. With personal websites, however, you are definitely obtaining a biased view. This is something to consider when using such lists as selection tools. Talking to vendors at professional conferences can likewise be informative to the selector of library materials (again, realize that vendors are there to sell, so take what they say as you would take that of any salesperson). Lastly, demonstrations of tangible items and/or tutorials can also be helpful as selection tools. If you are able to actually work with what you are considering for purchase or can really understand how that item functions, your selection may be influenced.

Next we consider library materials selection criteria.

Selection Criteria

Selection criteria are developed by school librarians every day, and most school library manuals or handbooks have a segment that states sample specifications. It may be a general statement in the policy section and/or specific criteria in a procedures section (Bowling Green Area Schools, n.d.; Indian Prairie Community Unit School District 204, 2006). General school library selection criteria, asked of possible items to be added to the library collection, may include

- relevancy in today's world;
- curricular support/expected outcomes;
- quality (literature, information, illustrations, etc.);

- support of national, state, and local standards;
- subject area appropriateness;
- age, grade, learning style, and so on suitability;
- user appeal;
- agency of author;
- publisher/producer reputation;
- currency;
- factuality;
- bias;
- cost. (American Library Association 2013b; Baltimore County Public Schools, n.d.)

Specific criteria often address a particular resource (or piece of equipment) in terms of the curriculum it may support, the students and teachers who will use the item, the medium's format, or even the facility where it will be housed and/or used. Sample specialized criteria are listed here in question form:

- Does this item support the 6th grade science curriculum?
- Can the students in Mrs. Jones's second grade class understand the material in the book?
- What is the length of the video? Is it too long for the middle school special needs students?
- Does this website support the special needs students in Mrs. Carr's classroom?
- Is this medium in a format that can be accessed by elementary school students?
- Is the reading/listening/viewing level of this multimedia product appropriate for freshman English students?
- Would audio books work for low-reading students?
- Can we access web pages on breast cancer with our school filter on?
- What is the bandwidth for this database?
- Is federal government information accessible via this database virtual or finite; that is, will it be brought up to date on a regular basis?
- How often does this newspaper database get updated?
- If we subscribe to this streaming service, will we have enough money in the budget to purchase other commercial Internet products?
- Are these federal government websites free for use in the school?
- Is there help available online, if a high-interest, low-reading student does not understand how to retrieve the material on this website?
- How expensive is this DVD? Can the library afford it?
- Will this e-book provide the information the social studies teacher is requesting?
- Can more than one person use this CD-ROM at the same time?
- Can we pay for the e-books the Spanish teacher requested?
- Does this online instructional tool keep track of a student's progress?

- If a teacher wishes to copy parts of this book and share it with others, will he or she be breaking copyright law?
- Is this app free?
- Do we have the hardware in the library to support this item?
- Do the tablets we wish to purchase for the library have warranties?
- Does this medium have documentation, stating what we can and cannot do with it?
- Can we store the software on the regular library shelves; that is, is it a shape that will sit on a shelf?
- How durable is this DVD collection?
- Does this company archive articles?
- Is there enough information in this statistics software to make it worthy of purchase?
- What special features are there to this biographical video; that is, does it include an interview of the real-life person portrayed in the movie?
- Will these apps work with the autistic children in Mrs. Ames's class?
- Is the book organized so that third graders can find the information they need in the table of contents, glossary, and appendixes?
- We have a number of ELLs (English language learners) in our building. What materials can we find to support their needs (any format)?
- Can we use this computer software with a classroom full of students or is this for individual use only?
- Mr. Adams's technology lab is completely surrounded by windows. Are the computer screens we want to purchase able to adjust to extreme lighting?

Specific criteria addressing particular resources are often the result of faculty recommendations as to what is needed to support a class, administrative suggestions, or student requests. You, as the school librarian, may also find holes in the collection that you feel need to be filled.

Figures 3.1 to 3.4 depict four fictional selection scenarios. Each includes a flowchart presenting specific selection criteria of a particular medium. Please note that criteria in any of these flowcharts can be substituted or deleted, depending on your actual situation. School libraries, their communities, and their clientele may vary; therefore, specific selection criteria may also do so.

Scenario 1 (figure 3.1) deals with book selection. In this case, the school librarian has been asked by a high school biology teacher to order a book on bugs that eat bodies for a forensic science unit he plans to teach with high school juniors. (Please note that depending on what you find, you may have a short set of selection criteria, as is demonstrated here.)

Scenario 2 (figure 3.2) focuses on DVD selection. Here an elementary school librarian is looking to update old antibullying videos with DVDs. Her student body is primarily Spanish speaking.

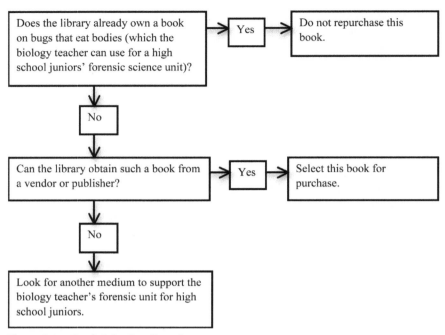

Figure 3.1.   Book Selection Flowchart

Scenario 3 (figure 3.3) is concerned with the selection of a website to support seventh grade technology education (specifically how to make a model airplane).

Scenario 4 (figure 3.4) covers selection of hardware, in this case a set of tablets for student use in a K–9 library.

Next, due to their importance in today's schools, diversity selection criteria are emphasized separately.

Diversity

The American Library Association (ALA) states in Article II of the Library Bill of Rights, "Libraries should provide materials and information presenting all points of view on current and historical issues. Materials should not be proscribed or removed because of partisan or doctrinal disapproval" (American Library Association 2013c, 1). This statement reinforces the concept that "library collections must represent the diversity of people and ideas in our society. . . . Librarians have an obligation to select and support access to materials and resources on all subjects that meet, as closely as possible, the needs, interests, and abilities of all persons in the community the library serves" (American Library Association 2013a, 1). The community the school library serves is

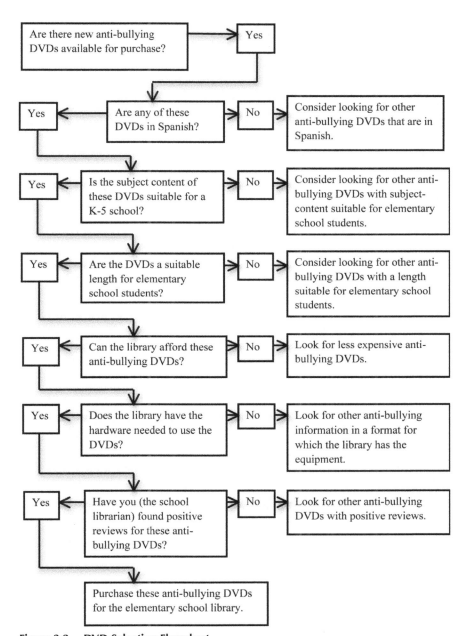

Figure 3.2. DVD Selection Flowchart

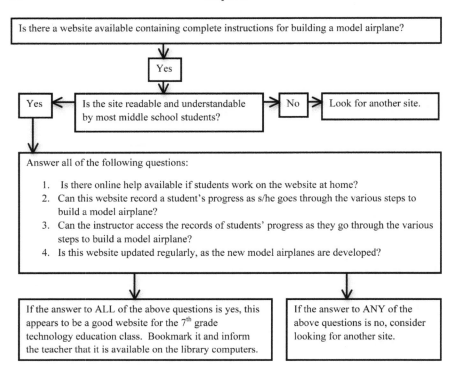

Figure 3.3. Website Selection Flowchart

most likely composed of students, faculty, administration, and parents who could hail from any number of diverse groups including those of varying social and economic status, culture and ethnicity, race, religion, age, language, sexual orientation, handicaps, and more. With that in mind, it is important that all these groups receive representation. Textbox 3.1 offers sample criteria that might be used by the school librarian when selecting library materials for diverse audiences.

As current and/or future school librarians, let us remember here that "diversity . . . is about inclusion of ideas, lifestyles, races, religions, abilities, socioeconomic classes, languages, employee status and age. It means everyone gets to sit at the table" (Culpepper, 2005, 32).

Materials Evaluation

Much of the evaluation of future library resources and equipment comes under selection criteria as covered earlier. To illustrate, a particular medium under consideration for purchase needs to fit the needs of the projected audience (in this case, students and faculty). This may mean looking at reading/viewing/listening levels of the medium; its

Answer the following questions:

1. Are these tablets simple enough to be used by very young students as well as older ones?
2. Are these tablets affordable for the school library?
3. Are these tablets durable (e.g. can they be used by many students for many years without needing repair)?

If the answer to ALL of the above questions is yes, continue below.

If the answer to ANY of the above questions is no, look for another set of tablets.

Answer the following questions:

1. Do the tablets have a warranty?
2. Do the tablets have clear directions for use either in print and/or on the Internet?
3. Are the tablets light enough for students to carry in their backpacks?
4. Is there a carrying case provided for each tablet?
5. Are these tablets large enough for all students to be able to read the print on them?
6. Are these tablets in color and with sound?
7. Can the students take pictures and videos with these new tablets?
8. Are these tablets readable in direct sunlight?
9. Can these tablets handle a variety of operating systems?
10. Do these tablets have a USB port?
11. Do these tablets have quick response time?
12. Are the tablets WiFi compatible?
13. Is there a wide variety of educational apps for these tablets?
14. Are these educational apps free or inexpensive?

If the answer to ALL of the above questions is yes, consider purchasing a set of these tablets for your K-9 school library

If the answer to ANY of the above questions is no, consider looking for another set of tablets.

Figure 3.4. Hardware Selection Flowchart

format; how the item fits with the learning styles, cultural backgrounds, maturity, and interest levels of the intended audience; how faculty plans to use the item in question; and how students might access the medium. Let's use an example of high school seniors in a career and technology class as an example. These students (the audience) have a wide range of learning styles, cultures, reading levels, and so on. So we know that whatever the medium obtained, it must be able to meet a variety of learner conditions and skill sets. Next, the instructor is asking his students to obtain information on careers of interest to each of them (how faculty plans to use the item in question). Thus, the

TEXTBOX 3.1
SAMPLE SELECTION CRITERIA: DIVERSITY

Does this medium characterize a particular group of people?

Socioeconomic
Cultural/Ethnicity
Race
Religion
Language
Sexual Orientation
Exceptionalities (Disabilities—Physical and Mental, Illnesses, Gifted)
Age
Geographical
Etc.

Is the medium a positive or negative representation of a specific group or community and its values?

Does this medium reinforce a belief in equality? Address a distinct group and its connection to society at large?

Is the medium biased? Bias free? That is, how does this medium's creator handle diversity?

Is the medium in the needed language?

Does this medium also offer information on other dissimilar populations?

Is the medium written in a minority-neutral manner?

Are there federal, state, or private grants or other funding sources available for the purchase of this and similar media?

Are there organizations or individuals available to support the use of this medium and/or discuss it with your students?

Once the item has been read/heard/viewed, are there museums (for example, the National Underground Railroad Freedom Center), archives, or other field trips that might supplement the information obtained through use of this item?

Are supplemental materials for this particular subject area/group available (through bibliographies, diversity organizations, etc.)?

Can this medium be used with more than one diverse group?

Does this medium show a diverse group interacting with other diverse groups?

Are interactions among/between this group's members portrayed in a realistic or stereotypical manner?

Are the history, settings, characters, illustrations, language, and story depicted in this work represented in a positive and accurate manner?

Human beings can be a member of more than one diverse group. What groups are represented in this medium, and are any of the identified individuals portrayed as being diverse in more than one way?

Are multiple perspectives recognized in this medium?

Are diverse individuals, as pictured in this medium, the problem, the solution, or both?

Who is shown in this work—a group's heroes or common people?

Is this item written by a member of the group depicted in the work or by an individual of another culture, ethnicity, age, race, or other diversity? Does who wrote the medium influence how characters, and so on, are portrayed; that is, are the diverse individuals in the medium portrayed as tokens or as real people with real problems and issues?

Source: Bishop 2005; Butler and Cunningham 1996; KidsSource Online 2009; Kwanzaa 2013; National Underground Railroad Freedom Center 2012.

format of the resource must be able to support knowledge acquisition on careers that the seniors are considering for their future. Since these careers can also vary widely, a good format for such information might be a career database, accessible in the library and/or at home online on the library's web page. In this case, the school librarian would now use these generated criteria to search for a database that might support all the requirements of the class. Subsequently, when evaluating a library's current collection, more specifications may be added.

It is easiest for the school librarian to automatically appraise the current collection as he or she works with it. In that way, obsolete or deteriorating media can be removed (see the Weeding section later in this chapter) as soon as possible, and the value of the item to the collection (what is being currently used as compared to what is just taking up space on the shelf) can be determined quickly (through circulation statistics and observations of in-library or online use).

Next, we look to the actual procurement process.

ACQUISITION OF LIBRARY MATERIALS AND EQUIPMENT

"Acquisitions is the process of selecting, ordering, and receiving materials for library or archival collections by purchase, exchange, or gift" (American Library Association

2013a, 1). When looking to acquire library materials and/or equipment, questions to consider once we know what we want include the following:

- How are we planning on acquiring this medium: purchase, interlibrary loan, through networking?
- Have we found a trusted vendor who can provide this item to us?
- Do we already own the item?
- Did we previously order it?
- Is it available for purchase at what we consider to be a reasonable price?
- Is there money in the budget to purchase this item?
- Do we have all the correct information (author, title, model number, ISBN, or whatever is necessary) to order the exact item that we want?
- Can we purchase this medium already cataloged and/or processed?
- When will we be able to receive the item?
- Have we kept records of all acquisition information?
- If hardware, can we obtain a contract to send back or have repaired any equipment that may suffer damage or become broken?

In addition, once the item has been ordered and received, we would want to check it against the original order to make sure that we received what we asked for, and also to make sure that we received the item in optimum condition.

MAINTENANCE OF LIBRARY MATERIALS AND EQUIPMENT

Oftentimes when we think about maintenance, we think of the hardware housed and used in the library: computers, handhelds, projectors, and more. However, we can also look at this in terms of our face-to-face (print and nonprint collection) and digital materials.

Proactive or preventive media maintenance involves retaining all warranties, purchasing information, manuals, and any other records about a particular medium in an easily accessible place for future reference. Additionally, it entails inventorying all items periodically, training faculty and staff to use hardware and software properly, repairing all damaged media, and keeping media in the proper storage bins, on the right shelves, and so on (i.e., storing them properly).

Given the repair issue and various mediums, for example, a projector might need to be sent out for repair either to the vendor or to a district technology person, while a print item could be repaired by the library assistant with book binding tape. It is also possible that the technology specialist would be contacted to turn off the filter so that certain websites needed to support a class were accessible to said class. While not really a repair as such, this last example demonstrates something that needs fixing or changing in order to obtain the desired selection. Although what is maintained and how it is maintained can vary based on the school district and library and what media is used, housed, or accessible within its boundaries, the criteria for maintenance are also something that may be found in school library policies and procedures manuals.

WEEDING

Another important section of the library policies and procedures manual is that which deals with weeding. Items in the school library collection (no matter the format) are usually weeded for similar reasons: they are outdated, in poor physical condition, no longer used in the curriculum, inaccurate, or not age appropriate (or inappropriate for your school clientele on another basis), or they have not been checked out for a long period of time (usually several years). Items likely to be retained in the collection (even though some of the preceding criteria might apply) include classics; state, regional, and local history; school yearbooks and similar publications; and media in need of reclassification. Hardware, such as computers and projectors, can also be weeded (or saved, as in the case of a piece of antique equipment).

The following figures illustrate general reasons a school librarian might consider when weeding a book (figure 3.5) or movie (figure 3.6), deselecting a website (figure 3.7), and removing hardware, in this case a VCR (figure 3.8), from the school library collection. Please note that criteria in any of these figures can be substituted or deleted, depending on your particular situation. All school libraries, their communities, and their clientele are not the same; therefore, weeding criteria may also differ.

In addition when weeding, it is best to

- always officially withdraw every weeded item from the collection. This includes revising your online catalog and marking the physical copy in such a manner that all who see it will recognize that it is no longer part of the library collection.
- document why you are weeding an item—no matter the medium. This will come in handy when a diligent community member spies half an old science book in the school trash, rescues it, and returns it to you, even though you have written "withdrawn" in large capital letters all over the book!
- recognize that not all items deserve to remain in the school library, even if they are in good shape.
- discard the withdrawn item in a suitable manner. This may be throwing it away, sending it to a more appropriate school environment (for example, sending a resource from the elementary to the middle school, if elementary students are not deemed mature enough to handle the item), giving it to teachers who still want to use it, or selling it.

Weeding is not a bad thing; it is important for the growth of the school library collection. Shelves full of unusable items mean a less-used library with little room to store any newly purchased resources.

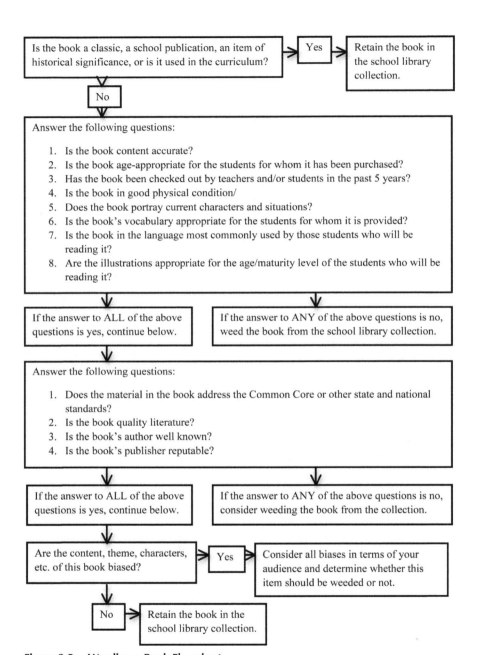

Figure 3.5. Weeding a Book Flowchart

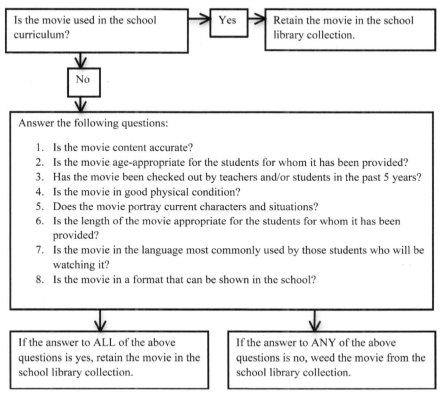

Figure 3.6. Weeding a Movie Flowchart

TECHNOLOGY PLANS

A technology plan centers "on integrating technology into the teaching and learning process to transform the way teachers teach and students learn" (Missouri Department of Elementary and Secondary Education 2013, 1). Thus, teaching and learning may be enhanced by the use of technological tools and students prepared to better function in a technology-focused world (Picciano 2011). While such a plan is normally separate from a library policies and procedures manual, it is included here (1) to illustrate the similarities between the two, (2) because a school librarian is often a member of a technology planning committee, and (3) because the school library of the 2000s is commonly a major area for access to and the use of technology in the school.

Customary items in a school technology plan include the following: mission statement or introduction, technology needs assessment, goals and objectives, hardware and software plan(s) (selection, evaluation, acquisition) and budget(s), needed

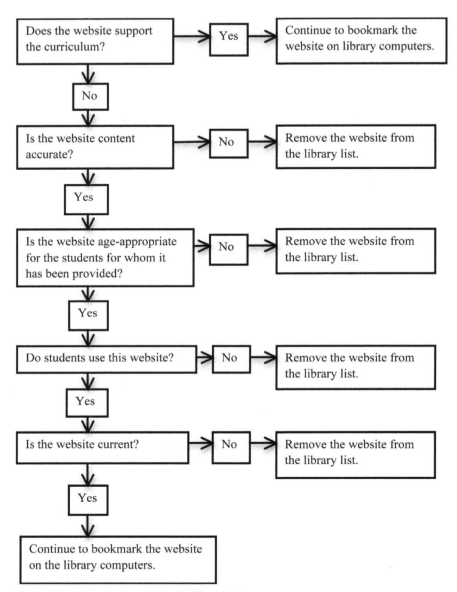

Figure 3.7. Deselecting a Website Flowchart

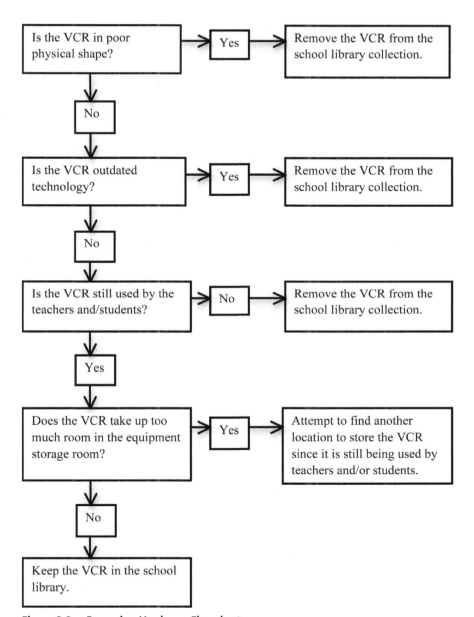

Figure 3.8. Removing Hardware Flowchart

personnel and descriptions, staff development, acceptable use policy (AUP), specialized growth strategies, process for plan evaluation, and how the plan will be communicated to all stakeholders (school administration, technology specialists, school librarians, faculty, and interested others) (Missouri Department of Elementary and Secondary Education 2013; Network Support Services Branch 2008; Picciano 2011; WhatIs.com 2013). You will note that several of those items in the technology plan (for example, selection/evaluation plans and budgets, and, in some cases, an AUP) are also included in many school library policies and procedures manuals (see discussion earlier in this chapter).

KEY CONCEPTS FROM THIS CHAPTER

- All school libraries need a policies and procedures manual.
- The policies and procedures manual sets forth those things needed to run all (or most) aspects of the school library.
- Common parts of a policies and procedures manual include
  - introduction/mission statement;
  - goals and objectives;
  - collection development policy, which includes
    - selection tools and criteria,
    - acquisitions,
    - gifts,
    - maintenance, and
    - weeding;
  - acceptable use policy.
- All types of media (print, software, hardware, and digital) can be selected and evaluated for inclusion in the school library collection.
- An important selection tool is the review.
- Other selection tools include
  - commercial catalogs (print and online);
  - advertisements (print and online);
  - word of mouth;
  - lists (from organizations and individuals);
  - demonstrations;
  - tutorials.
- Selection criteria vary depending on the
  - format;
  - subject;
  - audience;
  - creator/author;
  - quality;

- ○ currency;
- ○ cost;
- ○ durability;
- ○ whatever the prospective user and/or school librarian believes is necessary in that item.
- Recognition of diversity in collection, audience, and all programming and services is essential in today's school library.
- Library media are often evaluated according to selection criteria.
- Library acquisitions represent the selection, purchase, and receipt of media.
- Be a proactive media maintenance person.
- School library materials and equipment are weeded because the media are
  - ○ obsolete;
  - ○ damaged;
  - ○ no longer taught in the classroom;
  - ○ have not been checked out for a long period of time;
  - ○ erroneous;
  - ○ inappropriate for the age/maturity level of the school's audience.
- Technology plans deal specifically with the school's technology needs. They are similar in scope to the school library policies and procedures manual.

Coming in chapter 4: "Follow the Money."

DISCUSSION QUESTIONS

1. Why does a school library need a policies and procedures manual?
2. What criteria might you use to support the weeding of six copies of *Dr. Zhivago* from the high school library?
3. Identify how technology planning is accomplished in a school district with which you are familiar. Who are the main participants in the planning process? How might the planning process for this district be improved?
4. Should a school library inventory be done in an open (where collection remains in use during inventory) or closed (where collection is closed to all users during inventory) environment? Why?

ACTIVITIES

1. Break into small groups by the type of school library you are in or would like to be in: K–12, elementary, middle school, high school. Choose a medium (book, e-book, DVD, Internet site, computer software, multimedia). Develop a set of criteria that you would use in your selected school library environment,

in order to select the best medium possible. Take about 10 minutes to discuss this in small group. Take notes. Report in large group.

2. Select a K–12 school library or computer lab. Observe students interact with technology in this area for at least one hour. Consider how what you have observed might impact future technology purchases.

3. View an educational video online or from your local school library. Evaluate the video, answering the following: (a) bibliographic data (author, copyright date, title, place of publication, publisher); (b) brief summary of video; (c) video genre (your opinion); (d) outstanding features of video; (e) ages/grade levels you recommend view this item; (f) why students might like/dislike the video; (g) whether you would recommend it to students and faculty and/or purchase it for your school library; (h) anything else you consider important about this medium. You may also choose to look for published reviews of said video; compare what real-life reviewers say to your opinion/video evaluation.

4. In small groups, discuss what makes your student body (or one that you are familiar with, if you are not currently in a K–12 school setting) diverse: (a) Rural or urban? (b) Cultures/ethnicity? (c) Religions? (d) Exceptionalities? (e) Gender/sexual preferences? (f) Other? Report in large group.

REFERENCES

Abel, M. 1979. "What Makes a Good Review? Ten Experts Speak." *Top of the News* (Winter): 146–152.

Alabama Department of Education. 2008. "Alabama's School Library Media Handbook for the 21st Century Learner." alex.state.al.us/librarymedia/Library Media Handbook.pdf.

Amazon. 2013. "Books at Amazon." http://www.amazon.com/s/ref=nb_sb_noss?url=search-alias%3Dstripbooks&field-keywords=

America Reads Spanish. 2009. *Essential Guide to Spanish Reading for Children and Young Adults*. Coral Gables, Florida: Trade Commission of Spain.

American Library Association. 2013a. "Acquisitions." http://www.ala.org/tools/atoz/profresourcesacquisitions/acquisitions.

———. 2013b. "Diversity in Collection Development: An Interpretation of the Library Bill of Rights." http://www.ala.org/advocacy/intfreedom/librarybill/interpretations/diversity collection.

———. 2013c. "Library Bill of Rights." http://www.ala.org/advocacy/intfreedom/librarybill.

Arizona State Library, Archives and Public Records. 2015. "Collection Development Training Policies." http://apps.azlibrary.gov/cdt/colldev.aspx.

Association for Library Service to Children. 2013. "Caldecott Medal and Honor Books, 1938–Present." http://www.ala.org/alsc/awardsgrants/bookmedia/caldecottmedal/caldecotthonors/caldecottmedal.

Baltimore County Public Schools. n.d. "Selection Criteria for School Library Media Center Collections." bcpslis.pbworks.com/w/file/fetch/68240711/.

Bishop, Kay. 2005. "Multicultural Literature and the School Library Media Center." *Educational Media and Technology Yearbook 2005*. Westport, Conn.: Libraries Unlimited: 171–176.

Bound to Stay Bound. 2011. "Bound to Stay Bound Bookstore." http://www.btsb.com/.

Bowling Green Area Schools. n.d. "Instructional Materials Selection Policy." bgcs.noacsc.org/LinkClick.aspx?fileticket=KaAyA3GG9FA=&...

Bradshaw Primary. n.d. "Day to Day in Bradshaw Library." http://www.schools.nt.edu.au/bradshaw/bradbasics/library/libday.html.

Butler, Rebecca P. and Cunningham, Catherine. 1996. "The Tortoise and the Hare or CD-ROMs vs. the Internet." *The Proceedings of the Consortium of College and University Media Centers.* San Diego, Calif.: The Consortium of College and University Media Centers: 5–22.

Carter, Betty. 2000. *Best Books for Young Adults.* 2nd ed. Chicago, Ill.: American Library Association.

Culpepper, Gwenne. 2005. "Perspective: Diversity Matters." *University of Northern Iowa Today: Learning to Make Things Better for Others* 89 (2): 32.

Discovery Education. 2014. "Transforming Teaching and Learning: Who We Are." http://www.discoveryeducation.com//who-we-are/about-discovery-education.cfm .

Ford, Deborah B. 2013. "Some of the Best Books, K–12: An Internet Hotlist on Best Books of the Year." http://www.kn.att.com/wired/fil/pages/listbestboode.html.

Indian Prairie Community Unit School District 204. n.d. "Library Media Center." http://clow.ipsd.org/lmc_program.html.

———. 2006. "Library Media Center Policy and Procedure Manual Indian Prairie Community Unit School District 204." http://r.search.yahoo.com/_ylt=A0LEVvdWqfxUuE0A2z MnnIlQ;_ylu=X3oDMTEzMW0yNTZkBHNlYwNzcgRwb3MDMQRjb2xvA2JmMQ R2dGlkA1lIUzAwMV8x/RV=2/RE=1425873366/RO=10/RU=http%3a%2f%2fclow. ipsd.org%2fdocuments%2flmc_manual_revisions%2fLMC_Procedure_Manual.pdf/ RK=0/RS=zNdWnxFj8Geu98yN4SNSkunofsU-.

KidsSource Online. 2009. "Gender Issues in Children's Literature." http://www.kidsource.com/education/gender.issues.L.A.html#contents.

Kwanzaa. 2013. "Fundamental Questions about Kwanzaa: An Interview." http://www.official kwanzaawebsite.org/faq.shtml.

Library Media Connection. March/April 2015. "Featured Reviews." http://www.librarymedia connection.com/lmc/?page=featured_review.

Library Media Services. 2005. *Marion County School Library Media Handbook.* Ocala, Fla.: Marion County Public Schools.

Merriam-Webster Online. 2013a. "Mimeograph." http://www.merriam-webster.com/dictionary/mimeograph.

———. 2013b. "Policy." http://www.merriam-webster.com/dictionary/policy.

———. 2013c. "Procedure." http://www.merriam-webster.com/dictionary/procedure.

Missouri Department of Elementary and Secondary Education. n.d. "Six-Step Process in Creating a Technology Plan." http://dese.mo.gov/quality-schools/education-technology/six-step-process-creating-technology-plan.

NASA. 2014. "NASA Education: For Educators." http://www.nasa.gov/audience/foreduca tors/#.VKBpOf8w6U.

National Underground Railroad Freedom Center. 2012. Home page. http://freedomcenter.org/.

Opensource.com. n.d. "Discover an Open Source World: What Is Open Education?" http://opensource.com/resources/what-open-education?sc_cid=70160000000dW5rAAE.

Pappas, Marjorie L. 2005. "Virtual School Library Media Center Management Manual." *School Library Media Activities Monthly* XXI (5).

Picciano, Anthony G. 2011. *Educational Leadership and Planning for Technology.* 5th ed. New York, N.Y.: Pearson.

Quail Valley Middle School. n.d. "Library." http://campuses.fortbendisd.com/campuses/qvms/ActivityDetail.cfm?ActivityIndex=10295.

School Library Journal. 2013. "SLJ Reviews." http://www.slj.com/category/books-media/reviews/.

———. 2015. "SLJ Reviews." http://www.slj.com/category/reviews/.

Thomson, A. 1991. "How to Review a Book." *Canadian Library Journal* 48: 6.

VOYA. 2015. "VOYA's Perfect Tens 2014." http://www.voyamagazine.com/2015/01/24/voyas-perfect-tens-2014/.

"Wake County Public Schools Internet and E-Mail Permission Form." n.d. http://www.ncsu.edu/ligon/au.policy.html.

Welch, Rollie James. 2011. *A Core Collection for Young Adults.* 2nd ed. New York, N.Y.: Neal-Schuman Publishers.

WhatIs.com. 2013. "Acceptable Use Policy (AUP)." http://whatis.techtarget.com/definition/acceptable-use-policy-AUP.

4

Follow the Money

In the school library, as in almost all 21st century institutions (educational and otherwise), money and materials continue to be important factors in maintaining and improving programming, services, resources, personnel, and even library supplies. How to obtain the money to support the library may be the purview of the school administration, but you, as the school librarian, may also have a part in this. Ways to obtain the funds and items necessary to support the library can come from (1) a budget (most often controlled by the school administration), which could include general fund money, capital outlay (budgeted money for projects), or special state and federal funds; (2) grant monies; (3) monetary gifts from community, parent-teacher organizations, and others; (4) librarians earning extra money running book fairs, a school store, a student coffee shop, and/or similar activities; and (5) librarians scrounging up "freebies" from federal and state governments, community and professional organizations, and, in some cases, purchasing things needed for the library with their own money. This chapter focuses on three of the primary ways to obtain money or materials and equipment: budgets, grants, and gifts.

BUDGETS

In the 21st century, many school librarians are finding their budgets diminishing. This can result in fewer resources and services, decreased library work days, and attempts to siphon off library money for other needed school resources. Thus, a good budget is a must—whether the administration or business office oversees its use, or you, as the school librarian, are in control of it (a less likely scenario). The next few pages briefly go over some of the budget types that may be used in your school library. (Please note that these are listed starting with those most commonly used.)

Line Item

The line item budget assigns definite amounts of money to particular areas or lines. Thus, for the school library, there might be an amount assigned for books, another for online databases, a third for DVDs, and so on. There is little flexibility with this type of budget; however, it is a detailed budget that lists those resources necessary to successfully run a school library in a given year, and it is common in many school libraries. Figure 4.1 is an example of a line item budget.

Books	$2000.00
Periodicals	$500.00
DVDs	$700.00
Online Databases	$1000.00
Equipment (new)	$5000.00
Equipment (repair/replacement)	$1500.00
Supplies	$500.00
Furniture	$1500.00
Membership to Professional Organizations (librarian)	$300.00
Conferences (librarian and/or paraprofessional)	$500.00
Total	$13500.00

Figure 4.1. Sample Line Item Budget

Object/Expenditure

Object or expenditure budgets are actually detailed line item budgets. Figure 4.2 demonstrates such a budget, using new hardware as an example.

New Technology Budget, 2014-2015	
Circulation Computer	$1500.00
5 iPads with Retina Displays	$2500.00
40-inch LCD Television	$600.00
Flat Panel Television Cart	$400.00
Total	$5000.00

Figure 4.2. Sample Object/Expenditure Budget

Lump Sum

A lump sum budget (see figure 4.3) is simply when the administration and/or school board awards a sum to the school librarian to use as he or she sees fit. In this case, the librarian chooses how much to spend on books, databases, needed equipment, even oftentimes supplies, furniture, and so on. While less complicated to the administration, this can be difficult for a new librarian, who may have no idea how much will be needed in certain areas. For example, a new librarian might decide that the print collection is adequate for the next year and choose to spend the entire sum on technology. This may seem fine, for example, until a classroom teacher asks for print support for a particular project (and none is available), the newly funded Internet and database sources are formats that do not work well for certain students, or there is little or no print material available during an electrical outage. On the other hand, when a library is inundated with a particular resource, having a budget that will allow the librarian to focus on acquiring other things during a particular year can be quite helpful.

School Library Budget 2014-2015 School Year	$13,500.00

Figure 4.3. Sample Lump Sum Budget

Program

Program budgets (see figure 4.4 for an example) stress programming/activity needs, rather than individual resources. Library resources normally seen in budgets, including technology (hardware and software), print materials, supplies, and even conferences, may thus be built into each of the program areas (speakers, public library visits, poetry slams, etc.) listed in this budget type.

Author Visit #1	$1200.00
Author Visit #2	$700.00
Illustrator Visit	$1800.00
Poetry Slam	$300.00
Coffee House Fridays	$1000.00
Busing to Public Library of Students to Obtain Library Cards	$500.00
Second Language-Learner Literacy Initiative	$5000.00
Art in the Library Activity	$300.00
Winter Holiday Reading Festival	$700.00
Summer Reading Program	$1500.00
International Day	$500.00
Total	$13,500.00

Figure 4.4. Sample Program Budget

Performance

While not commonly used in most school libraries, the performance budget "relates units of output (accomplishments) with inputs (budgeted resources)" (Georgia Department of Education, n.d., 6). This means that the results of library endeavors are grouped into distinct tasks and then related to a library's materials, equipment, facility, and so on. Figure 4.5 shows a sample of a possible school library performance budget.

Task	Resource	Cost per Resource	# of Resources per school year	Total
Programming	Library Events	Varies from $200.00 to 1500.00	15	$5000.00
Reference/Information/Teaching	Student and Teacher Questions and Requests to Librarian and Paraprofessional	$10.00	600	$6000.00
Selection and Acquisition	Materials, Equipment, and Internet-Based Items	50	20	$1000.00
Other	Supplies	$10.00-$100.00	75	$1500.00

Figure 4.5. Sample Performance Budget

Zero Based

With zero-based budgets (ZZBs), each department or area of a school (in this case the school library would be seen as a department) must consider its goals and objectives in relation to the funds that it believes are needed for the coming year. Thus, the school librarian might use a ZZB to put forth ways to reach the library's goals and objectives. The school administration would then rank all departments' ZZBs and make a decision as to how much money is allotted each area. With the ZZB, departments are judged on merit; thus, they compete for the same pot of money and can be awarded any amount that the administration determines is needed (Georgia Department of Education, n.d.; Government Finance Officers Association, n.d.; Holmes 2011). Figure 4.6 show a sample zero-based budget.

School Department: School Library

Benefits of School Library Proposal: This budget proposal allows for school library growth in print and non-print resources, as well as services, to update and expand on curriculum and supplementary needs that support our school mission. This is for all school library clientele: students, faculty, administration, staff, and (in some cases) community members.

Proposal Costs:
    Print Materials: $2500.00
    Software and Internet Resources: $1700.00
    Technology/Equipment: $6500.00
    Supplies/Facilities: $2000.00
    Librarian/Paraprofessional Dues and Conferences: $800.00
    Total: $13,500.00

Results of Denying Proposal: The school library would be in maintenance mode, which means that there would be no new support to student curriculum, student and faculty services, or supplementary needs for school clientele.

Figure 4.6. Sample Zero-Based Budget

Performing, Programming, Budgeting System

Planning, programming, budgeting systems (PPBSs) have been around since the 1950s. Often used by federal government agencies, PPBSs can also be used in school situations, although this is less common. There are four basic stages to a PPBS. According to Lunenberg (2010, 4) the first stage, Specifying Goals, is "analyzing and specifying the basic goals in each major activity or program area . . . [answering] . . . such questions as "What is our basic purpose or mission?" and "What, specifically, are we trying to accomplish?" Stage 2, Search for Relevant Alternatives, focuses on "total costs and benefits of various [programming] alternatives." The third stage, Measure the Cost of the Program for Several Years, involves just that; it is basically a form of the long-range budget. The last stage, Evaluate the Output of Each Program, "enables school administrators to compare program proposals, relate them to current activities, evaluate them in terms of priority, and then to increase or decrease allocations of resources to them." A question that is answered with this stage might be "How effectively and efficiently are we achieving our goals?" (Lunenberg 2010, 4). School administrators and librarians who wish to tie the school library's goals and objectives, as well as planning and programming needs, completely into funding may find the PPBS their budget of choice. However, this can be a complicated and time-consuming budget to use (Khan 2010). See figure 4.7 for a sample PPBS budget.

Budget Planning Additions

Long-range planning can be applied to almost any type of budget. Basically, the budget planners estimate how much funding will be needed in the next several years, and that estimate is built into a particular budget. Using a long-range planning budget can get complicated, since prices, funds, and so on can vary from those estimated when the plan was developed.

"Site-based management (SBM) is a general term for the reallocation of some decision-making authority from the district level to the school level" (Monk, Pijanowski, and Hussain 1997). To extrapolate this further to the school library, site-based management budgeting can be seen as the reallocation of selected monetary decision making from that of the school administrator to that of the library administrator/ school librarian. With site-based management budgets, the school librarian plans and defends his or her own budget for the library, highlighting current student and teacher needs, as well as postulating future needs. Such a budget could be applied to any other budget type; in this case, the librarian is creating the budget, rather than an administrator or the school board.

Formulas use "a customary or set form or method" (*Merriam-Webster Online* 2013, 1). Thus, a formula budget for a school library might assign a particular amount of money, per each pupil in the school, to the library for resources, services, and more. Thus, the student population, in this case, would define what the library budget would be. A formula budget could be applied to other budget types, including line, object/expenditure, and lump. Figure 4.8 demonstrates how a formula budget might work.

Author Visits' PPBS Budget, 2014-2019: $9500.00	
Goals	(1) Support school literacy initiative. (2) Introduce new authors to students. (3) Improve student reading scores.
Programming Alternatives	(1) Provide a series of literature-related events throughout each school year: media-talker (talks books, games, DVDs, etc.); book fair; gaming demonstration; publisher visit; field trip to an author's home; other as requested by students: $1900.00. (2) Bring in two authors per year; will encourage students to read that author's works and works of authors who write similar books: $1900.00. (3) Run a reading contest (broaden concept of reading to include books; magazines; newspapers; online video game directions, clues, etc.; visual reading [movies]; and more: $1900.00. (4) Combination of 1-3 above: $1900.00.
Long-Range Budget	$9500.00 ($1900.00 per year for five years)
Output Evaluation	(1) Consider each of the programming alternatives: literature-related events, author visits, reading contest, a combination of the three above. (2) Contrast them to current school library programming: librarian demonstrating new technologies and introducing new materials. (3) Prioritize alternatives: combination, author visits, literature-related events, reading contest. (4) Determine monetary allotments per alternative per year: combination ($1000.00); author visits ($700.00), literature-related events ($150.00), reading contest ($50.00).

Figure 4.7.   Sample PPBS Budget

Number of students in the school, 2014-2015 school year: 2700.
Amount of money assigned to the library per each student: $5.00
Total Library Budget for 2014-2015 school year: $13,5000.00

Figure 4.8.   Sample Formula Budget

Budget Levels

The level at which a particular budget is maintained is also of importance to the school library and can be applied to almost any of the budget types just listed. For example, a *maintenance or continuity budget* is on the low end of budgeted funds, in that its purpose is to maintain things the way they are. This budget level does not take into account new materials and equipment or the fact that technology evolves. With this budget level, worn-out equipment might be repaired but obsolete equipment would not be replaced with newer models. With the *incremental* level of budget, there is more money with which to work. The incremental level of budget "is . . . based on projected changes in operations and conditions. It tends to lead to budgetary increases over time, as it takes last years' budget as a starting point for the coming year" (*Maine Townsmen* 1993, 1). (FYI, an issue with incremental budgets is that, since they consider the previous year's budget as a good starting point, they may be faulty if the last budget was inadequate.) A third type of budget level is *expansion*. As with the other two levels discussed here, the expansion level can be applied to many budget types. Expansion is just what this budget does; it expands/is made bigger when there is a need for such. This budget works well for large projects (example: remodeling or building a library).

There will be pros and cons to whatever type of budget your school applies to the library. Usually as the school librarian, you will be told what the amount of your budget is and the type will become apparent either when you see the budget or when your administrator tells you how to apply it to the resources, supplies, and equipment that the school library needs. Chances are that you may not have a say as to budget type or amount. Whatever the case, make sure that (1) you maintain records of all that you have spent (item, date spent, cost, vendors); (2) all acquisitions and expenditures occur within a particular year's purchasing cycle; (3) you spend your budget amount, not under or over the amount assigned to the school library; and (4) no other department's or program's expenses have mistakenly been assigned to the library account. (These last three steps can be determined by checking periodically with the school's financial office to confirm payments posted to the school library account.) Finally, you may wish to prepare a budget, early in the financial year, accentuating new programming, curricular, and materials needs, even if not required by your principal. Doing so will inform your administration of projected school library needs as you see them and could possibly help influence the budget amount that the library receives.

GRANTS

Grants come in all shapes and sizes. Prospective grantors can be public or private organizations, your school district, even your friends or strangers looking to support a good cause via a charitable website such as DonorsChoose.org. There are a multitude of books, websites, magazine articles, and more written about grants. The information in this chapter attempts to summarize important grant information for school librarians, as interpreted by this author.

Sample Grant-Writing Steps

The directions for grants vary from grant to grant and grantor to grantor. However, there are several common steps to consider when writing a grant. The first, and most important one, is to *follow all directions exactly as they are stated*. Why? Because, especially with longer grants, there may be more than one reader, and all grant readers may not read the same sections. Thus, if you say, "Go to Section IIB for this information" a particular reader may not have that section. In this case, he or she will not have all necessary material in order to properly judge your grant application. In addition, there may be many applicants for a single grant. Therefore, grantors are often looking for reasons to drop applications from the process; not following directions could be such a reason. For example, if the grant states that monetary awards only go to organizations that are U.S. 501(c)(3) or in some other way tax exempt, do not apply if that does not fit your school's criteria. Another important step is to *submit your grant proposal on time* (or early). Grantors may not even bother to read late proposals. There are also several commonsense steps to follow when preparing a grant proposal: for example, *define specific terminology* that you use; *spell out all acronyms the first time* that you use them (remember that grant readers may not have the same background as you and may not know what you mean by a particular term or acronym); *keep records and copies of the proposal*; *use a consistent voice*; *provide examples*, when needed; and *edit the grant application and proposal*. (As a former reader for a major national library grant, I can tell you that grammatical, spelling, and formatting errors do matter. When there are many grants to read, those with several editing errors are easily tossed in favor of clean grant proposals.)

Following is a listing of some of the customary criteria asked for in many grant applications.

- Description of proposed project
- Project goals and objectives
- Plan of action
- Project personnel
- Project facility
- Possible local resources
- Budget (clear and detailed budgets are recommended.)
- Expected results
- Reporting of results to grantor (and possibly others)
- Project evaluation
- Letters of support
- Time line (this can include due dates, reading dates, mailing dates, etc.)
- Supporting documents
- Supervisor and applicant signatures
- How the awarding of the grant to an applicant might support the grantor's mission. (Developing and Writing Grant Proposals, n.d.; Gerli 2007; Office of Research and Sponsored Projects 2012)

Also important to remember is that some grants require the applicant to find matching contributions from another entity (Picciano 2011), whether it be the school, a community group, or another grant. If that is the case, only write the grant if you are also willing to find equivalent funds from another source.

Types of Grants

Public or Private Organizations

This grouping of grants represents the largest area for obtaining funding. Such grants can be from the federal, state, or local governments; from major corporations or individuals; from local stores; and more. For example, Bill and Melinda Gates Foundation grants could be several thousands of dollars (Bill and Melinda Gates Foundation 2013) while a grant from the local Walmart might range from $250 to $2,500 (Walmart 2013). Many of these grants are found online. For local commercial establishments, it may also be possible to walk into the store and ask for an application.

School District Grants

Oftentimes school districts may offer grants to their faculty, for example, through educational foundations. Such grants can be less complicated than some major grants, but the district type of grants may also not award as much money. That said, writing a school district education foundation grant is a good way to get started on the grant-writing process, and these grants are more likely to be awarded, due to fewer applicants and the fact that the applicants are often known by the grantor/ granting district. Examples of such granting opportunities include the Des Plaines District 62 Foundation (2014), the McHenry High School District 156 Foundation (FindTheCompany 2013), and the Chicago Foundation for Education (2011).

Charitable Websites

Here is an example of how a charitable website works: "DonorsChoose.org is an online charity that makes it easy for anyone to help students in need. Public school teachers from every corner of America post classroom project requests on our site, and you can give any amount to the project that most inspires you" (DonorsChoose. org 2013, 1). Another such website, AdoptAClassroom.org, states that they partner "donors with teachers so you can have funds to purchase critical resources and materials for your classroom" (AdoptAClassroom.org 2013, 1). With "grants" such as these, you may have several grantors. In actuality, these ways of obtaining funding are less like a grant and more like a gift.

Grants for Libraries

Grants that school libraries obtain can come under any of the previous three categories. Some federal grants include the Institute of Museum and Library Services'

Laura Bush 21st Century Librarian Program (2013) and the Laura Bush Foundation for America's Libraries (n.d.). A number of national grants—for instance, on the "Awards and Grants" page of the American Association of School Librarians website (2013), the LibraryWorks "Grant and Funding" page (n.d.), and the Grant Wrangler "Library Grants and Resources" page (2013)—can be found on the World Wide Web. There are also many statewide grants available, for example, from the Illinois State Library (n.d.) and/or from state professional organizations (Illinois School Library Media Association 2010).

Lastly, remember that there are many people who may be able to help you write a grant: colleagues, administration, the business manager, skilled community leaders, and so on. If you are unsure about your grant-writing skills, check around and see who might have written grants in the past or might be willing to work with you.

GIFTS

Library materials and equipment, whether print or nonprint, digital or analog, online or physically available, can be obtained in many ways, through purchase, interlibrary loan, rent (sometimes used for acquiring current or expensive technology), exchanges, free (example: U.S. federal government documents), or as gifts.

School librarians are often quite creative in how they obtain gifts. They may instigate a program where students, parents, and others can "gift" new books or DVDs to the library for someone's birthday or work out an agreement with a vendor that for every so many books sold during a book fair, the librarian gets to pick out one free one for the library. They may ask local business people for items, pick up freebies at professional conferences, or find online sites that will donate materials. Sometimes people just walk in to the library with a gift as well. Perhaps it is a collection of several years' worth of *National Geographic* to which they had a subscription; maybe they have just cleaned out a child's movie collection and feel that the school library could use some of those items. Who knows! The issue here is what do you do with those things that someone donates to your library?

The best way to handle gifts that you, the school librarian, have not planned on receiving is to be prepared with a gift policy. Sometimes gift policies are included in a school library policies and procedures manual, usually in the acquisitions section (more on policies in general can be found in chapter 3). Sometimes they are not. Some libraries have a form that the library and the giver fill out; again, some do not.

So, what should go in a gift policy? The simplest way to consider gifts to the school library is to apply the same selection criteria as that used for any other item obtained for the library in question. In addition, the following are important things that might be included in a school library gift policy: (1) physical conditions of items that the library will accept (example: the library will not accept books with missing pages); (2) formats of items that the library will accept (example: the school library accepts gifts of new books, DVDs, and hand-held readers but not used computer software or popular magazines); (3) how the gift will be disposed of, if the library is unable to make use of it (example: media that do not fit library selection policy criteria are offered to teachers to make use of in their classrooms, placed in a library sale, or thrown away, if no one in the school has a use for them); (4) a statement that the school/library does not provide tax appraisal forms for donation purposes (example: the school library does not appraise donations); (5) a record of the donation (example: the library documents all donations and the donor in a spread sheet maintained on the head librarian's computer); and (6) an acknowledgment of each gift (example: all accepted donations will be acknowledged with a written thank-you letter) (Ann Arbor Public Schools, n.d.; Cassell 2005; Mamakating Library, n.d.). FYI, it is best to set a limit as to when the library will acknowledge a gift, say two weeks, so that donors have a record of their donation. Also, since most school libraries do not provide tax forms or estimate the worth of a donation, a thank-you letter is recommended for all gifts accepted by the library.

Figure 4.9 shows an example of what might go in a gift form that the school librarian and donor would fill out, upon receipt of a gift.

The best way to work with gifts that you do not expect is to plan ahead for this possibility; hence the gift policy and/or gift form.

KEY CONCEPTS FROM THIS CHAPTER

- Three important ways for school librarians to find funding are through budgets, grants, and gifts.
- Budgets are most often controlled by the school administration.
- The line item budget is currently used the most often in school libraries.
- It is best to prepare a budget early in the school year.
- Always follow grant directions carefully and send in the proposals on time.
- Keep records and copies of all grant applications and any corresponding information.
- School district grants are usually less complicated to apply for than are major public and private organization grants.
- Public and private organization grants often award more money than do school district grants.
- Check for grants specifically for libraries.
- If you are not a grant writer, ask for help from school colleagues, administration, the business manager, and skilled community leaders.
- Ways to obtain freebies to include
  ○ instigating a program to gift items to the library for a student's birthday or another important event;

Sample School Library

Address

Phone Number

Email

Donor Name: _____

Address: _____

Phone Number: _____

Email: _____

Donated Item/s (Format and Author/Title): _____

Condition of Donated Items: _____

I understand that my donation is now the property of Sample School Library and that they may dispose of this donation as they see fit. I also recognize that my donation will not be appraised.

Donor Signature _____

Date _____

Figure 4.9. Sample Gift Form

- working out an agreement with vendors that for every so many items purchased, the school library gets something free;
- asking community leaders/local business people for items;
- picking up free media at professional conferences;
- searching the web for online sites that provide free material.

- Make sure that your school library has a gift policy, and if none is available, create one.
- Accept only gifts that truly support the library's collection, programming, and service needs.
- Thank all donors in writing as soon as possible.

Coming in chapter 5: "Facilities."

DISCUSSION QUESTIONS

1. Based on the readings in this chapter, determine what type of budget is best for your school library or a school library of your choice (in your opinion)? What are your reasons for this recommendation?
2. What is the single most important rule to grant writing? Why?
3. Where would you go to obtain free materials for your library? Be creative.

ACTIVITIES

1. In a small group, discuss the budget types used in your schools. Determine which, if any, best support the library and why. Report in large group.
2. Search the web for at least three places that you might apply for a grant to support some aspect of your school library. What makes these good grant choices?
3. Imagine that you are in a very poor school. A well-meaning family hears that the library is in dire need, and they clean out their attic, basement, garage, and so on, delivering the accumulation of books, magazines, videos, and DVDs to the library. They are certain you will be ecstatic with their donation.
   - How do you deal with this influx of material—some of which is valuable to your library and some which is not?
   - How do you deal with the fact that some of the material is in good shape and some is not?
   - How do you deal with givers who are so proud of their gifts that they come into the school to "visit" them?
   - What would go into a gift policy that could help in such a situation?

REFERENCES

AdoptAClassroom.org. 2013. "How the Program Works." http://www.adoptaclassroom.org/aboutus.aspx?id=4.

American Association of School Librarians. 2013. "Awards and Grants." http://www.ala.org/aasl/awards.

Ann Arbor Public Schools. n.d. "Collection Development Policies and Procedures: Gift Policy." http://www.aaps.k12.mi.us/ins.libmedia/collection_development.

Bill and Melinda Gates Foundation. 2013. "Awarded Grants." http://www.gatesfoundation.org/How-We-Work/Quick-Links/Grants-Database.

Cassell, Kay Ann. 2005. "Handling Gift Books in Libraries: A View from the US." *New Library World* 106 (9/10).

Chicago Foundation for Education. 2011. "Overview." http://www.cfegrants.org/about/about-cfe-overview/.

Des Plaines District 62 Foundation. 2014. "The Mini-Grants Program." http://www.d62.org/d62foundation/grants.html.

Developing and Writing Grant Proposals. n.d. http://www.nmfs.noaa.gov/trade/howtodograntts.htm.

DonorsChoose.org. 2013. "How It Works." http://www.donorschoose.org/about.

FindTheCompany. 2013. "McHenry High School District 156 Foundation Inc." http://nonprofit-organizations.findthebest.com/l/278394/Mchenry-High-School-District-156-Foundation-Inc Overview.

Georgia Department of Education. n.d. "Chapter 32—Preparing Operating Budgets." http://www.doe.k12.ga.us/Finance-and-Business-Operations/Financial-Review/Pages/LUAS-Manual.aspx.

Gerli, Merete F. 2007. *How to Develop and Write a Grant Proposal.* Washington, D.C.: CRS Report for Congress.

Government Finance Officers Association. n.d. "Zero-Base Budgeting: Modern Experiences and Current Perspectives." www.gfoa.org/downloads/GFOAZeroBasedBudgeting.pdf.

Grant Wrangler. 2013. "Library Grants and Resources." http://www.grantwrangler.com/librarygrants.html.

Holmes, Ronald W. 2011. "How Can School Districts Benefit from a Zero-Based Budgeting Model?" http://theholmeseducationpost.com/2011/12/how-can-school-districts-benefit-from-a-zero-based-budgeting-model-2/.

Illinois School Library Media Association. 2010. "ISLMA Lauretta McCusker, O.P., D.L.S. Professional Development Grant." http://www.islma.org/mccusker.htm.

Illinois State Library. n.d. "Grant Programs." http://www.cyberdriveillinois.com/departments/library/grants/.

Institute of Museum and Library Services. 2013. "Call for Applications: FY 14 Laura Bush 21st Century Librarian Program." http://www.imls.gov/call_for_applications_fy_14_laura_bush_21st_century_librarian_program.aspx.

Khan, Mohammad. 2010. "Planning, Programming, Budgeting System Models (PPBS)." http://www.articlesbase.com/personal-finance-articles/planning-programming-and-budgeting-system-models-ppbs-2926704.html.

The Laura Bush Foundation for America's Libraries. n.d. Home page. http://www.laurabushfoundation.com/index.html.

LibraryWorks. n.d. "Grant and Funding." http://www.libraryworks.com/LW_Grants/Grants_0310.aspx.

Lunenburg, Fred C. 2010. "Systems of Budget Administration." *Focus on Colleges, Universities, and Schools* 4 (1): 1–8.

Maine Townsman. 1993. "A Beginner's Budget Glossary." http://www.memun.org/Schools Project/Resources/Budget/budget_gloss.htm.

Mamakating Library. n.d. "Policies and Forms." http://mamakatinglibrary.org/policies-forms/.

Merriam-Webster Online. 2013. "Formula." http://www.merriam-webster.com/dictionary/formula.

Monk, David H., Pijanowski, John C., and Hussain, Samon. 1997. "How and Where the Education Dollar Is Spent: Site-Based Management." http://futureofchildren.org/publications/journals/article/index.xml?journalid=52&articleid=277&sectionid=1825.

Office of Research and Sponsored Projects. 2012. *Handbook for Principal Investigators and Project Directors.* Edinburg, TX: The University of Texas-Pan American.

Picciano, Anthony G. 2011. *Educational Leadership and Planning for Technology.* 5th ed. Boston, MA: Pearson.

Walmart. 2013. "Local Giving Program." http://foundation.walmart.com/apply-for-grants/local-giving.

5

Facilities

According to Element 5.3 (Personal, Funding, and Facilities) of the ALA/AASL Standards for Initial Preparation of School Librarians, those individuals being educated as school librarians are to

> apply best practices related to planning, budgeting, and evaluating human, information, and physical resources. Candidates organize library facilities to enhance the use of information resources and services and to ensure equitable access to all resources for all users. Candidates develop, implement, and evaluate policies and procedures that support teaching and learning in school libraries." (National Council for Accreditation of Teacher Education 2010, 17)

Element 5.3 speaks directly to the school library facility, the subject of this chapter, as does the ninth common belief fostering school library programming (American Association of School Librarians 2009): "School libraries are essential to the development of learning skills. School libraries provide equitable physical and intellectual access to the resources and tools required for learning in a warm, stimulating, and safe environment" (13). (See chapter 2, "Standards and Guidelines," for more information on national and state school library benchmarks.) Thus in this chapter, we look to the school library facility, whether it be in the form of a library, a learning resource center, a learning commons, and so on, as a physical resource. (Please note that a learning commons, in addition to physical spaces accessible in the school building, can be "virtual spaces, which may be accessed from the library or anywhere in the school or at home 24/7" [Hamilton-Wentworth District School Board 2014, 1]. Many school libraries are rapidly evolving in the direction of the learning commons concept as they add online databases, accessible 24 hours a day from a variety of school- and home-based computers and other electronic devices;

digital reference librarians; and more.) Throughout this chapter, we will consider criteria which might be addressed when building or remodeling school libraries. In textbox 5.1, we look to the questions one might ask when going through the design or redesign of an elementary school library.

TEXTBOX 5.1
SAMPLE QUESTIONS TO ASK WHEN BUILDING OR REMODELING AN ELEMENTARY SCHOOL LIBRARY

- How can we design the library so that there is line of sight throughout the entire library, when the librarian or aide is located at the reference desk?
- Can we make sure that the traffic patterns in the library are wide enough to accommodate several students at a time?
- How can we make sure our facility is ADA (Americans with Disabilities Act) compliant?
- Where should we keep air filters? Hand sanitizer? The first aid kit?
- How do we moderate the sound levels in this building?
- Where should we locate the library classroom within the library facility as a whole?
- How high should the shelving be? The charge desk?
- Where should we keep the teachers' professional collection—in the main library or in the library workroom?
- What colors should we paint the walls; that is, what colors work best with young children?
- Is it worth it to put in a courtyard; for example, how would we use it for the library?
- How high should the furniture be, given that some of our patrons may be very young and very small?
- Should the main traffic pattern go by the circulation desk *and* the story-time areas?
- Should we build to accommodate physically handicapped students, when there are none currently in the student body?
- What type of lights work best in winter?
- Where should we place emergency walkie-talkies?
- Do we need our entrance and exit doors alarmed?
- Do we need a separate computer lab?
- Should we have a glass wall in the computer lab, so that we can see in it from the circulation desk?
- Where do we place the Smart Board?
- What furniture will best display student hobbies, crafts, and other things we use to feature various classes?
- We have been given a bank of computers for research purposes. Where will we place them?

- How do we deal with sound issues, since our library is an open-space concept?
- Where should we locate the reference area?
- Should there be a bathroom in the library for the young students? A sink?
- Do we want a water fountain in the library?
- Is there a type of furniture that can help prevent echoing in our library facility?
- How can we stop the picture book covers from fading, since the "easy" section is near the windows?
- Do we want an aquarium or small animal cage in the library? If so, where?
- How high should the circulation counter be?
- What furniture is best in the elementary library: Plastic? Wood? Cloth?
- Do we want a story well, story stairs, story rug, or story tree?
- How do we ensure that all furniture is easily cleanable; that is, dirt, lice, and so on deterrent?
- Where do we place the librarian's office or desk?
- How many bulletin boards does the library need? Where should these be located?
- Are free-standing shelves safe for elementary students?

THE IDEAL SCHOOL LIBRARY

What is the ideal physical school library facility? It is possible that any of us who read this may see in our mind's eye our own ideal—and such dreams may be similar or wildly different. I know that my personal ideal of a school library is a very large and tastefully decorated facility, with complete line of sight (for student supervision; to determine possible patron needs, based on observed actions; for facility use/information and statistics; etc.) for the librarian, no matter where he or she is standing. It is on one floor; is situated in the middle of the school; has a centrally located entrance and exit; has a separate workroom for the librarian; has lots of materials arranged in between reading spaces and tables; has all the technology that any school could possibly want; has great indoor and outdoor lighting through skylights and the newest in electrical illuminations; has comfortable and easy-to-clean furniture; has an outside wall that can be taken out for future expansion; has a fireplace; has a waterfall (yes, a waterfall—flowing water can be calming [Ebner 2005]!); and has the serenest, most pleasant and studious students and teachers a school could possibly have. Is this a dream? Well, probably! Let's look at what a school library facility is and can be, as well as steps in the design and building (or redesign and rebuilding) of a school library facility. See figure 5.1 for an example of a hand-drawn high school library floor plan.

DESIGN AND DEVELOPMENT

The school library facility is normally seen as that physical place within the school where library resources and equipment are accessed, used, and stored. Depending on the school building itself, the library facility can be large or small; planned and designed

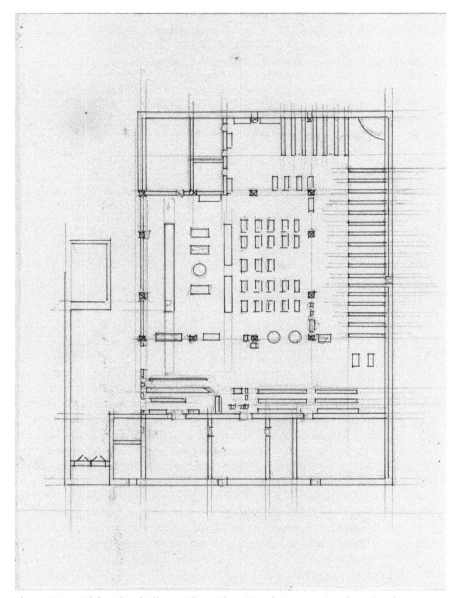

Figure 5.1. High School Library Floor Plan (Hand Drawn). *Stephen Condren, 2014, East Leyden Nardini Library, Franklin Park, Illinois*

for the school community (North East Independent School District 2014) or placed in a former classroom, a basement workroom, or another unused space within the building; created with future technological growth in mind or focusing primarily on print sources; and so much more. It could even be a bank of computers (given those who believe anything can be obtained through the Internet and that other resources are not necessary) or a librarian pushing a traveling cart from classroom to classroom (with a storage room that he or she can access for needed materials when necessary to a specific library lesson or request from a particular student, teacher, or class). These last two illustrations exclude the ideal and are not stressed in this chapter, as they are less likely to take into account various learning styles of students, needs of classroom teachers, and the fact that the digital divide still exists in some American homes (thus even if information were digitally available during the day via computers and tablets, students might not be able to access what they needed outside of school). Additionally, facilities must support library programming and services; for example, a school library with flexible access, which varies given curricular needs, might have furniture and equipment arranged to meet the requirements of more than one class being in the library at a time, and/or small and large groups simultaneously working on projects or checking out materials, as well as a traffic flow pattern designed to circumvent disruption. Therefore, this chapter considers the school library as a physical facility. See textbox 5.2 for questions one might ask when going through the design or redesign of a middle school library.

Steps in the Design and Building or Redesign and Remodeling of a School Library

Whether designing a brand-new library facility or remodeling that which is already in the school, there are certain steps that need to be addressed and/or considered. Let's

TEXTBOX 5.2
SAMPLE QUESTIONS TO ASK WHEN BUILDING OR REMODELING A MIDDLE SCHOOL LIBRARY

- Should we replace the flooring with carpet or vinyl?
- How many doors does the library need?
- How do we make the library feel inviting?
- Do we need a quiet study area?
- What type of shelving should we use for the graphic novel collection?
- Should library signage also be in braille?
- Does the library need its own storage area?
- Do we need round or square or oblong tables, or some of each? Where should these be placed? How many do we need?
- Can we put in a fireplace?
- Where do we put the popular novels?
- How big should the student and faculty production lab be, and where do we want it, in conjunction with the main library?
- Will we allow video gaming in the library? If so, should we designate specific computers for research and others for gaming purposes?
- Can we tint the outside window glass, so that there is less glare in the library?
- How many full classes can this library accommodate?
- How much and what type of space do we need for small group work?

imagine you are the librarian at a school that is constructing a new building. Part of the new building will include a modern, technologically ready library. Where do you start?

One of the first things to do is to establish a steering committee composed of library stakeholders. These might include a member of the school board, administrator, librarian (yourself), teacher, student, library aide/assistant, parent, and possibly an interested community member. The purpose of this committee is to meet and discuss what the members believe are the functions, programming needs, physical and technological needs, and so on that will be supported by the new library. In addition, it is best if this group also remembers to consider the school and library's mission statements, curricular support for all students and faculty, and any other possible functions that the library will have in the new school and surrounding community. In order to gain a better perspective on the new library, this stakeholders committee might also visit other school libraries—preferably new ones and/or those considered successful.

The school librarian (in this case—you) involved in the building of a new school library also needs to be assertive. Make sure that the school administration, school board, architectural firm, and builders realize that you plan to be a part of the design and creation of the new library, reporting on determinations of the stakeholders committee, and participating in designing the facility that you will eventually administrate. As part of this, provide the architect (as early as possible) with such information as whom the library will serve (students, teachers, and administration will top this list), approximate numbers of these individuals who will be served daily and annually, and the types and quantities of resources (hardware and software, print and nonprint) to be housed in the library. Remember, "If it isn't described to the architect, if it isn't in the construction drawings, it won't be in the finished project" (Marion 1997, 48). Figure 5.2 represents

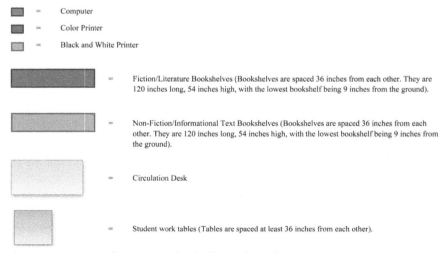

=   Computer

=   Color Printer

=   Black and White Printer

=   Fiction/Literature Bookshelves (Bookshelves are spaced 36 inches from each other. They are 120 inches long, 54 inches high, with the lowest bookshelf being 9 inches from the ground).

=   Non-Fiction/Informational Text Bookshelves (Bookshelves are spaced 36 inches from each other. They are 120 inches long, 54 inches high, with the lowest bookshelf being 9 inches from the ground).

=   Circulation Desk

=   Student work tables (Tables are spaced at least 36 inches from each other).

Figure 5.2.   Upper Elementary School Library Floor Plan. *Megan Knops, 2013, ETT 533 Facilities Project, DeKalb, Illinois*

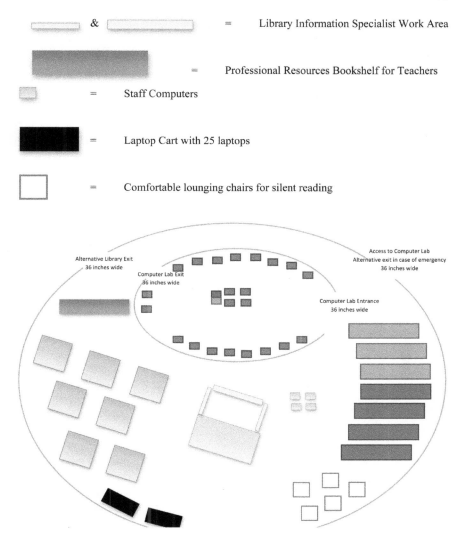

= Library Information Specialist Work Area

= Professional Resources Bookshelf for Teachers

= Staff Computers

= Laptop Cart with 25 laptops

= Comfortable lounging chairs for silent reading

Figure 5.2. (*Continued*)

a sample upper elementary school library floor plan; figure 5.3 illustrates a model of a middle school library floor plan.

Furthermore, be sure to apprise the architect of what technology the library currently has and how the design of the library may be informed by that technology. Remember that it is difficult to "guess" what will be the next educational technologies to develop in the future; neither you nor the architect or builders can truly design and build for technologies that do not yet exist. Therefore, argue for a design that works for what you have today, with the idea that changes/revisions will occur in the facility as technologies evolve in the future. See figure 5.4 for a view from a middle school library charge desk.

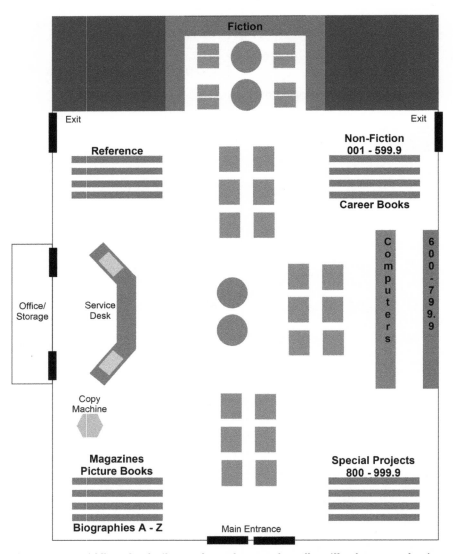

Figure 5.3. Middle School Library Floor Plan. *Mark Melka, Jill Johnson, and Kristy Gaynor, 2013, ETT 533 Facilities Project, DeKalb, Illinois*

Figure 5.4.   View from Charge Desk. *Michelle Johnson, 2014, Still Middle School, Aurora, Illinois*

In addition, consider walking through the facility at various times throughout the building process. This walk-through could be done by you alone, with other members of the steering committee, accompanied by the architect, or some combination of these. This way, you can see if your requests are being met. It is important to do this relatively often and from the earliest stages of the project to facilitate easy and timely change to the project if necessary. (This could involve you obtaining a hard hat.) Textbox 5.3 contains representative samples of the types of questions that might be asked by the school librarian, administration, architect, builder, and other stakeholders when considering the design or redesign of a high school library.

Moreover, study the floor plans and advise the architect of what happens in the library on a typical day. Remind him or her of such things as the

- location of the library within the school (example: in the middle of the school building, near those who will use it most);
- need to be able to turn on light switches immediately upon opening up the library door (therefore, light switches should be close to the entrance);
- importance of line of sight for student supervision throughout the library, particularly when you are standing at the circulation desk (this includes ensuring

TEXTBOX 5.3
SAMPLE QUESTIONS TO ASK WHEN BUILDING
OR REMODELING A HIGH SCHOOL LIBRARY

- How early do we want the library open in the morning? Is there a space to put in a coffee shop?
- Are the aisles wide enough for wheel chair access?
- Are security mirrors available so that we can see into areas where line of sight is an issue?
- How can we re-design the entrance, so that students are kept from "jumping" the gate?
- What brand of furniture is most durable yet soft seating for the reading area?
- Where can we put the open mike area?
- Can we create an area to display student art?
- How do we stop students from passing books and other library media "over the fence" to other students standing in the hall?
- Where should we situate library computers with catalog access?
- What is virtual library space, and how can we make sure that our library has it?
- Where do we put the really tall shelves?
- What is better in the library—natural or artificial light?
- What brand of sound tile will make for the best library acoustics?
- Do we place telephones only near the supervisor's desk?
- How many laptop carts can be stored in the library equipment room?
- How many movable tables, chairs, and shelves do we need in order to be able to use the library for presentations and open mike times?
- Do we want a bank of windows in the library?
- Should we have the library be on more than one floor?
- How many seating areas do we need? Should some be "easy reading" versus tables and chairs for studying?
- Should we make the library Wi-Fi available?
- How much seating do we want in the fiction area?
- Do we need a spot for patrons to plug their BYOT (bring your own technology)? If so where and how big should this spot be?
- How many classrooms does the high school library facility need?
- How many conference rooms should the library have?
- Do we want plants in the library?
- Do we want display cases?
- Where should outlets be placed?

that the library is on a single floor, rather than multiple stories) (see figure 5.5 for a line-of-sight example);
- requirement that materials needed for answering reference questions (computer terminal and reference media) be easily accessible to you;
- necessity that electrical outlets, computer monitors, network access points, file servers, switching and routing equipment, cords, ventilation systems, telephones,

Figure 5.5.   Line of Sight. *Sara Meyer, 2014, Plank Junior High School Library, Oswego, Illinois*

and so on be placed in spots where they are available to those who need them, yet not in the way of library traffic flow patterns;

- need for reading/study/story areas available for large and small groups of student patrons, as well as individual students (depending on the age of the students, this may mean tables, reading areas with comfortable seating, a reading nook, study carrels, or a story well) (figure 5.6 shows a middle school reading area);
- necessity for sound absorption tiles/good acoustics, so that those working in the library will not be bothered by other patrons or outside noise;
- need for (or lack thereof) an outside door for before and after school activities;
- desirability of restroom facilities, drinking fountains, backpack storage units, or security systems near the library entrance or exit or in the library itself;
- importance of both large-group (classroom-sized) and small-group teaching areas;
- preferred location of library computers and/or a computer lab or library classroom;
- age/size of your main patrons (i.e., to determine the optimal shelving sizes and where they might best be located);
- need to comply with ADA requirements, since the library must be available to all patrons;
- desired traffic patterns (including if students will pass through the library in between classes);
- locating reading and study areas away from high traffic areas;

Figure 5.6.   Middle School Reading Area. *Bethann Pries, 2014, Maple School Library, Northbrook, Illinois*

- providing adequate and proper lighting (best if natural, nonglare, or full spectrum);
- necessity of an area that can be darkened for presentation needs;
- need for pleasing esthetics, such as coordinating colors or materials (in walls, on floors, etc.), to encourage patron use of the library;
- recommendation that display areas (for student art, new books, library activities, and more) be near areas with high traffic flow;
- desirability for a library workroom and/or office for the librarian;
- need to provide areas for students and teachers to use technologies (such as laser printers, scanners, digital cameras and recorders, and more) housed in the library;
- availability of a book/media drop for times when the library is not open;
- availability of storage for library equipment, resources, and supplies;
- need for building code compliant fire exits, tornado or earthquake safety areas, and so on. (Bailey and Bruyere 2001; DesignShare 2006; Formanack 2005; Johnson, "Changed," n.d.; Johnson, "Designing," n.d.; Johnson, "Some" n.d.; Johnson 2012; Kollie 2006; Lenk 2002; Library Alive! n.d.; Lumenistics 2012; Mitchell 2002; Morris 1992; Picciano 2011; Sannwald 2001; YA Spaces of Your Dreams 2009)

Figure 5.7 is a photo of a theme-based elementary school library computer station.

Figure 5.7. Elementary School Library Computer Station. *Lisa Daugherty, 2014, Good Shepherd Catholic School, Frankfort, Kentucky*

In addition to those things to be brought to the attention of the architect, the librarian planning a new school library also has a number of other issues to consider. While these can vary from school to school, and be things as large as where to place a white board or as small as should there be hand sanitizer available, there are several points of concern to almost all school librarians working with a new facility. One instance is that of the furniture. Ideal library furniture is comfortable, easily cleanable, and hardy—students can be rough on the furnishings. Let's look at chairs as an example. Questions to ask might consist of the following: What kinds of chairs are best for this new library: stacking, rocking, folding? Should they be low or high? Big or small? Is it better to purchase chairs that purport to have an extended life (those that have two or three positions, thus accommodating those students who try to tilt the chairs back or sit on two legs) (Demco 2013)? Similar considerations can be extended to other library furniture. Below (figure 5.8) is an example of furniture that might be found in a middle or high library reading/browsing area.

Another subject is that of weeding. The old collection must be weeded before the move. There is no purpose in moving unused or deteriorating items to a new facility, unless they are archival in nature (see chapter 3 for more information on weeding).

An additional point the school librarian needs to think about is how all the library materials and equipment will be moved into the new facility. Is it worth the extra

Figure 5.8.   School Library Furniture. *Michelle Johnson, 2014, Still Middle School, Aurora, Illinois*

money to hire a library moving company? Can students and community volunteers carry stacks of books and other materials from the old library to the new with little breakage or loss?

Still more details for the librarian to contemplate:

- Programming needs: The services and activities that are planned for the library can greatly influence its physical space. For example, a school with primary students might wish to add a story well with a small stage or risers and colored squares on which students might sit or a K–9 building might design an area specifically for young adults, in a café-style atmosphere.
- Signage: Directional and informational signage—in a legible font, with as few words as possible for the needed directions/information, containing clear contrasts between lettering and background colors (red is good, as is the contrast between yellow and black), and securely mounted in a place easily attracted to users' gaze (Barclay and Scott 2012)—allows library patrons to find those items or areas they request or need more easily.
- Food and drink: Are you going to allow students and faculty to carry in foodstuff or beverages? Have you thought about having a "library coffeehouse" in the early mornings or on special occasions? (See figure 5.9)

Figure 5.9. School Library Coffee House. *Cheri GoGo, 2014, Lyons Township High School Library, La Grange, Illinois*

- Meetings and other nonlibrary services and activities: Keep in mind that if you have many tables in one area or a large open space that could hold rows of chairs, you open the library up to meetings, testing days, study halls, and more (Johnson, "Designing," n.d.).
- Charge desk: Locate this in a main traffic flow area; ensure that its height makes it accessible to all library patrons; and ensure that a book return is nearby. A photo of a high school library circulation desk can be found in figure 5.10.
- Flexibility: It is best to build in flexibility; that is, as technologies, programming, and services evolve, so too might the library facility—for instance, moveable shelving and furniture, the ability to expand the library by co-opting a nearby classroom or storeroom, and if adding OPAC (online public access catalog) computers means the addition on a blank wall of a waist-high counter (Mueller 2012; Myerberg 2002; Simpson 2002).
- Wall space: That wall space not covered with shelving or signage could be used for displaying student work, literacy posters, a student-developed and themed bulletin board, and other items particular to your school and library (Taney 2003).
- Learning styles: Students do not all learn in the same ways. There are visual, audio, verbal, logical, social, individual, and tactile learners, for instance; plus

Figure 5.10.   High School Library Circulation Desk. *Cheri GoGo, 2014, Lyons Township High School Library, La Grange, Illinois*

those who learn through practice, inquiry, reading, and/or conversation. The library design and collection needs to reflect the varied learning styles of students (Felder, n.d.; Learning-styles-online.com, 2014).

When designing your school library, be aware that there is a lot of help available through books, magazine articles, and websites (see earlier in this chapter), specialized architects and builders, and so much more. Just remember to differentiate between what is needed for the library and what you want. You may not get everything on your list, so prioritize. Remember to list and file away those items not included in the original/updated construction. They make an excellent starting point for future annual facilities budgets. Just because you can't afford everything now doesn't mean you won't be able to pay for these things in the future. Occasionally funds become available at the end of a budgeting cycle, and because such funds must be spent somewhat quickly, those projects already planned often get the money.

KEY CONCEPTS FROM THIS CHAPTER

- National standards and guidelines speak to good school library facilities design.
- The school library facility is normally a physical space allocated within the school.
- Before design and building begin, establish a committee of school library stakeholders for information and advice.
- Be assertive; make sure that the needs of the library, yourself, and your clientele are known to the architect and builders.
- Walk through the facility every week or so during construction or remodeling.
- Consider all aspects of library use, clientele (ages, curriculum, learning styles), programming and service needs, and materials and equipment storage in the design and construction of the school library.
- Prioritize needs over wants.
- List wants for future available facilities monies.

Coming in chapter 6: "Relationships and Personnel."

DISCUSSION QUESTIONS

1. What sorts of programming and/or service needs might influence the physical facility of an elementary school library? Middle school? High school?
2. Argue for a separate work area within the library, including a door that closes, for the school librarian. Argue against such a work area.
3. Can a school library facility be planned for future but unknown trends? Discuss how this might occur.

ACTIVITIES

1. Observe for an hour in a school library of your choice. Look especially at the following:
   - Organization/layout
   - Use of directional and other signs
   - Traffic patterns
   - Areas of supervision
   - Number of exits
   - Location of collection
   - Height of shelves
   - Print and nonprint collection access
   - Location of library computers
   - Ease of accessibility for students
   - Furniture—for example, carrels, small group work areas, conference rooms, and classroom accommodations
   - Accessibility to classrooms
   - How many students the Library Media Center (LMC) can accommodate
   - Suitability for technology applications for present
   - Suitability for technology applications for future
2. Given your observations, is this library facility representative of an ideal 21st century school library? If not what needs to change and why?
3. Design or redesign a school library of your choice. Write down your ideas for wall and floor colors, lighting purchases, environmental schema, theft prevention, shelving (size and construction), furniture, and so on. What is absolutely necessary for this library? What things would make this a pleasant library for students and faculty? What things would make this an enjoyable working environment for the school librarian?
4. Diagram a floor plan of the school library you designed in activity 2. Be sure to include traffic flow, seating areas, shelving and storage room locations, exits and entrances, and line of sight (supervision of the school library by the librarian and aides/assistants).

REFERENCES

American Association of School Librarians. 2009. *Empowering Learners: Guidelines for School Library Media Programs.* Chicago, Ill.: American Association of School Librarians.

Bailey, Nell and Bruyere, Susanne M. 2001. "Assistive Technology, Accommodations, and the Americans with Disabilities Act." http://digitalcommons.ilr.cornell.edu/edicollect/18/.

Barclay, Donald A. and Scott, Eric D. 2012. "Directions to Library Wayfinding." *American Libraries* 43 (3/4): 36–38.

Demco. 2013. "Library." http://www.demco.com/goto?PNHL19&intcmp=CN_L19.

DesignShare. 2006. "Imagining the Future of the School Library." http://www.designshare .com/index.php/articles/school-library-future.

Ebner, Kevin. 2005. "Health and Healing through Water." Eugene, Ore.: University of Oregon Scholars Bank.

Felder, Richard. n.d. "Learning Styles." http://www4.ncsu.edu/unity/lockers/users/f/felder/ public/Learning_Styles.html.

Formanack, Gail. 2005. "Designing a Facility: Making It a Place Where Every Student Succeeds." http://www.ala.org/aasl/sites/ala.org.aasl/files/content/conferencesandevents/conf archive/pittsburgh/DesigningaFacility.pdf.

Hamilton-Wentworth District School Board. 2014. "The System Learning Commons." http:// www.hwdsb.on.ca/llrc/about/what-is-a-learning-commons/.

Johnson, Doug. n.d. "Changed but Still Critical: Brick and Mortar School Libraries in the Digital Age." http://www.doug-johnson.com/dougwri/changed-but-still-critical-bricks-and-mortar-libraries-in-th.html.

———. n.d. "Designing Digital Libraries." http://www.doug-johnson.com/dougwri/designing-digital-libraries.html.

———. n.d. "Some Design Considerations When Building or Remodeling a Media Center." http://www.doug-johnson.com/dougwri/some-design-considerations.html.

———. 2012. "What Spaces Do Libraries Need?" http://doug-johnson.squarespace.com/blue-skunk-blog/2012/10/9/what-spaces-do-libraries-need.html.

Kollie, Ellen. 2006. "Acoustics Take the Lead in Classroom Design." http://webspm.com/ articles/2006/02/01/acoustics-take-the-lead-in-classroom-design.aspx.

Learning-styles-online.com. 2014. "Overview of Learning Styles." http://www.learning-styles-online.com/overview/.

Lenk, Mary Anne. 2002. "FAQs about Facilities: Practical Tips for Planning Renovations and New School Library Media Centers." *Knowledge Quest* 31 (1): 27–31.

Library Alive! n.d. "A New Look for the Future." http://www.cla.ca/slip/library-alive.pdf.

Lumenistics. 2012. "What Is Full Spectrum Lighting?" http://lumenistics.com/what-is-full-spectrum-lighting/.

Marion, Breck. 1997. "Facilities Design for Beginners and Blueprints 101." *Proceedings of the Consortium of College and University Media Centers*. San Diego, Calif.: Consortium of College and University Media Centers.

Mitchell, Lynnette. 2002. "Transformation of a School Library Media Center." *Knowledge Quest* 31 (1): 9–10.

Morris, Betty J. 1992. *Administering the School Library Media Center*. 3rd ed. New Providence, N.J.: R.R. Bowker.

Mueller, Charles G. 2012. "The Once and Future Library." *American Libraries* 43 (3/4): 39–41.

Myerberg, Henry. 2002. "School Libraries: A Design Recipe for the Future." *Knowledge Quest* 31 (1): 11–13.

National Council for Accreditation of Teacher Education. 2010. "ALA/AASL Standards for Initial Preparation of School Librarians." http://www.ncate.org/Standards/ProgramStandardsandReportForms/tabid/676/Default.aspx.

North East Independent School District. 2014. "Welcome to the Douglas MacArthur High School Library." http://neisd.libguides.com/MacLibTranformation.

Picciano, Anthony G. 2011. *Educational Leadership and Planning for Technology*. 5th ed. Boston, Mass.: Pearson.

Sannwald, William W. 2001. *Checklist of Library Building Design Considerations.* 4th ed. Chicago, Ill.: American Library Association.

Simpson, Carol. 2002. "Information Technology Planning: Computers in the School Library—How Many Are Enough?" *Knowledge Quest* 31 (1): 23–26.

Taney, Kimberly Bolan. 2003. *Teen Spaces: The Step-by-Step Library Makeover.* Chicago, Ill.: American Library Association.

YA Spaces of Your Dreams. 2009. "Teen Rooms in Worthington Libraries." *Voice of Youth Advocates* 31 (6): 512–515.

6

The School Librarian, Relationships and Personnel

In this chapter, the focus is on school librarians, their relationships with administration, faculty, and students, as well as those personnel who more commonly may work in or with the school librarian in a supportive role (library assistants or aides); technology, literacy, and additional teacher-coaches; and student, parent, and community library volunteers.

THE SCHOOL LIBRARIAN

So, you want to be a school librarian? The modern model school librarian is a wonder. He or she wears a wide assortment of hats:

- Information specialist
- Teacher
- Collaborator
- Technology coordinator
- Library advocate
- Web page designer
- Ethics go-to person (intellectual freedom, intellectual property, and privacy)
- Technology troubleshooter
- Facility administrator
- Policy maker
- Selector and evaluator of information resources, both print and digital
- Supervisor

- Literacy (reading, technology, visual, data, etc.) specialist
- Accountant
- Curriculum preparer
- Researcher
- Communicator
- Standards follower and interpreter
- Test creator
- Library club organizer
- Literature expert
- Cataloger
- Materials processor
- New facility designer
- Furniture arranger
- Book-shelving helper
- Grant writer
- Teacher/trainer
- Partnership developer
- Acquisition specialist
- Reference/information access person
- Abstract writer
- Disciplinarian
- Entertainment specialist
- Diversity promoter
- Crisis handler
- Committee member
- Copyright expert
- Library services, resources, instruction, and so on, evaluator
- Collection developer
- Problem solver
- Manager
- Media reviewer
- Policy writer
- Equitable access proponent
- Trends champion
- Internet safety specialist
- So much more!

In addition he or she might be handling extra responsibilities; for instance, hall monitor, yearbook adviser, or after-school judo instructor (who knows what extra knowledge or skills the librarian has)! For a sample high school librarian job description, see textbox 6.1.

Now, let's add on the fact that sometimes school districts employ *district librarians*. Such individuals normally maintain a district office in the school district administration building or work in one library—say a high school—as the head librarian, in addition to their district-level responsibilities. So, how do the district duties vary from those of the building-level school librarian? Well in most cases,

TEXTBOX 6.1
SAMPLE HIGH SCHOOL
LIBRARIAN JOB DESCRIPTION

POSITION DESCRIPTION

The high school librarian will serve as a "Leader . . . Instructional Partner . . . Information Specialist . . . Teacher . . . [and] Program Administrator" in the school (American Association of School Librarians 2010, 1–4) and will work with students in grades 9–12 to achieve the following four library skills benchmarks:

1. "Inquire, think critically and gain knowledge.
2. Draw conclusions, make informed decisions, apply knowledge to new situations, and create new knowledge.
3. Share knowledge and participate ethically and productively as members of our democratic society.
4. Pursue personal and aesthetic growth." (American Association of School Librarians 2009, 98–101)

SUGGESTED ROLES AND DUTIES
OF THE HIGH SCHOOL LIBRARIAN

- Be responsible for library programing
- Provide library services
- Collaborate with subject-specialist teachers for delivery of research and information literacy skills instruction and library materials to students, grades 9–12
- Select and evaluate library materials and equipment
- Work with school administration to maintain library budgeting agenda
- Oversee reference and referral with outside agencies
- Develop and/or administrate the high school library website
- Join and contribute to high school curricular and activity committees
- Uphold national and state school library program standards and guidelines
- Promote reading
- Create and maintain attractive physical and digital library spaces
- Manage and assess library staff and services
- Follow and model for high school students, staff, and faculty proper ethical and legal actions, for issues such as intellectual freedom, copyright, access to information, privacy, and more (Irvine Unified School District 2004; Illinois School Library Media Association 2010).
- Other duties as assigned by school administration

REQUIRED

"A master's degree from a program accredited by the American Library Association . . . [and] appropriate state certification as a school librarian and . . . a teacher preparation program and/or educational degree" (American Association of School Librarians 2010, 1).

similar responsibilities are necessary, although on a wider (district) level. Here are some examples:

- Director of all building-level school librarians
- Writer of grants
- Technology leader
- Coordinator of the district library budget
- Trainer of building-level school librarians (new skills and technologies)
- Organizer of district-wide school library meetings
- Manager of all new materials processing for district
- Evaluator of building-level school librarians and clerical staff
- Selector and assessor of district-level professional library collection
- Go-to person for intellectual freedom challenges across the district
- Internal copyright expert
- Overseer of library and technology trends
- Supervisor of district-wide cataloging and classification of all library materials
- Partnership advocate
- Liaison between school libraries and local community
- Communication specialist
- Other school library-related responsibilities as needed in the district (Butler 2009; Illinois School Library Media Association 2010; Irvine Unified School District 2004) (See textbox 6.2 for an example of a possible school library district coordinator position description.)

Wow! Are school librarians busy or what? Clearly, fulfilling all of these responsibilities requires that they establish strong working relationships with others. Let's take a look at some of these connections.

TEXTBOX 6.2
SAMPLE SCHOOL LIBRARY DISTRICT
COORDINATOR POSITION DESCRIPTION

POSITION DESCRIPTION

"Responsible for library services, acquisitions (ordering of books), and organization within the district" (Market Data Retrieval 2010, 1). "Coordinates district-level programs and resources in support of school library media centers . . . provides leadership in the development, implementation, and evaluation of the school library media program to promote student learning and teacher effectiveness for the benefit of the district's total educational program" (Irvine Unified School District 2004, 1).

RESPONSIBILITIES

- "Assume responsibility for oversight of the district-wide school library program
- Work with building level library staff to improve library services
- Design and implement collaborative lesson plans with teachers in the elementary grades
- Provide instruction to students in information literacy as needed
- Plan library staff development including monthly staff meetings and district-wide staff development days
- Supervise the selection, ordering, processing, and cataloging of school library materials for all school sites
- Coordinate the development of district school library media program standards, policies, and procedures
- Work with other administrators to establish district library budgets
- Work to integrate library services into district's educational and staff development plans
- Encourage effective use of the resources and services available from state and county agencies, and other libraries
- Develop and oversee the district's professional development collection
- Lead the development, annual review, and revision of the district school library plan to meet approval of the state board
- Promote reading and assist library staff, teachers and administrators in developing school reading motivation programs
- Participate on the district's technology committee to ensure that library media information and communication technologies are fully incorporated into the district's technology plan
- Provide regular updates for the school library media section of the district's Website and assist library media teachers in developing their own school library media Website" (Berkeley Unified School District, n.d., 1)
- Other duties as assigned by district administration

EDUCATION AND EXPERIENCE

Full-time experience in a school library setting.
Master's or bachelor's in library science from an accredited institution.

DESIRED

Administrative experience and/or accreditation (Berkeley Unified School District, n.d.; Irvine Unified School District 2004; Market Data Retrieval 2010).

(Please note: This position description is crafted from several real school library district coordinator job narratives and, when needed, with fictional places, times, dates, etc.)

RELATIONSHIPS

Colleagues

Who are the school librarian's colleagues? One could argue that these individuals are fellow librarians; technology specialists; technology, literacy, and other coaches (one-on-one support staff [Picciano 2011]; these may be full-time positions or classroom teachers with extra responsibility); and subject-expert and grade-level teachers. The school librarian may serve as (1) a partner to fellow librarians and technology specialists/coordinators/coaches; (2) a leader and expert resource to the classroom teacher (in terms of such things as information ethics, technology coordination, reading expertise, etc.); (3) a collaborator (e.g., classroom teacher, technology specialist); or (4) all of the above, depending on the situation and the individuals involved. Thus, the librarian may help coordinate a district library event, work with the school technology specialist on a web-filtering issue, lead a workshop for classroom teachers on copyright law, collaborate with an English teacher on a research unit for high school juniors, and more. The roles performed by the school librarians when working with these individuals will vary, depending on services, information, and access requested or needed. Regardless, it will surely require that he or she establish and maintain strong interpersonal bonds with colleagues. Ideally, he or she will be recognized by these individuals as a critical member of the education team at the school.

Administration

"Perhaps the greatest impact the principal can have is on integrating the library program into the school program" (Donham 2013, 66).

While the librarian may be an information expert or technology coordinator to the administrator, the librarian is also the administrator's employee. And common sense dictates that in as much as the librarian supervises his or her library and those who work in it (e.g., school librarians are "mini-administrators" in that they supervise a particular entity in the school), so too do the administrators do the same for school and district. All this means that the school librarian is usually seen in a supporting, or sometimes collaborative, role by and to the administration. One thing to keep in mind when working with administration is that in some ways, they are like you. For example, like you, the principal may be the only one of his or her kind in the school; thus the two of you may share a "separateness . . . both . . . concerned with all the teachers and students in the school" (Donham 2013, 57). This can be a bond if the librarian and principal share the same vision for the library. Developing a sound interpersonal relationship with the principal will help create an environment where there is open communication between the two of you. This, in turn, allows the school librarian a voice in creating the library vision.

Students

Without students, there would be no need for the school or its library. The librarian's main role is normally that of supporting students' needs and wants in terms of learning, information, and literature. With students, the librarian is usually a leader, teacher, information specialist, and/or supervisor. He or she creates an environment that allows students to see the library as a valuable resource and to enjoy using it as such. In a large respect, the librarian's ability to create this environment will depend on his or her ability to develop positive associations with colleagues as discussed before. This will allow him or her to be aware of what the students are working on in their classrooms at any given time and, therefore, make materials available for support. It would also be helpful for the librarian to be as involved as possible with other student activities (e.g., clubs, music programs, athletic events, etc.). By participating in such activities, the librarian will be viewed, by the students, as a key member of the faculty, rather than as a peripheral person.

Other ways that librarians can support their students are through acknowledging that students' perceived needs and requests (Smith 2012) are not always those that educators feel are important. For instance, students may want access to some "fun" library materials; things such as video games, skate-boarding magazines, or directions on how to knit the school mascot emblem onto a sweater. Textbox 6.3 illustrates some of the questions that a librarian might ask the students in order to become informed as to their needs and wants, their interests and concerns.

Consider what you see students searching for when they are in the library; what the student deems as important library materials may not be that which the adults in the school find necessary.

PERSONNEL

In this section we look at personnel in terms of those, other than the librarian, who work in the school library.

Library Support Staff: Aides, Assistants, and Secretaries (Paraprofessionals)

Recruitment of library support personnel (aides, assistants, and/or secretaries, sometimes called paraprofessionals) can come through advertisements in appropriate media (local newspapers, school websites, and professional listings), recommendations, college and university employment centers, and so on. When working with such individuals, the school librarian usually acts in the role of supervisor. As such, it is best to think of what responsibilities are yours, as the school librarian, and what responsibilities you are willing or able to delegate to your staff. In this supervisory role, the librarian "integrates the program's goals and objectives into staff duties, identifying tasks required for each activity, and

TEXTBOX 6.3
QUESTIONS A SCHOOL LIBRARIAN MIGHT
ASK OF HIS OR HER STUDENTS IN ORDER
TO BETTER UNDERSTAND THEIR NEEDS
AND WANTS, INTERESTS AND CONCERNS

- Who do you admire most? Why?
- Who do you admire least? Why?
- What is the most significant challenge that you see in the world today?
- What might be some solutions to this challenge?
- If you could go anywhere in the world, where would you go and what would you do?
- What is the most important problem in our school? How can we solve it?
- If you could be a teacher or the school principal, what would you do differently than what they do? The same?
- What are you most afraid of? Why?
- What do you most like to read? Give examples.
- What kinds of movies do you prefer? Why?
- What apps do you use the most? What do they have or do that makes them important to you?
- Do you watch the news on television or read it online or in a newspaper?
- What do you find most important in the news?
- Where do you obtain your reading materials? Movies? Apps? Music? Other media that you use?
- Would you rather go to a bookstore, the school library, the public library, or online for your reading/viewing/listening materials? Please explain why.
- Are you on any social networks? Why do you participate in them?
- What are you studying now? What do you like about that subject? Dislike?
- What do you think is the most important media in the school library? Why?
- Are there materials that you would like in the school library that we do not currently have? If so, what and why?
- Are there materials in the school library that you think should not be there? If so, what are they and why do you think this?
- Should the school internet be filtered? Explain your answer to this question.
- What do you like best about the school library? The least?
- Phrase other questions to fit each student.

Source: Butler 2014; Hopkins 1998

assigning them to building-level library media staff" (American Association of School Librarians 2009, 32). For example, the librarian working with a new library aide might prepare a plan, develop the appropriate training and assign performance standards, designate responsibilities, and provide guidance as needed. As the supervisor, the librarian also needs to ensure that the aide (or other employee) feels welcome, has a safe environment in which to work, is a team player (he or she will not be working in isolation in a school library), and is able to perform the duties required and/or learn new duties. (Please remember that as the school librarian, you are both a supervisor and an employee; you may not have control over all aspects of the library or the library paraprofessionals.) Be aware that it pays to remain respectful and courteous to those working for you. Develop clear and attainable goals and expectations, provide frequent feedback, let them know that what they do is important, and share how this work contributes to the success of the library and the school. If those who work for you are happy, they will work harder and longer, and the library can be the smoothly operating machine that you wish it to be.

It should be noted here that a special set of personnel issues/opportunities exists for the school librarian who divides his or her time between more than one school. In this case, there might be an aide at each of the schools, who is there every day, while the librarian may only be at the school one or two days per week. In cases like this, the rest of the staff at the school may see the aide as the librarian since that person is there every day (Dickson 2006). In such a case, the librarian could be seen as an outsider, while the aide possibly might see him- or herself as the librarian. This may mean that the actual librarian must spend more time and effort developing his or her collegial and leadership roles; those so important for success.

Possible duties for an aide or assistant in the school library include

- checking books and other media in and out (circulation);
- helping maintain circulation statistics;
- shelving books;
- creating bulletin boards and other displays;
- mending books and other media;
- answering simple technology questions;
- taking inventory;
- answering simple reference questions;
- collecting more difficult reference questions for the librarian to answer;
- pulling requested teacher materials;
- running errands;
- dusting;
- answering the phone;
- rearranging furniture;
- weeding deteriorating and outdated library materials;
- reading shelves;
- photocopying or scanning needed items;
- supervising student/volunteer help.

Below (textbox 6.4) is an example of an employment description for library support staff.

TEXTBOX 6.4
LIBRARY SUPPORT STAFF:
EMPLOYMENT DESCRIPTION

REQUIREMENTS

The candidate must "possess at least a high school diploma or equivalent. . . . Memorization and research skills are extremely useful for assisting patrons" (Education Portal 2014, 1).

PURPOSE

The support staff "helps librarians . . . organize materials and make them available to the public" (McKay 2014, 1).

GENERAL RESPONSIBILITIES

- "Assists with the circulation and storage of all library resources
- Processes new materials
- Assists students and staff in finding and using the library resources
- Prepares correspondence, reports, resource lists, newsletters, and requisitions requested by the school library information specialist
- Implements efficient office procedures
- Assists with inventories and withdrawal of materials
- Assists in preparing instructional materials, exhibits, and displays
- Collects data as requested by the librarian
- Participates in work-related training
- Helps maintain an attractive and inviting school library environment
- Promotes a positive relationship with students, staff, and community
- Performs other duties as assigned" (Illinois School Library Media Association 2010, 64)

ANNUAL SALARY RANGE

$17,080 to $38,290 (Education Portal 2014, 1)

Volunteers

Volunteers are different from paid personnel. The title says it all—they are volunteers; that is, not paid. Library volunteers are often students, parents of students, or community members and/or others just interested in being a part of the school library. Because they are not paid, they may receive only on-the-job training and can elect to come or not—depending on their schedule. The result is that although they can and may do similar chores to those assigned to library paraprofessionals, we often see them as less skilled and less dependable. Yet, they can serve a very important function in a library with little or no paid staff—that of the person who

- welcomes patrons to the library;
- shelves books;
- runs errands;
- checks library materials in and out;
- mends library materials;
- demonstrates simple technologies to library patrons;
- decorates the library facility;
- moves furniture;
- helps with inventory;
- collects reference questions for the librarian to answer;
- generates PowerPoint slides;
- creates library displays;
- works additional clerical-type jobs vital to the library. (Bridge School Library 2011; Clay Elementary School Library Media Center 2013; Francis Howell School District 2013; Waukegan Public Library, n.d.)

It is important that the work of volunteers be consistent with the goals and objectives of the library. So keep volunteers in the loop. Create clear and attainable expectations, keep them informed, and ask for their feedback just like you would with a paid employee. Remember, while you may hold them accountable for coming in on time, doing the work that you request, and responding in a positive and pleasant manner to all school library patrons, in fact—unless volunteering for the library is very popular—there is little you can do should they decide to skip work or quit altogether. Therefore, appreciate your volunteers; they are working of their own volition.

TYPICAL SCHEDULES OF SCHOOL LIBRARY PROFESSIONALS AND VOLUNTEERS

While the schedules of those who most commonly work in school libraries can vary exponentially and depend on the specific library in which they work, it is possible to point out what might happen on a weekly, daily, or hourly basis. This section illustrates examples of weekly activities for district, high school, middle school, and elementary librarians; daily activities of a library aide; and hourly commitments for a library volunteer.

District Librarians

Not all school districts hire a district-level librarian. Such an individual will normally report to the district administration, rather than that in a particular building, and will handle school library matters on a district level. Sometimes when a particular district cannot fund building-level librarians in all buildings, the district librarian will also function as a traveling school librarian. See textbox 6.5 for sample duties of a district librarian.

High School Librarians

High school librarians' weekly commitments can range from library supervision to after-school basketball or speech-team coaching and more. For additional examples, see textbox 6.6.

TEXTBOX 6.5
POSSIBLE ACTIVITIES IN A WEEK:
DISTRICT SCHOOL LIBRARIAN

- Find grants for the K–12 librarians to use to support their budgets
- Work with the building-level librarians to write grants for their libraries
- Select new materials to supplement the district professional library collection
- Train all building-level library personnel on how to handle a challenge to library materials
- Travel to all the elementary school libraries in the district to observe, answer questions, and handle issues with which the librarians feel they need help
- Travel to all the middle school libraries in the district to observe, answer questions, and handle issues with which the librarians feel they need help
- Travel to all the high school libraries in the district to observe, answer questions, and handle issues with which the librarians feel they need help
- Hire an outside trainer to work with all of the school librarians in the district to learn, keep, and uphold privacy compliance
- Maintain all purchasing records for school libraries in the district
- Retain all equipment repair and replacement records for school libraries in the district
- Coordinate all school library cataloging, K–12
- Meet with the district technology director as necessary to coordinate library technology with school and district technology labs and needs
- Attend statewide meetings for school librarians
- Serve on the district technology committee
- Participate with district administration on committees that support or are important to the district's school libraries
- Function as a go-to person for the building-level librarians
- Advocate for your constituency: district-wide K–12 librarians
- Keep up with school library and technology trends, and impart this information to the building-level people
- Create and update on an annual basis policy and procedure manuals for all of the district's libraries
- Model ethical behavior at all times

TEXTBOX 6.6
POSSIBLE ACTIVITIES IN A WEEK:
HIGH SCHOOL LIBRARIAN

- Teach research classes for an English teacher
- Collaborate with the industrial arts teacher to bring a speaker to the high school campus
- Attend a district copyright compliance meeting
- Instruct a student on how to use a particular database
- Advise the school yearbook staff
- Order new library computers
- Create a pathfinder for the Future Medical Careers Club
- Go to the social sciences curriculum meeting
- Share new library materials with faculty and staff
- Meet with principal to determine library programming during testing week
- Book-talk nonfiction materials to a science group
- Write a grant for new iPads
- Chair the school technology committee
- Promote Teen Read Week
- Select new teen paperbacks
- Host an open mike night
- Operate a "library store" during the school day
- Supervise library aides and parent volunteers
- Work with district librarian in the creation of a district-wide professional collection
- Design a coffee house for students who come to the library before classes begin for the day
- Open library computer lab after school for students who do not own personal computers
- Teach a one-semester-hour course on library information to interested students
- Advocate for use of the library with the school community
- Introduce a new Hispanic author to the Spanish classes
- Evaluate web pages for use of the history department, given a unit on World War II

Middle School Librarians

While I use the terminology here of *middle school librarian* to mean a building-level librarian for a school of grades 6–8, 7–8, 6–9, or a similar combination, there are also schools where the library serves multiple grades, such as K–9, K–12, 6–12, and so on. Most commonly, however, a middle school library serves the same/similar population of the older termed *junior high* school. For sample responsibilities, see textbox 6.7.

Elementary School Librarians

Elementary school librarians can have fixed or flexible teaching schedules and may be in one school or travel between two or more. Sample responsibilities they may

TEXTBOX 6.7
POSSIBLE ACTIVITIES IN A WEEK:
MIDDLE SCHOOL LIBRARIAN

- Establish a graphic novel club for interested middle school students
- Open the library during the lunch periods for students who desire access
- Participate on the school technology plan committee
- Design a series of lessons, in conjunction with the seventh grade math teachers
- Attend a building teachers' meeting
- Set up the library for an evening parent-student open house
- Work with the technology specialist to develop instruction on use of school building technology
- Draw up a floor plan for a possible new library and share with the building administrators
- Launch an annual book fair for the school
- Troubleshoot technological issues for a panicky classroom teacher
- Provide room for art displays in the library
- Add some plants to make the library feel more home-like to students
- Teach literacy skills to the sixth graders
- Invite a local authors' group to present on their works during a library-sanctioned book fest
- Work with small groups of students when they are sent to the library
- Introduce an interested student to the Percy Jackson books
- Collaborate with teachers on a literature unit
- Start a student library club
- Work with the German teacher on a school Oktoberfest celebration for his class
- Create a series of flipped library classes
- Chaperone a trip to Hoover Presidential Library in West Branch, Iowa
- Prepare a set of questions and answers on each of the Harry Potter books, in order to keep the eighth graders quiet on a school bus trip
- Help the vocal music teacher obtain copyright clearance for a piece of music for a middle school concert
- Keep the library open every day after school for an hour for those students who need it
- Select educational games, movies, books, and software to support classroom curriculum

deal with can be found in textbox 6.8. A sample advertisement for an elementary librarian is included in textbox 6.9.

Library Aides

Although paid staff, library aides, whether part time or full time, may also be asked to work outside of the library in another staffing position when needed. The types of "outside" activities the aide might be required to do include bus duty, hall supervision, and overseeing fourth (or another) grade recess. See textbox 6.10 for more clarification on a library aide's possible duties.

TEXTBOX 6.8
POSSIBLE ACTIVITIES IN A WEEK:
ELEMENTARY SCHOOL LIBRARIAN

- Teach library skills to every elementary class at a set time every week
- Read a story to the kindergarten classes
- Evaluate library materials for use with special education students
- Handle an intellectual freedom challenge
- Present on a school night, about new library media, to the Parent Teacher Organization
- Bring in an author to speak to the students
- Create a library web page
- Pull books for a sixth grade class unit
- Prepare lessons on web searching for the third graders
- Collaborate with the fourth grade teachers on a unit about forestry
- Communicate with the principal about a rowdy student
- Order library supplies
- Model copyright compliance to the school community
- Supervise students using the in-house television studio
- Work with the technology coaches to help familiarize students with the new library laptops
- Supervise community and student volunteers
- Evaluate web pages for a fifth grade research lesson
- Select library materials
- Attend a children's literature conference
- Shelve library materials
- Select print and online magazines for elementary school children
- Design a story well in the library for preschool and lower elementary use
- Create new library signage
- Move library furniture
- Clean up the library at the end of each day

TEXTBOX 6.9
SAMPLE JOB ADVERTISEMENT:
ELEMENTARY SCHOOL LIBRARIAN

DETAILS

Starting Date: August 5, 2015
Application Deadline: May 1, 2015

JOB DESCRIPTION

"As a leader, the school librarian creates an environment where collaboration and creative problem solving thrive. The school librarian is an excellent communicator who instills enthusiasm in literacy and demonstrates this as a visible resource within the school community. . . . The candidate should be energetic, flexible, and able to provide library enrichment to students in an urban setting" (SchoolSpring 2014, 1). Additionally, candidate must be able to coordinate early elementary literacy programming, teach technology classes, and work with administration and architects to design new elementary library facility.

QUALIFICATIONS

Education and Licensure/Certification

"Master's Degree in Library Science required" (SchoolSpring 2014, 1).

Experience

At least one year of previous experience in a library or technology center is preferred.

SALARY RANGE

"$49,000.00–$61,300.00 / Per Year" (Sheldon Independent School District 2014, 1).

EQUAL OPPORTUNITY EMPLOYER STATEMENT

Our school "is committed to maintaining a work and learning environment free from discrimination on the basis of race, color, religion, national origin, pregnancy, gender identity, sexual orientation, marital/civil union status, ancestry, place of birth, age, citizenship status, veteran status, political affiliation, genetic information or disability, as defined and required by state and federal laws. Additionally, we prohibit retaliation against individuals who oppose such discrimination and harassment or who participate in an equal opportunity investigation" (SchoolSpring 2014, 1).

CONTACT INFORMATION

Lucas Everyman, Principal
111 Spring Green Street
Quietville, Alabama 30758
1-344-798-2046
everyman@ala.edu
Send letter of application, résumé, and official college transcripts to Principal Everyman by May 1, 2015 (SchoolSpring 2014; Sheldon Independent School District 2014). (Please note: This advertisement is crafted from several real elementary school library advertisements and, when needed, with fictional places, times, dates, names, and more.)

**TEXTBOX 6.10
POSSIBLE ACTIVITIES IN A DAY:
SCHOOL LIBRARY AIDE**

- Show students how to use the circulation computer to check out books
- Check in and re-shelve books
- Create and put up a bulletin board
- Walk interested student over to the poetry section
- Write up overdue notices
- Supervise lunch room
- Collect library passes
- Put away CDs
- Repair print-based books and magazines
- Help new student start up a Chromebook
- Neaten up the library

Library Volunteers

Because library volunteers are most apt to come to the library on a limited basis, whether for half a day, two-hour blocks, or whatever the agreement is per a weekly or monthly period (agreement between the school administrator, librarian, and the volunteer), textbox 6.11 describes what a library volunteer might be asked to do during an hour-long period.

As you can see, school librarians are busy people with a multitude of commitments and responsibilities. Being a school librarian can be fulfilling and challenging; certainly such a person wears many hats and is a dedicated educational professional.

KEY CONCEPTS FROM THIS CHAPTER

- The 21st century school librarian has many job responsibilities.
- School librarians work with students, faculty, and administration.

**TEXTBOX 6.11
POSSIBLE ACTIVITIES IN AN HOUR:
SCHOOL LIBRARY VOLUNTEER**

- Shelve books
- Dust shelves
- Rearrange magazine collection
- Make bookmarks

- School librarians can be leaders, partners, and collaborators with their colleagues.
- District librarians supervise building-level school librarians and/or clerical staff.
- Administrators and school librarians often share "separateness," in that they both work with the entire student body and faculty.
- The main role of the school librarian is to support student learning.
- School librarians are mini-administrators, in that they manage a library, its resources, and oftentimes personnel.
- What students consider important library materials may not be the same as those which their teachers find necessary.
- Paid paraprofessionals help support the role and mission of the school library.
- Library volunteers often have similar responsibilities as the paid library aides, assistants, and secretaries, without the benefit of a salary.
- All those who work in school libraries, whether district librarians, high school librarians, middle school librarians, elementary school librarians, library aides, or library volunteers, have many varied tasks and obligations.

Coming in chapter 7: "Services."

DISCUSSION QUESTIONS

1. For an elementary, middle school, or high school library, list the responsibilities you might see a librarian performing on a given day.
2. What role do you see your principal playing in terms of school library services? Programming? Technology? Discipline? Other?
3. How can we create and maintain a pleasant school library, one where volunteers would like to come and help us out—for free?

ACTIVITIES

1. Interview a practicing school librarian. What position does he or she hold in technology integration and digital information access in the school? To whom does he or she go for advice, technological and otherwise?
2. Observe in a school library of your choice for an hour. What do you see students doing? How are they most likely to come to the library—in full classes? Small groups? Individually?
3. Volunteer to work in a school library for half a day. Reflect on your experience; would you do this again? Why or why not?

REFERENCES

American Association of School Librarians. 2009. *Standards for the 21st-Century Learner in Action.* Chicago, Ill.: American Library Association.

———. 2010. "Sample Job Description: Title: School Librarian." http://www.ala.org/aasl/education/recruitment/learning.

Bridge School Library. 2011. "Volunteer Manual 2011–2012." http://lps.lexingtonma.org/cms/lib2/MA01001631/Centricity/Domain/232/Volunteer_Manual.pdf

Butler, Rebecca P. 2009. *Smart Copyright Compliance for Schools: A How-To-Do-It Manual."* New York, N.Y.: Neal-Schuman.

———. 2014 "Young Adult Interviews' Assignment." *ETT 523: Media for Young Adults.* DeKalb, Ill.: Department of Educational Technology, Research and Assessment, Northern Illinois University.

Clay Elementary School Library Media Center. 2013. "Volunteer Handbook 2013–2014." http://www.cobbk12.org/clay/Media%20Center/Clay%20Media%20Center%20Volunteer_handbook_new.pdf.

Dickson, Gail. 2006. "The Question . . . Should I Correct Those Who Refer to My Library Clerk as the Librarian?" *Knowledge Quest* 35 (1): 60–61.

Donham, Jean. 2013. *Enhancing Teaching and Learning: A Leadership Guide for School Librarians.* 3rd ed. Chicago, Ill.: Neal-Schuman.

Education Portal. 2014. "Library Clerk: Requirements, Salary Info and Career Outlook." http://education-portal.com/articles/Library_Clerk_Requirements_Salary_Info_and_Career_Outlook.html.

Francis Howell School District. 2013. "Volunteer Handbook." http://fhsd.sharpschool.net/community/volunteers/volunteer_handbook/.

Hopkins, Dianne. 1998. "Young Adult Literature Assignment." *SLIS 631: Young Adult Literature.* Madison, Wis.: School of Library and Information Studies, University of Wisconsin-Madison.

Illinois School Library Media Association. 2010. *Linking for Learning: The Illinois School Library Media Program Guidelines.* 3rd ed. Canton, Ill.: Illinois School Library Media Association.

Irvine Unified School District. 2004. "Library/Media Coordinator." https://www.iusd.org/human_resources/job_descriptions/libmedcoord.htm.

Market Data Retrieval. 2010. "K–12 Job Titles and Descriptions." www.schooldata.com/pdfs/111110_Webinar_Q&A_JobTitles.pdf.

McKay, Dawn Rosenberg. 2014. "Library Assistant: Career Information." http://careerplanning.about.com/od/occupations/p/library_asst.htm.

Picciano, Anthony G. 2011. *Educational Leadership and Planning for Technology.* 5th ed. Boston, Mass.: Pearson.

SchoolSpring. 2014. "Job Posting: Elementary School Librarian." https://www.schoolspring.com/job.cfm?jid=877152&utm_content=MA&utm_campaign=Job+Search+Engines&utm_source=Indeed&utm_medium=organic.

Sheldon Independent School District. 2014. "Job Listings: Elementary Librarian." https://sheldontx.tedk12.com/hire/viewjob.aspx?jobid=625.

Smith, Nicole L. 2012. "Showing You Care: Suggestions for School Library Relationships." *Knowledge Quest* 40 (4): 18–21.

Victoria Independent School District. n.d. "Librarian—Elementary (5 Vacancies)." http://eweb.esc3.net/jobberbase/job/2768/librarian-elementary-5-vacancies-at-victoria-independent-school-district/.

Waukegan Public Library. n.d. "Volunteer Handbook." http://www.waukeganpl.org/sites/default/files/pr/Volunteer%20Handbook.docx.

7

Services

Chapter 7 covers services, both those supported by the school library and those used by this entity. Thus, in this chapter we embrace such things as how the district supports the building-level librarian, Internet services available to and from the school library, data-based decision making and why it is an important school library function, and the various types (and importance) of library scheduling (without which many services might not get completed).

DISTRICT-LEVEL SERVICES

There are many types of school districts. Some are huge entities with lots of schools in their orbit; others are small—the building itself could make up the entire district. Because of how these vary, those things that the district provides to the school library and librarian also may differ. For example, in a large district, a school librarian might send all orders (books, technology, supplies) in to a central office, which then

- prepares the purchase orders;
- receives the requested items;
- double-checks to make sure that every ordered item is there and in the condition requested;
- catalogs or otherwise processes said media for the particular school;
- sends the items out to the school.

In such a case, the school librarian has only to tell the central office what he or she needs for the library. On the other hand, in a much smaller district, the school librarian may be responsible for all or part of these duties.

The same procedure described for materials ordering and processing can also hold true for technology, curriculum, and more. This means, for instance, that in some districts all equipment requests/repairs might be done by a district-wide computer/technology repair person. This technician, whether housed in a central place or traveling from school to school, will then repair items, add the requested software or applications, and so on. Therefore, there is no need for someone in the school to do this work, unless in a smaller district, where no such central person exists.

With this in mind, also note that in a large district, there may be a district librarian or technology director, someone who in a manner similar to the building principal and/or vice principal, serves as another supervisor to the school librarian. However, it is also possible that you might find yourself as the only high school librarian in the only high school in the district. In such a case you could also discover that you are assigned as the library supervisor for all of the middle and elementary school librarians or as a supervisor to aides in these buildings, if no other school librarians exist. Since there does not need to be consistency among school districts, when considering your individual district and its own peculiarities, be prepared to function as you are needed/requested by those in charge; for example, your administration. Next, let's take a look at services and the local community.

COMMUNITY SERVICES

When it comes to community service, it is most likely that the community can, in some way, support the school library, whether through

- public libraries
  - providing sets of books on particular subjects to support class units (when the school library does not have any or enough of the requested material);
  - offering ILL (interlibrary loan) help (not all schools have their own interlibrary loan set-ups);
  - making after-school homework help available;
  - delivering summer reading programs either alone or in conjunction with a summer school program;
  - running young adult video gaming, manga, or fantasy reading programs;
  - referring information and help requests to community organizations, such as police departments, museums, and more (see also chapter 8, "Programming and Collaboration").
- businesses and corporations (more commonly local ones)
  - offering to fund particular school library activities or programming;
  - volunteering prizes for a reading contest;
  - developing something for the school or library that is in their area of expertise (for example, a local gardening supply store planting a vegetable garden outside

the library windows to supplement the hot lunch program, influence children to eat properly, and promote reading of nonfiction books about plants).
- community volunteers, who
  - could be parents or other family members of school students;
  - might be interested community members with a particular interest in libraries, computers, the Internet, volunteerism, or children and young adults. (See also chapter 6, "Relationships and Personnel.")

There are times, however, when the school library can also provide services *to* the community. For instance, in a rural area, the school library might also function as a supplier of books and other materials, access to technology, and information provider for the local community, where there is not a local public library available. Additionally, the local public might benefit from a Saturday Percy Jackson and the Olympians series festival or Thursday movie night that the library uses as an outreach activity, not only for the school students but also for students' family and friends. (For more on possible programming opportunities, see chapter 8, "Programming and Collaboration.") Another type of service that school libraries can receive and/or provide would include those that are web based.

WEB-BASED SERVICES

Any number of schools, K–12, establish their own library web pages. Frequently these are created and maintained by the school librarian, oftentimes with help from technology specialists, interested teachers and students, the library aides, and others. Such library web pages can usually be accessed 24 hours per day, seven days a week, thus providing the school's students and staff with online help and information in any number of ways. Among the services commonly offered on these web pages are

- online library catalogs.
- subscription database access.
- online encyclopedias.
- selected links to various sites of interest or need to students and staff (supporting curricular and entertainment demands).
- online reference services.
- homework help.
- resources for teachers.
- links to local public libraries, museums, and archives.
- lists of Internet access points to writing tools and writing help, including
  - various writing styles, such as APA (American Psychological Association), MLA (Modern Language Association), *Chicago Manual of Style*, Turabian, and so on;

- ○ citation examples;
- ○ numerous writing modes, including those needed for job applications; technical, creative, medical, and academic writing; recommendation letters; and so on.
- email a librarian or content area specialist.
- access to educational apps (applications for mobile phones and tablets).
- listings of social networking tools (possibly) allowed for use in a particular district.
- links for parent information.
- material for district librarians (on a website maintained by a district library director or his or her staff).
- so much more! (Chicago Public Schools 2014; Donham 2013; Middleton-Cross Plains Area School District 2014; Oakland High School 2013; Owl: Purdue Online Writing Lab; Warlick 2010)

In addition, the library in a *virtual* school is, well, virtual, which by its very essence is entirely online; or a traditional school or district may maintain a virtual library (essentially an advanced/very detailed library web page) for use by its students and staff. In a virtual library, a simple click on the correct graphic, subject, or link or listing of a search term in a search box can send the user where he or she wants to go; to obtain that which he or she wants or needs. This means that the user can be anywhere that his or her laptop, smartphone, or tablet device can pick up the Internet (Florida Virtual School 2008; Hillsborough County Public Schools n.d.; Library Media Services 2013). Oh, what a great world we live in, where information is truly only a tap or keystroke away!

From web-based services, we now turn to another service aspect of the school library of today—that of data-based decision making.

DATA-BASED DECISION MAKING

What is data-based decision making and why is it important to school libraries? Data-based decision making (sometimes called data-driven decision making) is "an ongoing process of analyzing and evaluating information to inform important educational decisions and actions" (Johns and Patrick, n.d., 2). Thus, data-based decision making collects data to evaluate systems, processes, procedures, tools, and so on. Through gathering such library data as circulation statistics, scheduling queries, technology demands, ILL requests, library programming activities, number of collaboration endeavors with fellow teachers, and so on, and providing this data to the school principal, the school librarian informs his or her administration as to what he or she *does* (services, programming, etc.) and (oftentimes) *needs* as far as more library materials, personnel, online databases, equipment, funding, and so forth. For instance, a simple sign-up sheet (available either in paper or online through the school intranet) for use of library-provided technology (in this case for one week, in a high school [see figure 7.1]) can inform the librarian, the technology director,

Name/Class	Date	Class Period/s	Technology
Brown/Soph. History	Monday, May 12	1 & 2	Laptop cart
Parry/Sr. English	Monday, May 12	2, 7 & 8	iPad cart
Garner/Automotives	Monday, May 12	3	Computer lab
Smith/Home Economics	Monday, May 12	4-6 & 8	Smart Board suite
Brown/Soph. History	Tuesday, May 13	1 & 2	Laptop cart
Lee/Technology Interns	Tuesday, May 13	½ hour before school	6 Chromebooks
Lewis/Jr. Sociology	Tuesday, May 13	6	iPad cart
Parry/Sr. English	Tuesday, May 13	3	iPad cart
Brown/Soph. History	Wednesday, May 14	1 & 2	Laptop cart
Reens/Library	Wednesday, May 14	During lunch	iPad cart
Cairns/Fr. Technology	Wednesday, May 14	5	iPad cart
Lee/Technology Interns	Wednesday, May 14	1 hour after school	iPad cart
Brown/Soph. History	Thursday, May 15	7	Laptop cart
Morris/planning period	Thursday, May 15	7	1 iPad
Anderson/Chess Club	Thursday, May 15	45 minutes after school	Computer lab
Caven/Farm Management	Thursday, May 15	2	iPad cart
Brown/Soph. History	Friday, May 16	1 & 2	Laptop cart
Vanisen/Government	Friday, May 16	3 & 7	iPad cart
Harrington/planning period	Friday, May 16	7	1 Chromebook
Hall/Industrial Arts	Friday, May 16	6-8	iPad cart

Figure 7.1. High School Library Technology Sign-Up Sheet

and the school principal as to possible future equipment purchases (that equipment signed up for the most).

In this way, data-based decision making supports the argument for the growth of the library and informs a principal, who is often more used to teachers and classrooms than to the distinct characteristics of the school library (Donham 2013), which sees more students less often and functions as a mini-administrative/resource and information provision entity in addition to that of an instructional unit.

Data-based decision making can also be used when the school librarian helps support student-based programming or other needs. For example, response to intervention (RTI) uses data-based decision making as the center of its four main components; essentially it drives the other three components of screening, progress monitoring, and multileveled instruction (Center on Response to Intervention n.d.).

Response to Intervention

"With RTI, schools use data to identify students at risk for poor learning outcomes, monitor student progress, provide evidence-based interventions and adjust the intensity and nature of those interventions depending on a student's responsiveness, and identify students with learning disabilities or other disabilities" (National Center on Response to Intervention 2010, 2). There are seven processes by which school librarians might not only influence student learning but also guide teachers—"getting started, training staff, planning interventions, assessing students, scheduling interventions, implementing interventions, and evaluating the RTI program"

(Robins and Antrim 2012, 1). Subsequently, many school librarians are involved in the RTI process; oftentimes in familiar roles, such as "providing appropriate reading materials for students, collaborating with teachers to create successful lessons, and finding new and exciting ways to employ technology in teaching" (Robins and Antrim 2012, 14). Thus, school librarians may serve as RTI consultants through curriculum collaboration with teachers; supplying technology, a variety of media, and in-service programs to fellow instructors; identifying student needs; and helping with such student assessment activities as working with and training other educators in the use of assessment software and subsequent reports (Robins and Antrim 2012). In these ways, RTI support is a service provided by the school library.

Next, we address scheduling and the school library.

SCHEDULING

Scheduling in the school library can be a contentious subject for school librarians and library staff, school administrators, and teachers. This is because most school librarians would prefer a flexible schedule, where teachers and classes (and/or individual students and small groups) come in to the library when they need help, information, research, or other training; wish to use library technology; or want to check out, return, or browse library materials. However, many school administrators (especially in elementary schools) see the weekly/cyclical school library class as a way to provide the teachers with another planning period. And many teachers are of a similar mind, if not having a library class means one less planning period per week or teaching cycle. Then, particularly in high schools or some middle schools, there may be a demand for another study hall. What a better place to put it than in the library! After all, there may be plenty of tables, a teacher (the librarian) to run the study hall, and all those materials and often a computer lab or bank of computers that students may use. But . . . a library study hall at the same time every day means a schedule with less flexibility (could be that no one other than those in that study hall can be in the library during that precise period[s]), and a librarian placed in the position of study hall monitor has less time to work with other classes, teach research skills, help find books, order materials, be a technology guru, and all the other services that he or she can and would like to provide to the school clientele. What to do? What is best?

Flexible Scheduling

Most school librarians will argue that a flexible library schedule is the best. Indeed, this is supported by the American Library Association (ALA) through the American Association of School Librarians' (AASL) "Position Statement on Flexible Scheduling" (remember, the AASL is the division of the ALA that is focused on school librarians; see chapter 1). This statement proclaims,

The library program is a fully integrated part of the educational program so that students, teachers, and school librarians become partners in learning. This integration strengthens the teaching and learning process so that students can develop the vital skills necessary to analyze, evaluate, interpret, and communicate information and ideas in a variety of formats. Inquiry skills are taught and learned within the context of the curriculum. . . . [This] requires an open schedule. Classes need to be flexibly scheduled into the library on an as needed basis to facilitate research, training, and utilization of technology with the guidance of the subject specialist, the teacher, and the process specialist, the librarian. (American Association of School Librarians 2011, 1)

A flexible schedule is indeed the ideal schedule for student learning. It means "eliminating a rigid schedule of regular library times for each class, allowing teachers to schedule their classes into the library as needed for appropriate lengths of time to suit the learning activity that was planned" (McGregor 2006, 1). For the librarian and library staff, this indicates that every day in the library can be different—some days might have two full classes where others may have four or five; some days could have small groups from a particular teacher other days may well see individual students coming in from several classes. However, flexible scheduling also implies that

- student library use and learning will be at times when it is needed and (due to repetition through classroom activities) will be retained;
- collaboration, between the librarian and his or her faculty and students, is more likely to occur;
- classes that need several days of library instruction for a complex skill will be able to obtain that which they need by coming in daily or biweekly, rather than waiting until the following week or for the fixed schedule cycle; and
- students may retain enthusiasm for, and see the relevance of (Donham 2013), what they are learning, since there is no lengthy break between library-related activities.

The timely library access found with flexible scheduling focuses on student learning, rather than on administrative convenience. It also means that school librarians are more likely to attend and participate in scheduled subject- and grade-level area meetings (because they are not teaching in the library at these times), thus ensuring that the librarian is aware of what curricular needs and requests he or she might be asked to provide to various students and faculty.

One major negative to library flexible scheduling is that it is possible some students might miss out on book selection and checkout, using library technology and resources, or just getting into the library, due to varying class interests, teacher disinterest in library instruction or dislike of the librarian, or other reasons. Thus, when adapting to flexible scheduling, the librarian, as well as the school principal and teachers, must be aware that *flexible* means still going to the library; just going when there is a requirement or interest, rather than on a cyclical basis.

A representative flexible schedule is found in figure 7.2. This sample schedule is for a high school with block-style scheduling. It represents one week in the scheduling for this particular secondary school.

While any school, K–12, can adopt a flexible library schedule, it still appears to most commonly occur at high school and middle school levels, with elementary schools still more likely to follow a fixed schedule approach.

Fixed Scheduling

A common type of library schedule, especially in many elementary schools across the nation, is that of the fixed schedule. With this type of schedule, the school librarian

	Monday	Tuesday	Wednesday	Thursday	Friday
Before School	Open for 45 minutes before school start.	Open for 45 minutes before school start.	Open for 45 minutes before school start.	Open for 45 minutes before school start.	Open for 45 minutes before school start.
Block #1	Data-base searching and strategies: Health and Human Sexuality/Mrs. Blue	Data-base searching and strategies: Health and Human Sexuality/Mrs. Blue	Data-base searching and strategies: Health and Human Sexuality/Mrs. Blue		
Block #2		Evaluating web sites: Technology/Mr. Larson		Research on social classes in the U.S.: Sociology/Ms. Patterson	Research on social classes in the U.S.: Sociology/Ms. Patterson
Lunch/ Tutor-ials,Clubs, Study Hall	Lunch/ Tutoring	Lunch/ Divergent series book discussion, book 1	Lunch/ Divergent series book discussion, book 2	Lunch/ Divergent series book discussion, book 3	Lunch/ Student Library Volunteers' Meeting
Block #3		Research on supply and demand of agricultural products: Economics/Ms. Thomas	Research on supply and demand of agricultural products: Economics/Ms. Thomas	Online searching/ republics: Government/ Mr. Smallfoot	
Block #4	Genetics: Biology/Mr. Quale Library Computer Lab	Genetics: Biology/Mr. Quale Library Computer Lab	Genetics: Biology/Mr. Quale Library Computer Lab	Genetics: Biology/Mr. Quale Library Computer Lab	Genetics: Biology/Mr. Quale Library Computer Lab
After School	Open for 1 hour after end of school day.	Open for 1 hour after end of school day.	Open for 1 hour after end of school day.	Open for 1 hour after end of school day.	Open for 1 hour after end of school day.

Figure 7.2.   High School Library Flexible Schedule

sees every class at a specific time. Usually, this time coincides with a classroom teacher's planning period, so he or she drops the kids off, uses his or her planning period, and picks up the kids at the same times each week (or school planning cycle). Besides giving the classroom teacher a period away from the class, the fixed library schedule also ensures that each elementary school child comes into the library on a regular basis for book checkout and library instruction. While the benefits of a fixed schedule may appear clear to the teacher getting a planning period or the administration trying to schedule such, it is less clear for the students (except in terms of scheduled book checkout), and as a result, the librarian. Why?

The most important reason is that students with a fixed library schedule are often taught library skills out of context. Because the librarian has a particular period (for example, between 20 and 40 minutes) each week/cycle for that particular class, during that time, he or she will choose a library skill to instruct the students on or read them a story and then allow book checkout. Such instruction may or may not coincide with what the students are learning in their classrooms. As a result, the instruction may have little meaning for the students, and without repetition, they may in time forget all or part of what they were taught. While one can argue that the librarian and classroom teacher can still collaborate for instruction beneficial to the student, in reality, with fixed scheduling this often does not happen. This can be because the librarian is so booked with classes that he or she has little time for the day-to-day responsibilities of the library; thus collaboration, attending grade level meetings, and so on, get set on the "back burner." Such collaboration is also less likely to occur when a district chooses to hire traveling librarians (again, most common with elementary schools), who are assigned a particular school only a few days a week. Because the traveling librarian is in and out of these schools, he or she not only knows the students and faculty less, but may be perceived by both groups as "not really a teacher" or "not quite part of the educational unit in the school." In such cases, the elementary school librarian is less likely to learn students' names (unless they are discipline problems), which results in the "You, there, in the red shirt," label for the students who actually may care or want to learn. This lack of recognition of the "good" students sometimes means that they choose not to focus on library instruction as much or try as hard to learn any information presented by the librarian. Indeed, fixed scheduling can be frustrating for both groups.

There are times when the administration may try to make the fixed schedule a bit more workable. This is sometimes done by requiring each class coming to the library to be accompanied by an aide or volunteer—the idea being that this extra individual can help with any disciplinary problems, and if the aide/volunteer also works in the classroom, it may also mean that there is some carryover with instruction. However, the only sure way of ensuring that students are learning in context is through collaboration between the teachers and librarians and/or teachers accompanying their students to the library and remaining throughout the entire library period. In this way, the teacher knows exactly what was taught and can reinforce these skills in the classroom. Figure 7.3 gives an illustration of what an elementary school library

Day	Before School	8:45-9:30	9:30-10:15	10:15-11	11-11:45	11:45-12:30	12:30-1:15	1:15-2	After School
Mon.	Library Open	3rd grade Murphy		4th grade Lewis	Lunch	4th grade Avery		Gifted Marsalis	Library Open
Tues.	Library Open		5th grade Arnez	K-2 Special Needs Falada		Lunch	2nd grade Pauls	5th grade Stewart	Library Open
Wed.	Library Open		K Smythe		3rd grade Jones	Lunch	2nd grade Fiere	K Potter	Girl Scouts
Thurs.	Library Open	1st grade Tannis	5th grade Lyman	3-5 Special Needs Linky	Lunch	2nd grade Bota		3rd grade Jordan	Teacher In-service
Fri.	Library Open		1st grade Milton	4th grade Hall	Gifted Lange	Lunch	1st grade Ferris	K Bell	Closed

Figure 7.3. Elementary School Library Fixed Schedule

weekly fixed schedule (K–5 with four classes of each, as well as gifted and special needs classrooms) might look like.

Figure 7.4 models how a traveling elementary school librarian's weekly fixed schedule might appear, if he or she had three schools (Dugan, Hartley, and Stone), K–6 with two sections of each class, plus one special needs classroom in Hartley. Please note that in both elementary school fixed schedule cases, a small amount of time (left blank) has been built in to do "other" library work; for example, materials selecting and ordering; circulation activities; technology troubleshooting; pulling materials for teachers; planning library lessons; cataloging; working with volunteers; attending meetings; lunch; and so on. Additionally, librarians may choose to work through all or part of their lunch hours.

Combination/Mixed Scheduling

Some school librarians and their administration choose a "combination" or "mixed" approach for scheduling classes in the library. This usually amounts to a set 10- to 15-minute time per week for each class/classroom to check out library materials, with a flexible schedule built in for collaborative units between teachers and the librarian. In this way, educators are assured that all students will get to the library on a regular basis, while inquiry and other research/library skills "are taught and learned within the context of the curriculum and may occur in the classroom, the library" (American Association of School Librarians 2011, 1). Such a schedule will vary from week to week, since the idea behind the combination/mixed approach is that the library truly becomes an extension of the classroom. (In addition, a school

Time	Monday	Tuesday	Wednesday	Thursday	Friday
Before School	*Hartley*	*Hartley*	*Dugan*	*Stone*	*Stone*
9-9:45	*Hartley* 1st grade Miller	*Hartley* 5th grade Nixen	*Dugan* 6th grade Lavender	*Stone* 2nd grade Johnson	*Stone* 2nd grade Malloy
9:45-10:30	*Hartley* Special Needs Arnold	*Hartley* 3rd grade Neeley	*Dugan* 5th grade Price	*Stone* 1st grade Gallagher	*Stone* 6th grade Daley
10:30-11:15	*Hartley* 2nd grade Talley	*Hartley* 4th grade Grivois	*Dugan* 1st grade Silipigni	*Stone* 3rd grade Valle	*Stone* 5th grade Zee
11:15-12	*Hartley* **Lunch**/3rd grade Bailey	*Hartley* 1st grade Mason	*Dugan* 5th grade Teale	*Stone* **Lunch**	*Stone* 1st grade Garth
12-12:45	*Hartley* 5th grade Crandall	**Travel Time/Lunch**	*Dugan* **Lunch**	*Stone* 4th grade Miley	**Travel Time/Lunch**
12:45-1:30	*Hartley* 4th grade Glenn	*Dugan* 4th grade Cash	*Dugan* 6th grade Greiman	*Stone* 3rd grade Topps	*H,D, or S every third week*
1:30-2:15	*Hartley* 6th grade Vance	*Dugan* 3rd grade Campbell	*Dugan* 2nd grade Smith	*Stone* 5th grade Kiefer	*H,D, or S every third week*
2:15-3	*Hartley* 2nd grade Arnison	*Dugan* 2nd grade Leigh	*Dugan* 1st grade Lattimore	*Stone* 4th grade Alvarez	*H,D, or S every third week*
3-3:45	*Hartley* 6th grade Streeter	*Dugan* 4th grade Lucas	*Dugan* 3rd grade Schultz	*Stone* 6th grade Prince	*H,D, or S every third week*
After School	*Hartley*	*Dugan*	*Dugan*	*Stone*	*H,D, or S every third week*

Figure 7.4. Traveling Elementary School Librarian's Fixed Schedule

practicing a collaboration/mixed library scheduling approach would also necessitate establishing procedures and passes for students who might be sent to the library individually or in small groups.) An example of what a combination/mixed library schedule week in a middle school library (with two each of sixth, seventh, and eighth grades) might look like can be found in figure 7.5. In this particular case, the book checkouts are 15 minutes in length and occur during the students' English classes. During scheduled classes (where the librarian and a teacher or teachers collaborate to teach a skill set or information to a classroom of students), as well as scheduled book selections and checkouts, the library is also open for other classes, small groups, and/or individual students. This is during the entire school day. Additionally, the library is open before and after school for an hour to accommodate those students who do not have computers at home or who need the time for curricular support or for entertainment reading.

	Monday	Tuesday	Wednesday	Thursday	Friday
Before School	Library Open	Library Open	Library Open	Library Open	Library Open
Period #1	6th grade Science: research skills lesson Thompson				6th grade English: 15 minute checkout Laughlin
Period #2		8th grade Spanish: research on Frida Kahlo Balboa	7th grade English: 15 minute checkout Gomez	6th grade Technology class: how to create a web page Beglinger	
Period #3	6th grade English: 15 minute checkout Fremont		7th grade History: research on WWII Richey		
Period #4	Library Open/ Lunch	Library Open/ Lunch	Library Open/ Lunch	Library Open/ Lunch	Library Open/ Lunch
Period #5	8th grade English: 15 minute checkout Levine		7th grade History: research on WWII Richey (second class)		
Period #6		7th grade English: 15 minute checkout Isles			8th grade Math: research on time management specialist, F.B. Gilbreth Neal
Period #7				8th grade English: 15 minute checkout Thomas	
After School	Library Open	Library Open	Library Open	Library Open	Library Open

Figure 7.5. Middle School Library Combination/Mixed Schedule

Library Master Schedule

For the librarian and his or her library staff, there is one more schedule that can be important to maintain—that of the library master schedule. This schedule would be similar to a flexible schedule in that it not only could change day to day, but even hour to hour, depending on how the day progressed. Things that could be in such a schedule might include

- pulling a cartload of materials for a teacher who came in before school started and requested the items by third period;

- adding a meeting with the principal over your lunch break to discuss an intellectual freedom challenge that came via email earlier in the day;
- arranging a time to get the iPad cart purchase order to the main office;
- finding a few minutes to run to a nearby classroom to help with a technology question;
- reserving the small conference room for a group of students working on a science project;
- creating a mini-tutorial session after school for three teachers who need some Chromebook expertise as soon as possible;
- establishing a library open mic event for the speech students;
- online conferencing with a parent about a student who cannot remember to return library materials.

The simplest way to keep a master schedule or calendar current—given that there can be any number of projects and responsibilities going on in the library at the same time—might be to reserve extra space on the library class schedule to add the other items. These items could then be penciled in as needed—or typed in, if the schedule is kept on an accessible library computer. See figure 7.6 for an illustration of a school library master schedule using the middle school combination/mixed schedule as an example. (Those items for the librarian or staff only are written in this example as italics. Also, please remember that this represents one week out of the year, and that the master schedule could vary daily, weekly, monthly, and so on, depending on needs and demands of faculty, staff, administration, and students.)

Online Schedules

Any of the schedules or calendars can also be done electronically through a wide range of commercial software and web applications (123 Contact Form 2014; Event Management Systems 2014; Google 2014; Michaelson 2014; Microsoft 2014; Professional Education Designs 2014; SchoolDude 2014; WordPress, n.d.). A few have been developed specifically for libraries, such as LibCal, which states that it "is an easy to use calendaring and event management platform for libraries" (Springshare, n.d., 1).

The school librarian has many responsibilities, ranging from student and teacher instruction and training to providing materials, serving as a technology specialist, and so much more. Keeping track of all these can be challenging. Maintaining a daily or weekly agenda, calendar, timetable, list, plan, whatever you want to call it, is so important to supporting the organized environment that the library is and should be.

KEY CONCEPTS FROM THIS CHAPTER

- District-level library services may vary from district to district.
- Community support for school libraries can be in the form of public library help, funding from local business, and parental volunteers.

	Monday	Tuesday	Wednesday	Thursday	Friday
Before School	Library Open *Librarian: prepare for 6th grade Science: research skills lesson in period 1* *Staff: Pulling teacher requests; supervising student volunteers*	Library Open *Librarian: Readying library for day; collaboration meeting with Industrial Arts teacher* *Staff: Pulling teacher requests supervising student volunteers*	Library Open *Librarian: Readying library for day; meeting with principal about disruptive student* *Staff: Pulling teacher requests; supervising student volunteers*	Library Open *Librarian: Readying library for day; reviewing professional periodicals for possible library purchases* *Staff: Pulling teacher requests; supervising student volunteers*	Library Open *Librarian: Readying library for day; reviewing professional periodicals for possible library purchases* *Staff: Pulling teacher requests; supervising student volunteers*
Period #1	6th grade Science: research skills lesson Thompson *Librarian: teach 6th grade science class lesson on research skills* *Staff: continuation of before school responsibilities*	*Librarian: grade 6 area meeting* *Staff: continuation of before school responsibilities*	*Librarian: grade 7 area meeting* *Staff: continuation of before school responsibilities*	*Librarian: grade 8 area meeting* *Staff: continuation of before school responsibilities*	6th grade English: 15 minute checkout Laughlin *Librarian: work with 6th graders; continue reviewing professional periodicals for possible library purchases* *Staff: circulation, book shelving, clerical work*
Period #2	*Librarian: work on ALA book grant* *Staff: supervise*	8th grade Spanish: research on Frida Kahlo Balboa	7th grade English: 15 minute checkout Gomez	6th grade Technology class: how to create a web page	*Librarian: work on ALA book grant* *Staff: supervise*

Figure 7.6.   Library Master Schedule

- School libraries sometimes also function as a de facto public library, when there is not one available in a particular community or area.
- School library web pages can often be accessed 24 hours per day, seven days a week.
- In a virtual school library, a simple click on the correct graphic, subject, link, or listing of a search term in a search box can send the user where he or she wants to go, to obtain that which he or she wants or needs.

- Data-based decision making supports the argument for the growth of the library and informs the principal, often more used to teacher/classroom requirements and requests than those of the school librarian/library.
- School librarians may serve as RTI consultants through curriculum collaboration with teachers; supplying technology, a variety of media, and in-service programs to fellow instructors; identifying student needs; and helping with such student assessment activities as working with and training other educators in the use of assessment software and subsequent reports (Robins and Antrim 2012).
- Scheduling in the school library can be a contentious subject.
- A flexible library schedule is the best for most students and school librarians.
- The timely library access found with flexible scheduling focuses on student learning, rather than on administrative convenience.
- Flexible means still going to the library; just going when there is a requirement (research, library instruction and/or book checkout) or interest, rather than on a cyclical basis.
- Flexible library schedules are most common in middle and high school libraries.
- Elementary schools are more likely to follow a fixed schedule approach.
- With a fixed library schedule, the school librarian sees every class at the same time, during the same day of the week or school cycle. Usually, this time coincides with a classroom teacher's planning period.
- The fixed library schedule ensures that each elementary school child comes into the library on a regular basis for book checkout and library instruction.
- Students, with a fixed library schedule, are often taught library skills out of context; thus, they may not retain what they were taught.
- A combination or mixed approach for scheduling classes in the library usually amounts to a set 10- to 15-minute time per week for each class/classroom to check out library materials, with a flexible schedule built in for collaborative units between teachers and the librarian.
- The idea behind the combination/mixed approach is that the library truly becomes an extension of the classroom.
- The library master schedule is similar to a flexible schedule in that it changes day to day, and hour to hour, depending on how the day progresses.
- Online and computer software scheduling applications are available for those who do not wish to create their own.
- Keeping track of all that goes on in the library on a regular basis can be challenging.

Coming in chapter 8: "Programming and Collaboration."

DISCUSSION QUESTIONS

1. What sort of a web presence do you anticipate for your library (or one of your choice) when you become a school librarian?

2. Describe how you plan to support RTI as a school librarian.

3. Imagine you are in an elementary school where the library class period has "always" functioned as a planning period for the classroom teacher. What arguments might you use to persuade the principal and classroom teachers that a library flexible or combination/mixed schedule is better for the students, and thus for everyone?

ACTIVITIES

1. In a small group, role-play the part of a high school librarian who has just been told by his or her administration that the physical library facility and all its materials are going to be replaced with a bank of computers; from now on only online informational materials, in the form of databases and regular Internet searches, will be available. Role-play both positive and negative responses to this information, as well as pro and con arguments to this news.

2. In a small group, role-play the part of an elementary librarian who has just been told by his or her administration that the physical library facility and all its materials will now be stored in an empty room in the school's basement, and that his or her new library will be in the form of a cart loaded with materials needed that day, which he or she will push to various classes during classroom teachers' planning periods. At these times, he or she will present, albeit possibly abbreviated versions, of the library activities these students would have received had they gone to the library, as in the past. Role-play both positive and negative responses to this information, as well as pro and con arguments to this news.

3. By yourself or with a partner, join Second Life or another virtual world. Create a small computer-generated school library (your choice—elementary, middle school, high school, K–8, or K–12). Give a tour of your library for the class once it is completed.

4. Create a library master schedule (one week) for a school library of your choice. Include collaborative units with other teachers; individual, small group, and classroom activities; administrative pursuits; and other responsibilities that you anticipate a school librarian in this library would have.

REFERENCES

123 Contact Form. 2014. "Create Google Calendar Events From a Web Form as Easy as 1-2-3." http://blog.123contactform.com/2013/09/create-google-calendar-events-from-a-web-form-as-easy-as-1-2-3/.

American Association of School Librarians. 2011. "Position Statement on Flexible Scheduling." http://www.ala.org/aasl/advocacy/resources/statements/flex-sched.

Center on Response to Intervention. n.d. "The Essential Components of RTI." http://www.rti4success.org/.

Chicago Public Schools, Department of Literacy: Library Media Services. 2014. "Information for Librarians." http://cpslibraries.wikispaces.com/libinfo.

Donham, Jean. 2013. *Enhancing Teaching and Learning: A Leadership Guide for School Librarians.* Chicago, Ill.: Neal-Schuman.

Event Management Systems. 2014. "Room Scheduling Software." http://www.dea.com/Solutions/Software-Solutions/Room-Scheduling-Software.aspx?mi=1.

Florida Virtual School. 2008. "Library." http://library.flvs.net/home.htm.

Google. 2014. "Google Calendar." https://www.google.com/calendar.

Hillsborough County Public Schools. n.d. "Library Media Services: Library Media Services Resources." http://www.sdhc.k12.fl.us/doc/list/library-media-services/resources/69-266/.

Johns, Suzy and Patrick, Jacquelin. n.d. "Data-Based Decision Making: What Our Numbers Are Telling Us." http://www.modelprogram.com/images/PPTDataBasedDecisionMaking.pdf.

Library Media Services. 2013. "Virtual Library." http://virtuallibrary.dadeschools.net/.

McGregor, Joy. 2006. "Flexible Scheduling: Implementing an Innovation." *School Library Media Research: Research Journal of the American Association of School Librarians* 9: 1–34. www.ala.org/aasl/slr.

Michaelson, Elizabeth. 2014. "Scheduling Software." http://lj.libraryjournal.com/2014/02/technology/scheduling-software/#_.

Microsoft. 2014. "Calendar I: Outlook Calendar Basics." http://office.microsoft.com/en-us/outlook-help/calendar-i-outlook-calendar-basics-RZ010100073.aspx.

Middleton-Cross Plains Area School District. 2014. "Online Resources Elementary/Middle Schools." http://www.mcpasd.k12.wi.us/students/library-media-centers/online-resources-elementary/middle-schools.

Oakland High School. 2013. "Welcome to the Oakland/SAMI/SOTA Online Resource Center." http://tpslib.tacoma.k12.wa.us/common/servlet/presenthomeform.do;jsessionid=92CBF6483CD16BDA394F8F086F22BE2F?l2m=Home&tm=Home&l2m=Home.

Owl: Purdue Online Writing Lab. n.d. "Site Map." https://owl.english.purdue.edu/sitemap/.

Professional Education Designs. 2014. "Facility Scheduler." http://www.pedesigns.com/fs.asp.

Robins, Jennifer and Antrim, Patricia. 2012. "School Librarians and Response to Intervention." *School Library Research: Research Journal of the American Association of School Librarians* 15: 1–16.

SchoolDude. 2014. "Facility Scheduling, Permit Processing and Event Management Software." http://www.schooldude.com/solutions/products/fsdirect.

Springshare. n.d. "LibCal: Complete Calendaring Solutions for Libraries." http://www.springshare.com/libcal/index.html.

Warlick, David. 2010. "Son of Citation Machine." http://www.citationmachine.net/.

WordPress. n.d. "Booking Calendar and Appointment Scheduler." https://wordpress.org/plugins/appointy-appointment-scheduler/.

8

Programming and Collaboration

In chapter 2, we addressed national and state standards and guidelines and how these influence the school library overall. In many of these standards and guidelines, various buzz words pop up, among them the following: collaboration, student achievement, inquiry-based learning, Common Core, and multiple literacies: information, technological, visual, digital, data, and textual, among others. The list can go on and on. Certainly a major part of library programming is influenced by standards and guidelines as well as by the needs and desires of school library patrons: students, staff, and sometimes the local community. This chapter looks to programming and collaboration in the school library. Programming for this chapter is interpreted broadly to include teaching and research, as well as curricular support and such things as author visits, poetry slams, homework help, and more. Collaboration in this chapter focuses on that between the school librarian and his or her faculty and staff, and possibly students.

STUDENT AND FACULTY NEEDS AND WANTS

What do our patrons, usually students and faculty, need and request from us? Well, that can depend on any number of things: the age, grade, maturity, and interest levels of our students; the curriculum; where the school/district is with technology; national and state standards and guidelines followed by the school/district; community resources; parental involvement; location of school to closest public library and bookstores; and so much more. Indeed, the criteria determining what programming a particular school library should focus on can be overwhelming. However, assuming that there are other venues for entertainment for your patrons, it is most likely that the library will have as its main charge the support of curricular needs of the students and those things that teachers request to assist in their instruction. For school librarians, the curricular needs and requests also then inform what they may be asked to teach to students or how they will collaborate with classroom instructors.

K–12 schools are divided up in any number of ways, most commonly, elementary, middle, and high schools. But there are also examples of K–9 schools, K–12, pre-K–6, and so on. In addition, there are public schools, private schools, charter schools, and so many more. All of these can have (and should have) school libraries. Let's now look at library instruction as a part of programming.

Curricular/Curriculum Integration and Library Instruction

Curricular/curriculum integration and library instruction can take many forms, depending on who is teaching or being taught, and the requested instruction. It can focus on research skills, literature circles, book care, web page creation, who knows! The school librarian of the 21st century needs a wide variety of knowledge in many areas to be able to support his or her clientele. With this in mind, many organizations have chosen to create lists of library skill sets that they believe students need to be taught. For example, *Standards for the 21st-Century Learner in Action*, a publication of the American Association of School Librarians (AASL 2009b), focuses primarily on the AASL (national) standards for the 21st century learner and how these can be taught to students through the combined efforts of the school librarian and the classroom teacher. As such, this book assigns library-related skills' benchmarks for each grade level, K–12, with illustrative lessons/instructional plans based on each standard. These lesson plan models may additionally include connections to state and local content standards, assessments, activities, and so on. One such example for students in second grade—"Standard 1: Inquire, think critically, and gain knowledge" (American Association of School Librarians 2009b, 72)—looks at how "students will apply the research process in a major project," learning how to "(1) develop questions that relate to and are of importance to their topic, (2) select a variety of resources to retrieve relevant information, (3) use a graphic organizer to organize the information collected, and (4) assess information to decide if it meets their needs" (American Association of School Librarians 2009b, 72). Another helpful tool when working with the national standards is the "Learning Standards and Program Guidelines Implementation Toolkit" from AASL.

State standards also play a role in students' library learning. In Illinois, for example, the Illinois School Library Media Association (ISLMA) promotes I-SAIL (Illinois Standards Aligned Instruction for Libraries), the purpose of which "is to empower, educate, and encourage school library information specialists to plan strategically with other teachers to incorporate information literacy skills in lessons and thereby provide college and career readiness for students" (Illinois School Library Media Association 2012, 1). For instance, the school library learning objectives for an 11th grader in an Illinois school, given "Standard 3: Use information accurately, creatively, and ethically to share knowledge and to participate collaboratively and productively as a member of a democratic society" (Illinois School Library Media Association 2014, 21) would be the following:

1. Analyze information and identify topics, subtopics, and relationships
2. Organize information in a logical sequence
3. Select an appropriate format for communicating ideas
4. Develop a formal outline or storyboard
5. Create a product that clearly expresses ideas
6. Use appropriate resources and technology in creating products
7. Revise and refine as necessary
8. Present, perform, or share information and ideas successfully
9. Evaluate product or presentation
10. Do not plagiarize
11. Observe copyright guidelines
12. Cite print and nonprint sources in a properly formatted bibliography
13. Respect intellectual freedom and recognize various viewpoints (Illinois School Library Media Association 2014, 21).

Please note that this particular set of state standards also aligns to the Common Core State Standards (n.d.) and the national standards from AASL (see earlier paragraph), with guidance from the second edition of the National Educational Technology Standards for Students (Illinois School Library Media Association 2014). Thus, when using standards to support teaching as a school library program area, any number of standards can be employed. (For more on state standards, see chapter 2.)

It is also possible that a particular community or school will have its own (local) standards that align library skill sets by grades.

Figure 8.1 shows a worksheet from a sample school library lesson plan entitled "Plagiarism and Copyright for Young Children."

Research, technology, and other skills taught to students in the library or by the school librarian are ideally not taught in isolation but as part of curricular support for a particular class or unit of instruction. This means that classroom teachers may also be involved.

Collaboration

"A collaborative approach to teaching . . . is most effective because process skills are best learned in the context of content learning, and content is most effectively learned when the necessary learning skills are taught at the same time" (American Association of School Librarians 2009b, 9). With this in mind, the school librarian, according to AASL directives,

- collaborates with a core team of classroom teachers and specialists to design, implement, and evaluate inquiry lessons and units;

Name _____   #_____

Writing Citations

Directions: Work with your partner. Choose four different items from the basket. Look carefully to find the title and author of the items. Record the information below.

Item 1	Item 2
Title: _____ _____ Author: _____	Title: _____ _____ Author: _____
Item 3	**Item 4**
Title: _____ _____ Author: _____	Title: _____ _____ Author: _____

Figure 8.1. Elementary School Library Lesson: Plagiarism and Copyright for Young Children

- collaborates with an extended team that includes parents, members of the community, museums, academic and public libraries, municipal services, private organizations, and commercial entities to include their expertise and assistance in inquiry lessons and units;
- works with administrators to actively promote, support, and implement collaboration;
- seeks input from students on the learning process. (American Association of School Librarians 2009a, 20)

Thus, K–12 learning in the 21st century is best supported by collaborative efforts between and among the classroom teachers, school librarians, administrators, students, and other interested individuals and groups.

Collaboration: School Librarians and Classroom Teachers

How can/do school librarians and classroom teachers work together? These two groups are most likely to pool resources when there is a unit in a particular classroom that needs (or can use) some sort of support that the library and/or librarian has to offer. Here are some collaboration examples.

- The high school librarian instructs senior English students in the use of a newspaper database during a research unit the English teacher has devised.

- An elementary librarian monitors fourth graders, playing an educational game called Let's Go to Mars (NASA 2011), on library computers, as part of a science unit.
- The middle school librarian teaches information graphics creation to a technology class, using the Internet.
- A K–9 librarian instructs a ninth grade class in the steps involved in print and online research, including how to use an online bibliography (reference) generator.
- An elementary librarian reads a picture book to a first grade class and then teaches how to find picture books on the shelf.
- A high school librarian teaches a unit on media literacy as part of a larger digital literacy unit for art students.
- A K–9 school librarian teaches Big6 (Big6 2013) and Super 3 (Lima Primary Library 2014) research skills to the students in his school as part of an all-school literacy unit.
- The middle school librarian coaches the eighth grade speech team on the value of primary sources as argumentative data.
- The school librarian and school technology coach unite to create a lesson on simple web page making for the after-school technology club.
- The school librarian partners with the technology specialist to train literacy coaches in the use of reading-related social networking tools, such as Shelfari and Goodreads.
- The elementary librarian collaborates with the reading teacher on a series of lessons where each teaches a different nonfiction book to a group of students with learning disabilities.

In support of collaborative efforts between school librarians and classroom teachers, please note that the AASL has released a position statement on the role of school librarians in reading and literature. In part, the rationale for this is as follows: "Reading is a foundational skill for 21st-century learners. Guiding learners to become engaged and effective users of ideas and information and to appreciate literature requires that they develop as strategic readers who can comprehend, analyze, and evaluate text in both print and digital formats. Learners must also have opportunities to read for enjoyment as well as for information. School librarians are in a critical and unique position to partner with other educators to elevate the reading development of our nation's youth" (American Association of School Librarians 2014, 1). As a school librarian states in *Knowledge Quest* (professional journal of AASL), "There are things that teachers can do in the classroom . . . and then things that classroom teachers and I can do together" (Conklin 2012, 46).

Here are some examples of media that a school librarian might provide to a teacher in need of materials for a class. In this way, the librarian may be supporting the curricular needs of the students, as well as assisting the instructor; thus, providing such materials can be seen as a type of collaboration between the librarian and the teacher and therefore within the realm of programming.

- Websites on advertising for a sociology class studying the influences of advertising on society
- Teacher's guide and accompanying CD of materials on President Lincoln, requested by an honors teacher
- Study materials in the form of flash cards obtained from an online site focused on the first amendment
- Lesson plans and activities, on red-tail hawks and found on the back of a library poster, for a science class
- Fiction book to teach math, found in the teacher's edition of *A Long Way from Chicago*; included in this volume is a section with math activities based on the story (Peck 1998)
- App called, "Shakespeare in Bits," obtained from iTunes
- Picture book entitled, *Razia's Ray of Hope,* for a third grade class talking about a girl's education in Afghanistan
- Illustrated copy of the Gettysburg Address for a special needs class
- Educational board game
- Educational video game
- Coloring book of prairie flowers, requested by a kindergarten teacher
- E-books for students in a 1:1 iPad classroom
- Books up for the state of Kansas's William Allen White Children's Book Awards
- URLs list of citation styles for a sophomore history class
- Two reading guide PDFs that assign Common Core Standards to various activities teachers may carry out with students, given the Narnia series of books
- Variety of Science, Technology, Engineering, and Math (STEM) sources off the web and off library shelves for a Parent Teacher Organization (PTO) program

Teacher/librarian collaboration can highlight the importance that the school library and librarian play in the school. "Collaboration with classroom teachers . . . has raised the visibility of our school librarians as instructional leaders in the district, increased their time in curricular work, and promoted their participation" in professional learning communities (Bilyeu 2009, 19).

Collaboration: School Librarians and an Extended Team

School librarians also sometimes work with those in the community to provide information and materials for elementary, middle, and secondary students. These individuals, groups, and organizations (AASL calls them the "extended team") may include the students' parents; other community members; museum and/or public or academic library staff; as well as community organizations such as the Rotary Club, the American Legion, Toastmasters International, and so on; police, fire department, and other local community services; neighboring shops and stores; and more (American Association of School Librarians 2009a). This extended team, based on particular skills, interests, media, and so on, may be able to support curricular requests or special interests and needs of individual students and/or certain student groups; for instance the Future Medical Careers Club, a high school auto safety class, the school newspaper staff. Such help, sometimes labeled as *reference and referral, information and referral,* or a similar term, is defined next.

A referral occurs when one reference person consults with another to help answer a patron's question. Referrals can happen in all formats of reference (in person, chat, email, telephone, etc.). Referrals include

- one reference person sending a question/patron to another for additional help and expertise, and ceasing his or her own work on the question;
- multiple reference personnel passing a question back and forth, with each contributing based on his or her expertise/knowledge of different aspects of the question.

A referral is a collegial way to meet a patron's information needs most effectively (University Library 2012, 1).

Following are illustrations of when the extended team might help the school librarian with certain requests:

- The driver education class wants to stage a mock accident and rescue. The school librarian works with the class to contact the local police, ambulance/hospital, and others who would support this activity.
- The agriculture teacher wishes to assign students to internships on dairy farms. The school librarian passes along this request to a regional farmers association.
- A group of high school students ask for a literature/lunch group focusing on fantasy novels made into young adult movies. The school librarian contacts a local service club, which then offers to create, staff, and run the literature/lunch activity.
- A student interested in meteorology asks the school librarian where he might learn more about this career. She directs him to the nearest National Weather Service Weather Forecast Office.
- A student career club wants help creating emoticons for its Facebook page. The school librarian puts the students in touch with a graphic design company that volunteers its help.
- The school librarian wishes to use social media (Dankowski 2013) to promote the many features of the school library to the extended team. She approaches a self-proclaimed "computer-geek" parent, who readily agrees to work on a You-Tube video of the library and then blog about it on the local community blog.

"Patrons often have needs that books alone will not meet. They need the services of special groups or agencies" (Ohio Library Council 2008, 1).

Collaboration: School Librarians and School Administrators

School librarians may also collaborate on occasion with school administrators (principals, vice principals, technology directors, superintendents, and others). Collaborative activities between these two groups might include

- creation of a school web page;
- participation in the writing of the school district technology plan;
- contribution to a school-wide grant project;
- composition of a new school handbook;
- formation of a district-wide Internet ethics panel;
- construction of a job center for district at-risk high school students.

Indeed, there are many ways that these two groups can work together in the school environment.

Collaboration: School Librarians and Students

"There are things that . . . I as the school librarian can do with students in the school library" (Conklin 2012, 46). Among such things could be some sort of teamwork. Perhaps the school librarian asks the sixth grade class to recommend Internet sites on dogs that he can then share with second graders; maybe a high school woodworking class is brought into the library to help build a new display case; conceivably a seventh grade English class could tutor remedial readers from the fourth grade as part of a literature unit held in the library; or a group of interested high school students could help create a school library Facebook page. There are many ways that students and school librarians might partner.

In addition to the types of collaboration already described, school librarians also collaborate with each other through sharing information and materials; an experienced librarian mentoring a new school librarian (Ricks 2013); coordinating programming, such as author visits; and more.

The Flipped Library

In the past few years, the concept of the flipped classroom has become recognized as a valid instructional method. A flipped classroom, in today's world, is one where instruction is filmed and placed on videos to be viewed online at home while classroom time is spent as "a place for talking, doing group projects, and getting individual help from teachers" (Springen 2013, 1). Additionally, "a flipped classroom inverts the traditional educational model so that the content is delivered outside of class, while class time is spent on activities normally considered 'homework.' For example, students may access instructional material through videos, podcasts or online tutorials before the class meeting. Then during class time, students work on activities which force them to apply what they have learned" (American Library Association 2014). School librarians can help support the flipped classroom model by doing the many types of support strategies mentioned earlier in this chapter—or can flip library instruction in a manner similar to that of the flipped classroom. For example, a school librarian may choose to videotape him- or herself teaching a particular set of library skills, for example, using a library database. Then, after students have viewed the video online at home (in their own time and at their own pace), the class may come in to the library to use that database—with the librarian's help and supervision. In addition, library flipping might also mean "remote instruction and the use of mobile tools, so applications that let students quickly add lesson comments and questions—via text, video, and audio" (Bayliss 2013, 1). There are currently flipping strategies, flipping Nings, rubrics for flipped classrooms, and so much more (Spartan Guides, n.d.). There is also available online a set of resources called, "Flip Your Library," where librarians can share materials (such as Power-Points) that they use for flipping purposes (Diigo 2013). Now, let's take a look at school library programming.

Programming Outside the Classroom

Library programming is in no way limited to that dealing with curricular support. Indeed, there are other types of collaboration, assistance, and so on, that can come under the heading of library programming.

Cooperating with Fellow Faculty

Here are some ways that the librarian might cooperate with his or her colleagues in the school:

- Provide space to display student art
- Offer an after-school club in tandem with and of interest to another faculty member
- Collaborate with school technology coaches, technology specialists, and so on, in terms of the teaching and training of faculty and students in new apps
- Feature library materials on STEM pursuits

Student Assistance

Programming for students, in terms of possible assistance needed, might include the following:

- Opening the library before and after school for research purposes
- Creating a graded library class for students interested in pursuing a career in this field
- Establishing a student library volunteer program
- Instituting a book or technology club
- Supporting the homework hotline

Exciting, Interesting, and Entertaining School Library Programming

Here is where much of the "fun" programming is listed; that is, what most of us think, when we consider library programming:

- Author visits
- Poetry slams
- Reader's theater
- Harry Potter day
- International festival (with food, fun, games)
- After-school and Saturday school library supported bus rides to the public library
- "Ask-a-librarian" online reference
- Writing award, created and participated in by students
- Library-sanctioned book sales
- Hobby displays
- Movie night
- Student-produced TV/school announcements
- Student-created video awards
- Student-produced websites, blogs, discussion boards, and so on, supported by the librarian and library resources
- Library coffee house

There are a multitude of activities and events that can be generated and sanctioned by the school library. Look to your clientele, their interests and needs; what ideas do you think might work? What interesting pursuits do you want to offer?

KEY CONCEPTS FROM THIS CHAPTER

- Standards play a role in library programming.
- Library programming can support the curriculum.
- Twenty-first century K–12 learning involves collaborative efforts between classroom teachers and school librarians.
- Teacher-librarian collaboration highlights the importance that the school library and librarians play in the school.
- Reference and referral is a type of cooperation between two entities (for example, the school librarian and a local business) in order to support the requests of school library patrons.
- Collaboration can also occur between the school library/librarian and his or her administration or students.
- Library programming is not limited to curricular support.
- Entertainment can be a function of library programming.
- Libraries, too, can be flipped!

- Library programming can be fun!
- Librarians can be creative people.

Coming in chapter 9: "Library and Ethics."

DISCUSSION QUESTIONS

1. Describe collaboration between a librarian and teacher. Give examples.
2. What are three types of library skills that you might teach in an elementary school library? Middle school? High school? Explain why these skills are important for this particular group of students.
3. List the steps involved in a library book sale.
4. How you would select a speaker for a library-sanctioned author event?

ACTIVITIES

1. Surf the web for two sites that support the teaching of research, literature appreciation, or support a class curriculum (sites that could be *used or taught in the library, by* you, *the librarian*). Share these with your classmates via a discussion forum, blog, or social media site.
2. Lurk or join a social media site for readers, such as Goodreads, Shelfari, LibraryThing, or BookCrossing. Discuss how you might use such a site with your students.
3. With a partner, discuss how you would set up a literature club for a group of your students. Consider what would be read and why; activities that would occur as part of the club meetings; when, where, and how often the group would meet; and other logistics of such an organization.

REFERENCES

American Association of School Librarians. 2009a. *Empowering Learners: Guidelines for School Library Media Programs.* Chicago, Ill.: American Association of School Librarians.
———. 2009b. *Standards for the 21st-Century Learner in Action.* Chicago, Ill.: American Association of School Librarians.
———. 2014. "Position Statement on the School Librarian's Role in Reading." http://www.ala.org/aasl/advocacy/resources/statements/reading-role.
American Library Association. 2014. "Keeping Up With . . . Flipped Classrooms." http://www.ala.org/acrl/publications/keeping_up_with/flipped_classrooms.
Bayliss, Sarah. 2013. "Flipping the Library: Tips from Three Pros: The Digital Shift 2013." http://www.thedigitalshift.com/2013/10/k-12/flipping-the-library-the-digital-shift-2013/.
Big6. 2013. Home page. http://big6.com/

Bilyeu, Linda. 2009. "Teachers and Librarians Collaborate in Lesson Study." *Knowledge Quest* 38 (2): 14–19.

Common Core State Standards. n.d. Home page. http://commoncorestandards.com/.

Conklin, Kerry Pierce. 2012. "Making the Case for Coteaching—the Evidence-Based Way." *Knowledge Quest* 40 (4): 46–49.

Cooley, Sarah. 2013. "Copyright for Young Children." Assignment for ETT 542. DeKalb, Ill.: Department of Educational Technology Research and Assessment, Northern Illinois University.

Dankowski, Terra. 2013. "How Libraries Are Using Social Media: Expanding Online Toolkits to Promote Advocacy." *American Libraries* 44 (5): 38–41.

Diigo. 2013. "Flip Your Library." https://groups.diigo.com/group/flip-your-library.

Illinois School Library Media Association. 2012. "I-SAIL 2011." https://www.islma.org/ISAIL.htm.

———. 2014. "11th Grade." Illinois Standards Aligned Instruction for Libraries. Galesburg, Ill.: Illinois School Library Media Association.

Lima Primary Library. 2014. "Super 3 Research: Plan Do Review." http://www.hflcsd.org/webpages/tpulver/super.cfm.

NASA. 2011. "Let's Go to Mars!" http://spaceplace.nasa.gov/mars-adventure/en/.

Ohio Library Council. 2008. "Information and Referral Services." http://www.olc.org/ore/4ir.htm.

Peck, Richard. 1998. *A Long Way from Chicago.* New York, N.Y.: Puffin Books.

Ricks, Joyce Jones. 2013. "Collaborating: An Effective Mentoring Program for School Libraries." *Knowledge Quest* 41 (4): 16–21.

Spartan Guides. n.d. "For Teachers: Flipping." http://sdst.libguides.com/flipping.

Springen, Karen. 2013. "Flipping the Classroom: A Revolutionary Approach to Learning Presents Some Pros and Cons." http://www.slj.com/2013/04/standards/flipping-the-classroom-a-revolutionary-approach-to-learning-presents-some-pros-and-cons/#_.

University Library. 2012. "Reference Referral Policy." http://www.library.illinois.edu/committee/ReferenceServices/policies/referral_policy.html.

9

Ethics, Intellectual Freedom, and Copyright

For a school librarian, the ethics and laws involved with the selection, use, borrowing, and evaluation of materials can be confusing and overwhelming. In chapter 1, we consider that the school librarian is seen as an expert in many areas, including those of copyright, intellectual freedom, privacy, and other ethical issues commonly found in the school library; in chapter 2, we study national and state professional standards and how these impinge on our ethical and legal views; and in chapter 3, we look at school library policies and procedures related to the ethics and law as seen in copyright, intellectual freedom, access to information, and more. As can be seen, ethics and law actually are woven throughout what we are responsible for in our roles as school library leaders.

Take a look, for example, at the Standards for the 21st-Century Learner as found in the American Association of School Librarians' *Standards for the 21st-Century Learner in Action* (2009b). Under the heading "Common Beliefs" can be found a statement on how school librarians need to teach their students ethical behavior in terms of diversity, responsible and safe use of social media, and information gathering and use (11). Responsibilities under all four of the main standards address legal and ethical concepts in terms of both creators/owners and users:

1. "Inquire, think critically and gain knowledge"
2. "Draw conclusions, make informed decisions, apply knowledge to new situations and create new knowledge"
3. "Share knowledge and participate ethically and productively as members of our democratic society" and
4. "Pursue personal and aesthetic growth." (American Association of School Librarians 2009b, 7)

For instance, four out of the five of Standard 1's responsibilities are

1.3.1 Respect copyright/intellectual property rights of creators and producers.
1.3.2 Seek divergent perspectives during information gathering and assessment.
1.3.3 Follow ethical and legal guidelines in gathering and using information.
1.3.5 Use information technology responsibly." (American Association of School Librarians 2009b, 13)

As can be seen, all of these speak to ethics and law. The same holds true for many of the responsibilities under the other three main American Association of School Librarians (AASL) standards (14–16).

Other professional organizations to which school librarians can belong (see chapter 1) may also address professional ethics and/or law. A case in point is the International Society for Technology in Education (ISTE). The fourth of ISTE's five standards is "Promote and model digital citizenship and responsibility" (International Society for Technology in Education, n.d., 2). The four parts of this standard stress "advocate, model, and teach safe, legal, and ethical use of digital information and technology . . . , equitable access to appropriate digital tools and resources . . ., digital etiquette and responsible social interactions related to the use of technology and information," and "engaging with colleagues and students of other cultures using digital age communication and collaboration tools" (International Society for Technology in Education, n.d., 2).

Another example is the Code of Professional Ethics of the Association for Educational Communication and Technology (AECT). This code, which addresses commitment to individuals, as well as the AECT profession and society as a whole, states, among other things, that members are obligated to "protect the individual rights of access to materials of varying points of view . . . conduct professional business so as to protect the privacy and maintain the personal integrity of the individual . . . seek to avoid content that reinforces or promotes gender, ethnic, racial, or religious stereotypes . . . engage in fair and equitable practices" and "inform users of the stipulations and interpretations of the copyright law and other laws affecting the profession and encourage compliance" (Association for Educational Communications and Technology 2007, 1; Sherry et al. 2008).

Indeed the support of professional standards and policies and procedures as well as our own individual morals and ethical beliefs are a big part of what lead us, as school librarians, to make the choices we do for materials selection and evaluation, how we deal with our school clientele, and so much more. Next, let's look to two important pieces of literature for us as library professionals, the Code of Ethics of the American Library Association (ALA) and the Library Bill of Rights.

LIBRARY CODE OF ETHICS

"As members of the American Library Association, we recognize the importance of codifying and making known to the profession and to the general public the ethical principles that guide the work of librarians. . . . Ethical dilemmas occur when values are in conflict. . . . We are members of a profession explicitly committed to intellectual freedom and the freedom of access to information" (Office for Intellectual Freedom 2010a, 303). The previous quotations are from the beginning of the ALA's Code of Ethics and "define the profession of librarianship into broad principles that may be used by individual members of that profession . . . as a framework for dealing with situations involving ethical conflicts" (Office for Intellectual Freedom 2010a, 305). While this code addresses all librarians, not just those in the school, the sentiments behind its statements reflect how our major professional association (ALA) encourages us as school librarians to conduct ourselves in our working lives. Now we look to another important document from ALA, the Library Bill of Rights.

LIBRARY BILL OF RIGHTS

The Library Bill of Rights is the premier intellectual freedom policy of the American Library Association. Its beginnings are in a 1938 statement from a public librarian at the Des Moines (Iowa) Public Library and have been revised by the ALA several times since its inception. Like the Library Code of Ethics, discussed in the previous section, the Library Bill of Rights is a general statement, covering all types of libraries. The current Library Bill of Rights, last updated in 1996, can be found at http://www.ala.org/ advocacy/intfreedom/librarybill. There are six points to this document. To summarize them briefly, they are library materials are to be provided for the clientele that the library serves, no matter what these materials represent; library resources are to present all points of view; libraries will challenge any censorship situations that occur as part of their provision of materials to their patrons; libraries will cooperate with all who are concerned with "resisting abridgment of free expression and free access to ideas" (Office for Intellectual Freedom 2010a, 49); no individual's right to use a library will be denied based on their circumstances, beliefs, and so on; and library spaces are available to all who wish to use them equally (Office for Intellectual Freedom 2010a).

In addition to the Library Bill of Rights, there are 22 interpretations of this document, ranging from "Access to Digital Information, Services, and Networks" to "Diversity in Collection Development" to "Labeling and Rating Systems" to "Restricted Access to Library Materials" (Office for Intellectual Freedom 2010e, 1). These interpretations are ALA policies. Several of these have especial meaning for school libraries, including "Access for Children and Young Adults to Nonprint Materials," "Access to Resources and Services in the School Library Media Program," "Free Access to Libraries for Minors," and "Minors and Internet Interactivity" (Office for Intellectual Freedom 2010e, 1). Let's take a brief look at these four next.

Access for Children and Young Adults to Nonprint Materials

Adopted in 1989 by the ALA Council and amended in 2004, this particular interpretation of the Library Bill of Rights (LBOR) focuses on (for the purposes of school libraries) the rights of students to access "sound, images, data, games, software, and other content in all formats such as tapes, CDs, DVDs, music CDs, computer games, software, databases, and other emerging technologies" (Office for Intellectual Freedom 2010b, 1). Some nonprint media (for example, movies and games) may have commercial ratings assigned to them; ALA, however, does not recognize such ratings and considers commercial, as well as any ratings assigned by librarians and libraries, to be unacceptable (Office for Intellectual Freedom 2010b).

Access to Resources and Services in the School Library Media Program

First adopted by the ALA Council in 1986 and amended several times after that, the latest being in 2008, this interpretation emphasizes that "all students have equitable access to library facilities, resources, and instructional programs" and school librarians "assume a leadership role in promoting the principles of intellectual freedom within the school by providing resources and services that create and sustain an atmosphere of free inquiry" as well as provide materials "that meet the needs as well as the developmental and maturity levels of students" (Office for Intellectual Freedom 2010c, 1).

Free Access to Libraries for Minors

This interpretation of the LBOR was first adopted in 1972 and amended four times, the last amendments being passed in 2008. "Free Access to Libraries for Minors" is, as its title asserts, a statement affirming that children and young adults also have First Amendment rights (i.e., the right of free speech and access to information in any format) and that the "American Library Association opposes all attempts to restrict access to library services, materials, and facilities based on the age of library users" (Office for Intellectual Freedom 2010d, 1).

Minors and Internet Interactivity

In school library terms the rights of K–12 school students, according to the "Minors and Internet Interactivity" interpretation is to "retrieve, interact with, and create information posted on the Internet" (Office for Intellectual Freedom 2010f, 1). It is one of the newer LBOR interpretations, having been adopted in 2009. Specifically this interpretation covers Internet filtering, including access to interactive sites (such as social networking sites). "In an effort to protect minors' privacy, adults sometimes restrict access to interactive Web environments. Filters, for example, are sometimes used to restrict access by youth to interactive social networking tools" (Office for Intellectual Freedom 2010f, 1).

As a current or prospective school librarian, it behooves you to read and understand the Library Bill of Rights, as well as those ALA interpretations just covered. These documents affirm the support of intellectual freedom in America's school libraries.

THE FREEDOM TO READ

"'The Freedom to Read,' the best known of the American Library Association's documents supporting the principles of intellectual freedom as embodied in the *Library Bill of Rights*" (Office for Intellectual Freedom 2010a, 208) finds support for its opinions in the U.S. Constitution (United States Constitution 1787) and the First Amendment (Illinois First Amendment Center, n.d.). ALA's statement has been revised several times since its first inception in 1953, the latest revision coming in 2004 (Office for Intellectual Freedom 2010a). However, the basic sentiments remain the same. Perhaps the first sentence of this document is among the most telling: "The freedom to read is essential to our democracy" (Office for Intellectual Freedom 2010a, 203). It is through texts such as this, as well as those who believe in them, that we as school librarians are able to find support for the intellectual freedom issues that can occur in our schools.

In addition to the Freedom to Read document, the Library Bill of Rights, and the Library Code of Ethics, the ALA has created and refined several other policy statements to support ethics and legal issues in American libraries. Among them are the following:

Libraries: An American Value

Guidelines for the Development and Implementation of Policies, Regulations, and Procedures Affecting Access to Library Materials, Services, and Facilities

Guidelines for the Development of Policies and Procedures Regarding User Behavior and Library Usage

Dealing with Concerns about Library Resources

Academic Freedom

Collections, Access and Challenges

Digital Information, Services, and Networks

Equity and Diversity. (Office for Intellectual Freedom 2010a, 224–253)

INTELLECTUAL FREEDOM

We have addressed ethical policies as written and adapted by the ALA, including two premier ones for intellectual freedom. Now let's look to intellectual freedom in the K–12 schools of the United States. Like many other issues found in school libraries, the subject of intellectual freedom has produced over the generations an overabundance of books, articles, websites, movies, and more. So, exactly what is intellectual freedom and why is it important in the school library?

According to the ALA, "Intellectual freedom is the right of every individual to both seek and receive information from all points of view without restriction. It provides for free access to all expressions of ideas through which any and all sides of a question, cause or movement may be explored" (American Library Association 2014b, 1). The concept of intellectual freedom is supported by three amendments to the U.S. Constitution, the first, fifth, and fourteenth. The First Amendment promotes the freedom of speech and the press, and the Fifth Amendment guarantees all people protection by invasion against the federal government; such protection also includes the privileges to speak and read freely. The Fourteenth Amendment obligates the states to respect the rights of all their citizens, in much the same manner as the Fifth Amendment does for the federal government through the due process clause (Kelly 2014; Constitution of the United States, n.d.).

Other terms of importance when studying intellectual freedom include censorship and challenges. Censorship is "a change in the access status of material, based on the content of the work and made by a governing authority or its representatives. Such changes include exclusion, restriction, removal, or age/grade-level access limitations" (Office for Intellectual Freedom 2010a, 106). A challenge is "a formal, written complaint requesting that library materials be removed or restricted." A challenge can be in the form of an "expression of concern . . . oral complaint . . . written complaint . . . public attack [or] . . . censorship" (Office for Intellectual Freedom 2010a, 417). Challenges and censorship do occur in American school libraries.

Intellectual Freedom and School Libraries

What do the Harry Potter series, *The Adventures of Huckleberry Finn*, *And Tango Makes Three*, *The Invisible Man*, and *The Giver* have in common? Well, for one thing, they have all been challenged or banned in American schools. Books, movies, web pages, software—almost any media can be challenged or banned, and many of them have been. Included among the reasons that individuals and/or groups often give for such actions are that the item in question is sexually explicit, profane or obscene, religious or the "wrong" religion, or violent; that the students who would read/view/listen to the work are too immature for it; that the work contains witchcraft, nudity, homosexuality, antifamily outlooks, suicide, drugs and alcohol, politics, or technical errors; or that the item may in some way be inaccurate (American Library Association 2014c; Hopkins 1991; Adams 2008, 2009).

John Milton (17th century poet), Judy Blume (21st century young adult author), Frank Zappa (20th century musician), Judith Krug (well-known former director of ALA's Office for Intellectual Freedom), and many more have come out in support of intellectual freedom in their time. On the other side of the coin are those who would censor or ban. Just as those who support intellectual freedom can be anybody, so too can those who would challenge or ban: your friend or neighbor, a fellow teacher or librarian, a politician or businessman. Likewise, because we are a large nation composed of numerous cultures, races, religions, and ideologies, what we will accept—or not—varies exponentially as well. Our school library collections need to reflect that diversity; after all, we are teaching our students about the world in which they live. They need to read/view/listen to media about themselves—and about those dissimilar to themselves.

Collection Development and Selection Policies

When a would-be censor (whether a parent, principal, student, or community member) tries to rid a school library of a particular item or restrict its use to those students who bring in a note from home or are in a particular grade, the librarian needs to have support for why that item is on the shelf (or on the web). One way is through the collection development policy. Part of a collection development policy is the selection policy, and part of the selection policy deals with selection criteria (see chapter 3). A basic criterion for purchase/obtaining of particular library media, for example, is that such media support the school curriculum. Other selection criteria (broad or specific) will also support why the library has (or has access to) a particular item. Here are some general examples (please note specifically the last point in the list):

- Materials integral to the instructional program
- Materials appropriate for the reading level and understanding of students in the school
- Materials reflecting the interests and needs of the students and faculty served by the media center
- Materials warranting inclusion in the collection because of their literary and/or artistic value and merit
- Materials presenting information with the greatest degree of accuracy and clarity possible
- Materials representing a fair and unbiased presentation of information. In controversial areas, the media specialist, in cooperation with the faculty, should select materials representing as many shades of opinion as possible, in order that varying viewpoints are available to students. (American Library Association 2014d, 1)

Thus, selection criteria can help when dealing with controversial materials, in that they demonstrate exactly why a particular medium was added to the library collection. However, there are other parts of a selection policy that also are needed, should someone decide that a library material is objectionable and "needs" to be removed from the library.

Controversial Materials Policies

A good school library selection policy will include a section on controversial materials and policies that support their placement in school libraries. In this section might be included such documents as the Library Bill of Rights, the Library Code of Ethics, the Freedom to Read text, and the First Amendment to the Constitution. There might also be a statement in this section from the local school district, school board, or school librarians supporting these policies (American Library Association 2014d).

Reconsideration of Materials

Another important section to a school library selection policy is one that states the procedures for handling a challenge to library materials. In this section are usually several parts:

- A listing of steps to be taken in light of a challenge. Such steps might include "asking the complainant to fill out a written complaint form . . . assigning a reconsideration committee to examine the materials in question . . . [and] requesting that the committee report their finding to the school board" (American Library Association 2014d, 1).
- Procedures to be taken, given the challenge—for example, all challenges are to be reported to the principal and school librarian, no matter who in the school originally took the complaint; an attempt will be made to informally settle the challenge (usually orally) before the written complaint and committee process steps occur; materials challenged will remain on the library shelves until the challenge process is complete; a letter or other recognition will be sent to complainants who have filled out a written challenge; and so on (American Library Association 2014d).
- Establishment of and instructions to the reconsideration committee. (While also a procedure, this issue is listed separately, due to the extensive discussion.) A school district/school board will often determine who will be on a reconsideration committee. Usual participants on such a committee include a school administrator, a school librarian, a teacher and/or student from the grade level/ subject at which the complaint was aimed, a local community member, other (as determined by the school district in question). (It is best if the school-based representatives come from a school of the same grade level as that at which the complaint occurred.) Instructions to such a committee comprise reading, viewing, or listening to the challenged item; taking into account published reviews of the item in question; examining the Library Bill of Rights, the First Amendment, and the school library selection policy in terms of the challenge; considering the whole challenged medium, rather than just the "objectionable" part; discussion; determination of a response; and the reporting of the decision to the school board, administration, school librarian, complainant, and others (American Library Association 2014d; Office for Intellectual Freedom 2010a).
- There are three possible responses to a challenge: to retain the item on the school library shelf, to restrict the item (e.g., student must have parental permission to check the item out, age limits on item use, item is shelved behind the circulation desk and a special request must be made to use it, etc.), or remove the item from the library.

The Written Challenge Form

Sample written challenge forms can be found in many places on the web, as well as in books and articles. School districts and school librarians also often create their own, to represent that which they feel is needed in their particular community and school. In general, the following items are likely to be found in a challenge form:

- Name and contact information of the challenger
- Material being challenged, including title, publisher, copyright date, and other bibliographic information
- Question determining if the challenger read/viewed/listened to the entire medium or just to the "objectionable" parts
- Question asking if the challenger read/accessed any published reviews of the item
- Concerns that the challenger has about the item under question;
- What the challenger would like to see done with the material, given the challenge (American Library Association 2014d; Illinois School Library Media Association 2010; Office for Intellectual Freedom 2010a)

Teaching Intellectual Freedom

School librarians and teachers can bring the principles of intellectual freedom and the right to read to their students through banned book week and banned website day activities; lessons on advocating for intellectual freedom or on specific challenged items, such as *Bridge to Terabithia, Blubber,* and *Julie and the Wolves,* and so much more (Adams 2008; Scales 2001). Indeed, students K–12 can—and should—learn what the First Amendment means and how this affects what they read, listen to, and view. For an example of part of a lesson plan that could be used by an elementary school librarian or a teacher, please view figure 9.1.

When you are introducing library-related concepts to your students, remember that ALA sponsors a number of campaigns and events throughout each year in

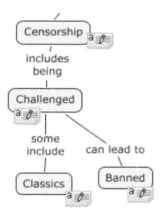
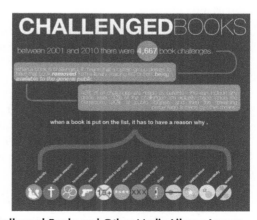

Figure 9.1. Intellectual Freedom/Challenged Books and Other Media Library Lesson

promotion of America's libraries. Among these are National Library Week, Library Card Sign-up Month, Teen Read Week, Picture Book Month, Digital Learning Day, Teen Tech Week, and Choose Privacy Week (American Library Association 2014a). In addition to School Library Month, two of importance to school libraries and intellectual freedom are Banned Books Week, "an annual celebration of the freedom to read . . . observed the last week of September" (American Library Association 2014a, 1) and Banned Websites Awareness Day, established by the AASL in 2011 and held during Banned Books Week. AASL's purpose behind this newer intellectual freedom event is "to bring attention to the overly aggressive filtering of educational and social websites used by students and educators" (American Library Association 2014a, 1). One way that school librarians can promote their libraries and reading is by setting up banned books/media displays during these celebrations. Many students are attracted to the controversial; watch the "challenged and banned" materials fly off the shelves!

Before we move to another set of ethical concerns often found in American schools and libraries, that of intellectual property, and specifically copyright law, let us note that there may be relationships between various ethical issues, in addition to the morality and law often involved. For example, there are those who argue "copyright is a monopoly on speech" (Doctorow 2014, 1), thus finding not only a connection but a conflict between the two. Is this the case? While such a question is beyond the purview of this book, it is important as school librarians that we recognize there can be conflicting opinions among our clientele, and sometimes contradictory laws between issues that affect us and those in the schools in which we teach. Now we turn to intellectual property.

INTELLECTUAL PROPERTY/COPYRIGHT

Intellectual Property

Intellectual Property is "a cluster of assets protected by federal or state law, including copyrights, patents, trademarks, and trade secrets" (Lipinski, 2006, p. xxx). The United States Constitution supports ownership of intellectual properties through the following statement: "Congress shall have the power . . . to promote the progress of science and useful arts, by securing for limited times to authors and inventors the exclusive rights to their respective writings and discoveries" (United States Constitution 1787, Art. 1, Sec. 8). Characteristics of intellectual properties include the fact that they are all "the fruit of one's intellect" (Wherry 2002, 1) and the laws representing them protect their owners and often cannot keep up with advances in technology. While school librarians usually find themselves occupied with those who want to use another's work, it is also possible that they will be working with the owner or creator of a particular intellectual property. In the school library, the most commonly addressed intellectual property is copyright.

Copyright

This chapter does not pretend to cover the plethora of materials available in print and online that support the concept of copyright in American schools. However, it is necessary to briefly address what copyright is, its importance to American school libraries and librarians, and how to be proactive in terms of copyright compliance. As defined by the United States' Copyright Office, "Copyright is a form of protection grounded in the U.S. Constitution and granted by law for original works of authorship fixed in a tangible medium of expression. Copyright covers both published and unpublished works" (United States Copyright Office 2014, 1).

The most commonly considered—and thus most often misunderstood—part of copyright law for K–12 schools is fair use. Most educators have heard of this statutory exemption (piece of the law) and believe that they grasp it. Some actually do— and, then again, others do not, including school librarians; thus a short explanation is included here.

Fair Use

There are four fair use factors. "The first fair use factor, purpose and character of use, looks at how those copying the work are going to use it. Works copied for educational, nonprofit, or personal purposes are much more likely to be considered within fair use than are those items that are copied with the intention of earning money. . . . Parodies and . . . commentaries" are also considered under this factor (Butler 2014, 14). This first fair use factor is the one most often misused and/or misunderstood in American schools, whether K–12 or higher education. Educators see the mention of education and assume that means they can borrow as they please as long as such use supports the curriculum and the students. This is not true, however. Copyright is written in "shades of gray," and only educational use by itself does not mean "free for all educators to borrow as they please."

"The second fair use factor, the nature of the work, deals with the work's characteristics: is the work fact or fiction, published or unpublished? Works most usable under fair use factor #2 are nonfiction published pieces" (Butler 2014, 14). Many times K–12 personnel do not realize that this factor is part of fair use and borrow fact or fiction indiscriminately. The "unpublished" part of this factor is a little more confusing, in that most materials that educators wish to borrow would be considered published. An example of an unpublished piece could be if someone found an old letter in an attic that had never (to their knowledge) even been read.

"The third fair use factor covers the quantity of work one plans to borrow. For example, do you want to use an entire hour-long movie or just five minutes of it?" (Butler 2014, 14). Factor 3 is measured two ways: quantitatively and qualitatively. The quantitative measurement is the easiest—only borrow exactly what is needed. If a teacher needs a two-minute movie clip, then that is what should be borrowed, rather than providing the whole movie because the kids might like to watch it.

The qualitative measurement is a bit more complicated. At issue here is whether the heart of the work is what is borrowed. This means no matter how small the item borrowed, if it is what the entire rest of the piece builds to, then to borrow this item is too much. An example of the "heart of the work" might be borrowing, "five minutes of an hour-long movie about computer science hackers" if "that particular five minutes was the heart of the recording; that is, showing exactly how the hacking was accomplished" (Butler 2014, 14).

"The fourth fair use factor features the marketability of the work. In essence, this means that if this work were to be copied and sold, either as part of a newly created item or by itself, would such a sale affect the amount of money that the owner or creator of the original work could earn from it?" (Butler 2014, 15). This particular factor is very important to owners of works, who often want the financial rewards that the use or borrowing of their works can generate.

Where some American educators have trouble with fair use (and by extension, copyright) is that they choose to believe using the first fair use factor, character of use, makes their borrowing of works legal. In reality the law wants us to follow *all four* of the factors; thus, if our use covers all of the fair use factors just mentioned, then we are using/borrowing another's work(s) in a legal manner. For more information on fair use, search the web for fair use tools; for example, the Fair Use Evaluator (Brewer and ALA Office for Information Technology Policy 2008) at http://library-copyright.net/resources/fairuse/ and others.

In addition to the fair use factors, U.S. copyright law covers such things as the public domain, classroom and library exemptions (the classroom exemption, for example, is what makes it legal to use many materials in a classroom setting), the DMCA (Digital Millennium Copyright Act), permissions, licenses, international uses, and so much more. Formats that can be registered by the U.S. Copyright Office include books, articles, newspapers, sheet music, and other print works; architecture, audio recordings, computer software, DVDs, games, photographs, sculptures, videos, and other nonprint items; and those things found on the Internet: email, web pages, blogs and vlogs, and other digitized works (Butler 2011).

Copyright versus Plagiarism

Copyright is not, as is often considered in the K–12 educational environment, "directly related to plagiarism" (Butler 2011, 59). Instead the two are indirectly linked in that both are engaged in the borrowing of someone else's work. Copyright considers whether permission has been granted to use another's work and/or a license agreed to or royalties paid. Plagiarism, on the other hand, focuses on whether the work's user gives credit (usually a citation) to the work's creator. Plagiarism is an ethical concern—sort of a "You will not pretend that you wrote something that you did not" issue. It is more likely to be taught in American schools than is copyright. Paradoxically, copyright is law—often misunderstood, not always followed, and often not taught, whether to students or teachers. Possibly through lack of knowledge, much of the education world is more willing to argue, "It is OK to borrow someone else's work for educational purposes; after all, we do not always have the money to purchase materials and the kids need them," rather than follow this law.

Copyright Compliance

Most school librarians do not wish to add the position of "copyright police" to the many hats they wear when working in the school library (see first page, chapter 6). Therefore, it is wise to encourage and model copyright compliant behavior to fellow educators and students. Follow the law, obtain the necessary licenses and permissions and pay royalties as needed, read the documentation that various media have available and that address copyright, consult your school or district's copyright policy and make it known to others, use material you have created yourself, and when in doubt—do not copy (Butler 2014, 234–235; Butler 2011)! An added option is to encourage your administration to work with you in creating a proactive copyright compliance program. The basic steps of such a program can be found in textbox 9.1.

Certainly this is a complicated law, and school librarians are often—perhaps because they work with numerous materials in many formats—one of the few individuals in the school to whom others may go with copyright concerns (the other usually being the school administrator and/or possibly the technology coordinator/specialist/coach). Thus, it is recommended here that school librarians obtain training in the basics of copyright law, whether by taking college or continuing education classes on this subject and/or by attending related conference presentations. In addition, currency can be maintained through reading professional books, journals, and websites. Certainly, a handbook or two on copyright and school libraries belongs on the professional bookshelf of any school librarian.

PRIVACY

Privacy is "the right of an individual to determine when, how, and what personal information may be shared with others and for what purpose" (Adams et al. 2005, 239). There are many federal laws that address privacy, among them the Privacy Act of 1974, the Health Insurance Portability and Accountability Act (HIPAA), the Family Education Rights and Privacy Act (FERPA), the Electronic Communications Privacy Act (ECPA), the Children's Online Privacy Protection Act (COPPA), the Children's Internet Protection Act (CIPA), and the USA PATRIOT Act (Adams et al., 2005; Federal Communications Commission 2014). In addition, states may and sometimes do enact privacy legislation. State privacy laws vary from state to state, with California the most committed state in regard to privacy legal code (Cooper et al., n.d.).

In school libraries, privacy is most likely to involve such things as circulation records, the Internet, and acceptable and responsible use policies. Of these, student

TEXTBOX 9.1
STEPS IN THE CREATION OF A PROACTIVE
COPYRIGHT COMPLIANCE PROGRAM

- "Establish and communicate a district copyright compliance policy.
- Establish and communicate the copyright compliance procedures.
- Analyze organizational impact.
- Determine copyright training needs.
- Provide necessary copyright training.
- Audit the copyright process for compliance.
- Provide feedback for copyright process improvement.
- Maintain copyright compliance."

Source: Butler 2009c, 4

circulation confidentiality is probably the most significant. The ALA "Policy on Confidentiality of Library Records" acknowledges

- "circulation records and other records identifying the names of library users to be confidential . . .
- such records shall not be made available to any agency of state, federal, or local government except . . . as authorized under the authority of, and pursuant to, federal, state, or local law." (Office for Intellectual Freedom 2010a, 255)

This policy is for all libraries, including school libraries. (Please be aware that the term *confidentiality* as used here is defined as "when a library is in possession of personally identifiable information . . . about users and keeps that information private on their behalf" [American Library Association 2014g, 1]).

In addition another ALA policy, the "Policy Concerning Confidentiality of Personally Identifiable Information about Library Users," states that library confidentiality (again, this includes school libraries) covers patrons' "database search records, reference interviews, circulation records, interlibrary loan records and other" (Office for Intellectual Freedom 2010a, 269). What this means, for school librarians, is that their student users also have rights of privacy and such rights include what those students check out from the library.

Considering privacy and school libraries, the AASL's "Position Statement on the Confidentiality of Library Records" (remember that AASL is a part of ALA) recognizes that "records held in libraries which connect specific individuals with specific resources, programs or services, are confidential and not to be used for purposes other than routine record keeping. . . . School librarians are advised to seek the advice of counsel if in doubt about whether their record keeping systems violate the specific laws in their states" and "eliminate such records as soon as reasonably possible" (American Association of School Librarians 2014, 1).

Another ALA document that supports privacy issues is the "Privacy Tool Kit," which includes information on privacy law and privacy principles, how to create or revise a privacy policy and do a privacy audit, and much more (American Library Association 2014f). Lastly, ALA's "Questions and Answers on Privacy and Confidentiality" contains several statements of importance to school libraries and privacy, including, "Each school library should have a privacy policy outlining how students' library records are protected and under what circumstances they may be released and to whom. . . . The privacy policy should reference and incorporate the state library confidentiality law and also incorporate FERPA guidelines . . . school libraries should also have a records retention policy detailing the types of records maintained, the length of retention, and a schedule for their destruction" and "Minors' records are best protected when minimal library records are maintained for the shortest period possible" (American Library Association 2014g, 1).

Thus ALA encourages us, as school librarians, to respect the privacy rights of our patrons—no matter their age. That encouragement notwithstanding, discretion in the sharing of K–12 students' circulation (or Internet use) records is often debated. For example, oftentimes parents and guardians wish to know what their children are checking out, especially arguing that a young child might not remember or be reliable in the returning of library materials without help from responsible adults. Then again, school administration may see its knowledge of library records in the same light as that of looking in a particular student's locker; that is, it may be school policy to do so. Bottom line is that while "there is no federal law protecting the confidentiality of library records for any library—school, public, or academic . . . the Family Educational Rights and Privacy Act of 1974 (FERPA) protects the confidentiality of 'educational records' of students in *any* school receiving federal funds and gives parents the right to inspect and review the minor student's education records" (minor students are considered those under age 18) (Adams et al., 2005, 102–103).

As mentioned earlier, states also have privacy legislation. Since state legislation may not always agree with that of another state (or, for that matter, with federal law), this indicates that it is possible one state will feel student library use is confidential while another state may not. So, what does all this mean for school librarians?

Following are a number of ways that school librarians can address student privacy and confidentiality:

- Become knowledgeable as to what privacy and confidentiality in the library are
- Read and recognize the main precepts of federal and your state's privacy laws
- Defend the relevant policies of the American Library Association
- Recognize the privacy and confidentiality rights of your student patrons
- Develop district school library privacy policies and place these in the library and school handbooks

- Add privacy concepts to the district's acceptable or responsible use policy
- Teach students about Internet safety, especially in terms of their privacy
- Inform library staff as to student privacy in all aspects of library usage, for both analog and digitally based media
- Stay current with federal and state government bills concerning privacy
- Model ethical library practices
- Protect library users' rights
- Create a privacy toolkit and displays for use in your library
- Maintain confidentiality of all library records
- Encourage adults in the local community to become aware of student privacy issues
- Respect others' privacy
- Seek legal and/or professional advice when questions dealing with privacy and confidentiality arise
- Become a school leader in privacy advocacy
- Send individual letters or emails to student's parents/guardians, when there is overdue media, instead of posting or announcing a list for all to see
- Advocate against the labeling (placing a reading level, age, or content label on books and other library materials, so that others can see what sorts of materials a patron is checking out) of library materials. (Adams 2008; Adams 2000; Adams et al. 2005; Caldwell-Stone 2012; Chmara 2012; Johnson 2003; Office for Intellectual Freedom 2010a; Scales 2009)

ACCESS TO INFORMATION

One of the nine common beliefs imbedded in the *Standards for the 21st-Century Learner* (American Association of School Librarians 2007) is "School libraries are essential to the development of learning skills. School libraries provide equitable physical and intellectual access to the resources and tools required for learning in a warm, stimulating, and safe environment" (American Association of School Librarians 2009a, 13). When considering both the physical and virtual learning spaces that make up the school library, the learning space guideline as found in the AASL's *Empowering Learners: Guidelines for School Library Media Programs* is as follows: "The school library media program includes flexible and equitable access to physical and virtual collections of resources that support the school curriculum and meet the diverse needs of all learners" (American Association of School Librarians 2009a, 33). This guideline concentrates on access, both physical and virtual—to information and materials—as provided in and by the school library.

Physical Access to Information

Physical access to information is achieved through the school library facility (see also chapter 5). This facility usually has several spaces—depending on the grade levels of the school. For example, an elementary library might have a story area for the grades K–2, a reading space for the older students, a classroom, a study/research section (with computers), a circulation area, and so on. A middle or high school library would not have a story area per se, but might have a large computer lab or area for plugging in iPads, Chromebooks, and other Internet-based devices and including wireless access; a reference section; a technology/production space; lots of tables and study carrels for group and individual work; space for recreational reading; perhaps a small group study room; and so on. The physical library facility needs to be able to assist in the many and varied needs of its student patrons, as well as teachers and support staff. Additionally, "physical access is best achieved through flexible scheduling, in which students and teachers are free to use the library facilities throughout the day. . . . [Flexible scheduling] . . . allows for collaborative planning and teaching to take place" (American Association of School Librarians 2009a, 33). Indeed student access to the physical library materials and equipment can be especially important to students unable to access technology or materials outside of the school day. Whether this is due to economics—for example, a student's parents are unable to afford a laptop and Internet access or other diverse issues (for example, a handicapped student needs a special reading device provided by the school or a new language learner has no access to books in English in his/her home)—the fact remains that "open access to the school library media center's information resources is essential to student learning" (American Association of School Librarians 2009a, 33).

Virtual Access to Information

"Virtual access allows students and teachers to take advantage of the school library media center's resources after hours and provides continual support for teaching and learning" (American Association of School Librarians 2009a, 33). Certainly the virtual school library space is Internet based, whether that means online reference services, access to digital databases, links to curriculum-supportive sites, pathfinders for particular class units, or wikis and discussion boards for online activities and communications (American Association of School Librarians 2009a).

Internet Filtering

Along with virtual access comes another list of issues. For instance, there is the equity matter, whereby schools use filtering software to restrict student access to certain websites, such as social networking sites, web pages with obscene language, and so on. Internet filtering became a very real concern in our nation's schools with the 2000 passing of the Children's Internet Protection Act (CIPA) by the U.S. Congress. "Designed to block adults and minors from accessing online images deemed 'obscene,' 'child pornography,' or 'harmful to minors' . . . by requiring public libraries and schools receiving certain federal funding to install software filters on their internet-accessible computers" (Batch 2014, 5), CIPA in today's world impacts elementary and secondary curriculum and school libraries much more than was originally intended by its authors. As the author of "Fencing Out Knowledge: Impacts of the Children's Internet Protection Act 10 Years Later" states, "the over-filtering that occurs today affects not only what teachers can teach but also how they teach, and creates barriers to learning and acquiring digital literacy skills that are vital for college and career readiness" (Batch 2014, 5). Indeed, the overfiltering that occurs due to " misinterpretations of the law, different perceptions of how to filter, and the limitations of internet filtering software . . . blocks access to legitimate, educational resources while often failing to block the images proscribed by the law" (Batch 2014, 5–6). Especially for American students without Internet access (or only entertainment access) in the home, this may mean a paucity of information that they need to stay abreast educationally with their more affluent and/or empowered peers.

Because filtering can also be interpreted as a type of censorship, this brings intellectual freedom into the mix. With this in mind, it would pay to keep an eye on Network Neutrality, "the concept of online non-discrimination. It is the principle that consumers/citizens should be free to get access to—or to provide—the Internet content and services they wish, and that consumer access should not be regulated based on the nature or source of that content or service" (American Library Association 2014e, 1). On February 26, 2015, the Federal Communications Commission (FCC) established new rules forcing Internet Service Providers (ISP) to provide the same broadband speeds to all users (Zolfagharifard and Prigg 2015). This and future federal legislation may possibly affect K–12 Internet access in the future.

Digital Divide

Another concern within the concept of virtual access to information is the "digital divide." Ten or more years ago, this was frequently represented by students whose parents or guardians could not afford a computer and web access at home. In the second decade of the 21st century, this now may mean the *type* of access available to students; that is, entertainment access via cell phones and gaming devices versus educational/empowerment access via any number of digital devices (Hertz 2011, 1). In addition, "another group that is often left out of the conversation are [*sic*] Americans with disabilities. The divide for these citizens has always been there, and assistive technologies have definitely made access easier (if the people who need them can afford them), there are no laws stating that websites need to be accessible to people with disabilities" (Hertz 2011, 1). Thus educators working with special education students, for example, may find their learners are unable to access needed materials available on the Internet. In such ways, intellectual freedom again becomes an issue, due to the fact that "the Digital Divide affects students' First Amendment right to receive information" (Adams 2008, 155).

Copyright, too, can become an ethical issue in virtual access (as well as physical access) to information, since without knowledge of how to work within that particular law, students and faculty alike may be infringing on the rights of those who own information. Furthermore, privacy concerns—whether it is the posting (or not) of children's names and photos on a school website or that of social networking and who can access what—can influence virtual access, or our (and our students') choices to use any of the innumerable websites and social networking tools now available. Accordingly, library ethics, or the lack thereof, may not be separate entities; it is possible for some to go hand in hand.

ACCEPTABLE/RESPONSIBLE USE POLICIES

Acceptable and responsible use policies in K–12 education are most often developed for the school community at large; for example, students, faculty, and staff. At times, they may also address parents and guardians, or even the local community, although that is uncommon. Such policies are for Internet and sometimes intranet ("a network operating like the World Wide Web but having access restricted to a limited group of authorized users" [*Merriam-Webster Online* 2014, 1]); for example, one could operate within a district or individual school environment) users' access to the World Wide Web and can be one to several pages in length. These usually contain signature and date lines; the idea being that after it is read and users sign off, they will abide by the policies and procedures located within the document.

An acceptable use policy (AUP) is essentially a contract or agreement between Internet users and the group/individual who is acting as their Internet service provider (ISP). In the case of K–12 schools, the school district often functions as the ISP in providing access to its students, faculty, administration, and staff. The types of things contained in AUPs may include

- preamble (declares why the AUP is needed);
- definitions (of key words in the AUP);
- rules or guidelines for appropriate use of the Internet or the school/district's intranet (this may include suggested Internet "manners" or online actions that should be avoided by the user);
- what school Internet access is to be used for; that is, "a description of the instructional values and approaches to be sustained by Internet access in schools" (Uhls and Peterson, n.d., 1);
- identity of the authorized users of the school network;
- laws or guidelines needed for legal Internet use—for example, copyright, licensing, privacy;
- consequences for inappropriate Internet use;
- instructions on how to report Internet violations and the recipient of these reports;
- Internet safety criteria;
- information on the school/district's Internet filtering;
- school district liability disclaimer;

- statement that use of the network may be monitored by the ISP;
- statement that access to the Internet through the ISP is an opportunity rather than an entitlement;
- sentence directing the user that the signing of the AUP means that he or she agrees to abide by the policies and procedures listed in the document;
- user signature line;
- signature of parent or guardian, if student is under age 18;
- date line (AUPs should be revised regularly, and once updated, reread and signed by all users);
- more as appropriate to a specific school district or school. (Uhls and Peterson, n.d.; Austin Independent School District 2011; Chicago Public Schools, n.d.; Education World 2014; Kentucky Department of Education 2013)

It is best if AUPs are accessible to the public as well as the school/district community. Places the AUP may be posted could be the school website, the library policies and procedures handbook, and the school technology plan. An understandable AUP is best written in a clear, nonjargon manner, with all terminology succinctly defined for the nontechnologist.

Please note that some schools/districts are beginning to adopt the term *responsible use policy* (RUP) instead of AUP. Instead of examples of violations and consequences, the RUP is more in the form of an agreement of the proper ways to access and use the Internet (Montgomery School 2013; Spotlight on Digital Media and Learning, n.d.). As such, it still includes much of what is found in the AUP, but presented in more positive language.

FYI, almost all K–12 schools, public and private, as well as institutions of higher learning and many commercial establishments, businesses, and corporations now have AUPs or RUPs. As such, there are many, many exemplars on the web. The school librarian may be tasked (or asked to be part of a committee tasked) at some point with updating the AUP/RUP in his or her school. To find illustrations of such policies and procedures, commonsense" search terms such as *acceptable use policy* or *responsible use policy* will pull up countless Internet examples.

KEY CONCEPTS FROM THIS CHAPTER

- Ethics and laws affecting school libraries and librarians can be overwhelming and confusing.
- School librarians need to teach their students ethical behavior in terms of diversity, social media safety, and information gathering and use.
- Professional standards and policies and procedures, as well as our own individual morals and ethical beliefs are a big part of what lead us, as school librarians, to make the choices we do for materials selection and evaluation and how we deal with our patrons.

- The Library Bill of Rights is the premier intellectual freedom policy of the American Library Association.
- "The freedom to read is essential to our democracy" (Office for Intellectual Freedom 2010a, 203).
- "Intellectual freedom is the right of every individual to both seek and receive information from all points of view without restriction. It provides for free access to all expressions of ideas through which any and all sides of a question, cause or movement may be explored" (American Library Association 2014b, 1).
- The concept of intellectual freedom is supported by three amendments to the U.S. Constitution—the first, fifth, and fourteenth.
- Books, movies, web pages, software, almost any media can be challenged or banned.
- Reasons for challenges include the following: sexually explicit, profane or obscene, religious or the "wrong" religion, violent; that the students who would read/view/listen to the work are too immature for it; that the work contains witchcraft, nudity, homosexuality, antifamily outlooks, suicide, drugs and alcohol, politics, technical errors; or that the item may in some way be inaccurate (American Library Association 2014c; Hopkins 1991; Adams 2008; Adams 2009).
- Collection development and selection policies can help the school librarian who is faced with a challenge.
- A good school library selection policy will include a section on controversial materials and policies that support their placement in school libraries.
- An important section to a school library selection policy is one which states the procedures for handling a challenge to library materials; this includes reconsideration of materials, written challenge form, and makeup of the committee who will hear and determine the outcome of the challenge.
- Many students are attracted to the controversial; watch identified "challenged and banned" materials fly off the shelves!
- Intellectual Property is "a cluster of assets protected by federal or state law, including copyrights, patents, trademarks, and trade secrets" (Lipinski, 2006, p. xxx).
- The most commonly considered—and most often misunderstood—part of copyright law for K–12 schools is fair use.
- Copyright and plagiarism are indirectly linked in that both are engaged in the borrowing of someone else's work.
- Copyright considers whether or not permission has been granted to use another's work and/or a license agreed to or royalties paid.
- Plagiarism focuses on whether or not the work's user gives credit to the work's creator.
- The school librarian can and should encourage and model copyright compliant behavior to fellow educators and students.
- In school libraries, privacy is most likely to involve such things as circulation records, the Internet, and acceptable and responsible use policies.

- School libraries provide both physical and virtual access to information.
- School acceptable use policy is essentially a contract or agreement between the students and teachers (Internet users) and the school, who is acting as the Internet service provider.

Coming in chapter 10: "Advocacy."

DISCUSSION QUESTIONS

1. Read the ALA Code of Ethics (pages 303–304 of *Intellectual Freedom Manual*). Part VII of the ALA Code of Ethics states, "We distinguish between our personal convictions and professional duties and do not allow our personal beliefs to interfere with fair representation of the aims of our institutions or the provision of access to their information resources" (Office for Intellectual Freedom 2010b, 304). Discuss how this statement might influence your selection of materials in a school library.
2. If a school's filter is overblocking Internet sites so that students are unable to get the materials they need for particular classes, is the school librarian justified in not following/by-passing the school/district filtering policy; for example, is Internet filtering a type of censorship?
3. At the end of each school year, the librarian gives a list of overdue items still checked out, to each student, in hopes of getting these back before summer break. His or her administration would like the list of items published on the school management software that they use, so that this list of overdue items is accessible to all administration, faculty, and parents. How should the librarian respond to this request from his or her administration? Do patrons, especially those under the age of 18, give up privacy rights by not returning library materials by the due date?

ACTIVITIES

1. Censorship interviews: Interview and report on a number of students or teachers (three or more) in your school to discover their views of challenges and censorship. Create your own list of questions to ask them. You may video/audio/digitally tape your interviews.
2. Develop a school copyright policy: Assume that this policy is to be placed in the school handbook. You may choose one of the following subjects for the policy: copyright and computer software; copyright and audio; copyright and video; copyright and the Internet; copyright and distance education (may include Internet, video, and audio); copyright and international media; copyright

and print; copyright and sheet music; a general copyright policy. (Remember that multimedia issues may be found under many of these subject areas.)

3. Create *two* separate items: (a) detailed policy of copyright dos and don'ts for your school (try to limit this to four pages) and (b) a *short* statement [with example(s)] of copyright dos and don'ts to be posted by or on computers and/ or other machines that make copies in your school. (Limit this to about one third or one half of a page.) Make this assignment practical for your library or a school library of your choice. You may borrow from copyright policies that you find in your school, on the web, or in books and articles. Cite all materials borrowed from other sources.

4. Teach an ethics library lesson/teacher training session: Develop a written lesson/training plan for a two-hour session, which includes the following: (a) an age/grade level or group for whom you are developing a lesson/training (e.g., a sixth grade class, an in-service for high school English teachers, and so on); (b) a particular area of intellectual property, intellectual freedom, privacy, Internet filtering, access, or other ethical concern you plan on teaching (e.g., an overview of the fair use guidelines, banned books for high school students, student privacy in the library, etc.); (c) why your chosen subject area is important to the intended audience; (d) objectives; (e) written explanation of how the lesson will be taught (e.g., instructional strategies, including media with which you will teach; you may include the policies and procedures [from school and library manuals] that this instruction will follow); (f) written explanation of how the lesson will be evaluated; (g) samples of teaching and evaluation worksheets/ criteria; and (h) resources used for this lesson (references/bibliography).

REFERENCES

Adams, Helen R. 2000. "The Internet Invasion: Is Privacy at Risk?" *Professional Development Series.* McHenry, Ill.: Follett Software Company.

———. 2008. *Ensuring Intellectual Freedom and Access to Information in the School Library Media Program.* Westport, Conn.: Libraries Unlimited.

———. 2009. "The Freedom to Question: Challenges in School Libraries." *School Library Monthly* 26 (3): 48–49.

Adams, Helen R., Bocher, Robert F., Gordon, Carol A., and Barry-Kessler, Elizabeth. 2005. *Privacy in the 21st Century: Issues for Public, School, and Academic Libraries.* Westport, Conn.: Libraries Unlimited.

American Association of School Librarians. 2007. *Standards for the 21st-Century Learner.* Chicago, Ill.: American Library Association.

———. 2009a. *Empowering Learners: Guidelines for School Library Media Programs.* Chicago, Ill.: American Library Association.

———. 2009b. *Standards for the 21st-Century Learner in Action.* Chicago, Ill.: American Library Association.

———. 2014. "Position Statement on the Confidentiality of Library Records." http://www.ala
.org/aasl/advocacy/resources/statements/library-records.

American Library Association. 1996. "Library Bill of Rights." http://www.ala.org/advocacy/
intfreedom/librarybill.

———. 2014a. "Celebration Weeks and Promotional Events 2014–2015." http://www.ala
.org/conferencesevents/celebrationweeks.

———. 2014b. "Intellectual Freedom and Censorship Q & A." http://www.ala.org/advocacy/
intfreedom/censorshipfirstamendmentissues/ifcensorshipqanda.

———. 2014c. "Missing: Find a Banned Book: Challenges by Reason, Initiator and Institution for 1990–99 and 2000–09." http://www.ala.org/bbooks/frequentlychallengedbooks/
statistics.

———. 2014d. "Missing: Find a Banned Book: Workbook for Selection Policy Writing."
http://www.ala.org/bbooks/challengedmaterials/preparation/workbook-selection-policy-
writing.

———. 2014e. "Network Neutrality." http://www.ala.org/advocacy/telecom/netneutrality.

———. 2014f. "Privacy Tool Kit." http://www.ala.org/advocacy/privacyconfidentiality/tool-
kitsprivacy/privacy.

———. 2014g. "Questions and Answers on Privacy and Confidentiality." http://www.ala.org/
Template.cfm?Section=Interpretations&Template=/ContentManagement/ContentDisplay
.cfm&ContentID=15347.

Association for Educational Communications and Technology. 2007. "Code of Professional Ethics." http://aect.site-ym.com/members/group_content_view.asp?group=91131&id=309963.

Austin Independent School District. 2011. "Austin ISD Acceptable Use Policy." http://www
.austinisd.org/technology/aup#education.

Batch, Kristin R. 2014. *Fencing Out Knowledge: Impacts of the Children's Internet Protection Act
10 Year Later.* Chicago, Illinois: American Library Association.

Brewer, Michael and ALA Office for Information Technology Policy. 2008. "Fair Use Evaluator." http://librarycopyright.net/resources/fairuse/.

Butler, Rebecca P. 2009c. *Smart Copyright Compliance for Schools: A How-To-Do-It Manual.*
New York, N.Y.: Neal-Schuman Publishers.

———. 2011. *Copyright for Teachers and Librarians in the 21st Century.* New York, N.Y.: Neal-
Schuman Publishers.

———. 2014. *Copyright for Academic Librarians and Professionals.* Chicago, Ill.: American
Library Association.

Caldwell-Stone, Deborah. 2012. "Ebooks and Users' Rights." *American Libraries* 43 (5/6):
60–61.

Chicago Public Schools. n.d. "Policy on Student Acceptable Use of the Chicago Public
Schools Network." alcottschool.net/.../network%20acceptable%20use%20form.pdf.

Chmara, Theresa. 2012. "Privacy and E-Books." *Knowledge Quest* 40 (3): 62–65.

Constitution of the United States. n.d. "Bill of Rights." http://www.ratical.org/co-globalize/
BillOfRights.html#1.

Cooper, Scott P., Soleymani, Navid, Davidson, Clifford S., and Forsheit, Tanya L. n.d. "Chapter 5: State Privacy Laws." www.pli.edu/product_files/booksamples/11513_sample5.pdf.

Doctorow, Cory. 2014. "Copyright Must Accommodate Free Expression." http://boingboing
.net/2014/01/19/copyright-must-accomodate-free.html.

Education World. 2014. "Getting Started on the Internet: Developing an Acceptable Use
Policy (AUP)." http://www.educationworld.com/a_curr/curr093.shtml.

Federal Communications Commission. 2014. "Guide: Children's Internet Protection Act." http://www.fcc.gov/guides/childrens-internet-protection-act.

Hertz, Mary Beth. 2011. "A New Understanding of the Digital Divide." http://www.edutopia .org/blog/digital-divide-technology-internet-access-mary-beth-hertz.

Hopkins, Dianne. 1991. *Factors Influencing the Outcome of Challenges to Materials in Secondary School Libraries: Report of a National Study.* Madison, Wisconsin: University of Wisconsin-Madison.

Illinois First Amendment Center. n.d. "The First Amendment in History." http://illinoispress .org/Foundation/1stAmendmentCenter.aspx.

Illinois School Library Media Association. 2010. *Linking for Learning: The Illinois School Library Media Program Guidelines.* 3rd ed. Canton, Ill.: Illinois School Library Media Association.

Johnson, Doug. 2003. *Learning Right from Wrong in the Digital Age: An Ethics Guide for Parents, Teachers, Librarians, and Others Who Care about Computer-Using Young People.* Worthington, Ohio: Linworth Publishing.

Kelly, Martin. 2014. "14th Amendment Summary." http://americanhistory.about.com/od/ usconstitution/a/14th-Amendment-Summary.htm.

Kentucky Department of Education. 2013. "Guidelines for Creating Acceptable Use Policies." http://education.ky.gov/districts/tech/Pages/Acceptable-Use.aspx.

Knops, Megan. 2013. "Intellectual Freedom/Challenged Books and Other Media." Assignment for ETT 542. DeKalb, Ill.: Department of Educational Technology Research and Assessment, Northern Illinois University.

Lipinski, Tomas A. 2006. *The Complete Copyright Liability Handbook for Librarians and Educators.* New York, N.Y.: Neal-Schuman.

Merriam-Webster Online. 2014. "Intranet." http://www.merriam-webster.com/dictionary/ intranet.

Montgomery School. 2013. "Responsible Use Policy: Responsible Use Policy Grades 3–5." http://www.montgomeryschool.org/program/lower-school/ls-curriculum/technology library/responsible-use-policy/index.aspx.

Office for Intellectual Freedom. 2010a. *Intellectual Freedom Manual.* 8th ed. Chicago, Ill.: American Library Association.

———. 2010b. "Access for Children and Young Adults to Nonprint Materials." *Intellectual Freedom Manual.* 8th ed. http://www.ifmanual.org/accesschildren.

———. 2010c. "Access to Resources and Services in the School Library Media Program." *Intellectual Freedom Manual.* 8th ed. http://www.ifmanual.org/accessslmp.

———. 2010d. "Free Access to Libraries for Minors." *Intellectual Freedom Manual.* 8th ed. http:// www.ifmanual.org/freeaccessminors.

———. 2010e. "Library Bill of Rights: Interpretations." *Intellectual Freedom Manual.* 8th ed. http:// www.ifmanual.org/part2section2.

———. 2010f. "Minors and Internet Interactivity." *Intellectual Freedom Manual.* 8th ed. http:// www.ifmanual.org/minorsinteractivity.

Scales, Pat R. 2001. *Teaching Banned Books: 12 Guides for Young Readers.* Chicago, Ill.: American Library Association.

———. 2009. *Protecting Intellectual Freedom in Your School Library: Scenarios from the Front Lines.* Chicago, Ill.: American Library Association.

Sherry, Annette C., Rothschild, Meagan, Kaliko, Kealoha, and Hagan, Pam. 2008. *The ABCs of Ethics for Today's Educators: An Adaptation of the Code of Professional Ethics of the Association for Educational Communications and Technology (AECT)*. U.S.A. Sherry and Association for Educational Communications and Technology.

Spotlight on Digital Media and Learning. n.d. "A 'Responsible' Approach to School Usage Policies on Internet Safety." http://spotlight.macfound.org/blog/entry/a-responsible-approach-to-school-usage-policies-on-internet-safety/.

Uhls, Max and Peterson, Jim. n.d. "Acceptable Use Policies." http://education.illinois.edu/wp/ www.sjfschool.net/whitepages/acceptableusepolicy.htm.

United States Constitution. (1787). Article 1. Section 8.

United States Copyright Office. 2014. "What Is Copyright?" http://copyright.gov/help/faq/ faq-general.html#what.

Wherry, Timothy L. 2002. *Intellectual Property in the Digital Age*. Chicago, Illinois: American Library Association.

Zolfagharifard, Ellie, and Mark Prigg. 2015. "New Neutrality Wins: FCC Passes Tough New 'Open Internet' Rules That Ban ISPs From Throttling Your Download Speed." http://www .dailymail.co.uk/sciencetech/article-2970703/D-Day-net-neutrality-FCC-votes-tough-new-open-internet-rules-ban-ISPs-throttling-download-speed.html?ITO=1490&ns_ mchannel=rss&ns_campaign=1490.

10

Advocacy

According to the American Association of School Librarians (AASL) Advocacy Committee, advocacy is an "on-going process of building partnerships so that others will act for and with you, turning passive support into educated action for the library program. . . . It begins with a vision and a plan for the library program that is then matched to the agenda and priorities of stakeholders" (American Association of School Librarians 2014e, 1).

Advocacy is important to school libraries for a number of reasons. There is the *very important fact* that numerous research studies (Lance, n.d.; Lance and Schwartz 2013; Library Research Service 2013a; Library Research Service 2013b) have found that schools with school librarians do better across the board when it comes to student test scores. Second, not all states, districts, or schools require at least one librarian per building; instead it might be one librarian for each high school with a part-time librarian for each elementary or middle school, one librarian per district, one librarian for five schools, or whatever. Third, when funding at one level (say, federal) is cut, those losses can trickle down to state and local budgets. This can affect school libraries across the board, in that oftentimes, where there is less money for the school or district, what some school boards or administrators consider the more "peripheral" educators (of which librarians are sometimes seen as one group) may be cut (American Library Association 2014; Gebeloff 2011; Johnson 2010). Because consistency fluctuates, this reflects in some parts of the country having stronger school libraries than others.

Another motive to advocate might be that you want to bring more patrons into the library. Let's illustrate this with an example. Imagine that you are a brand-new librarian in a middle school. You find that you have very few students or teachers coming in during the day and are puzzled—it is a nice facility, with lots of materials. In frustration, you approach a friendly teacher and ask why so few want to use the library. The response you get is that the old librarian was "mean," and did not like people making noise or "messing up" the library. Now people are out of the habit of coming in. OK, having few patrons is unacceptable! As a result, advocacy for increased student and faculty use of the library immediately becomes a high priority for your first year in the school. In some ways, you might actually be at an advantage since you now have the opportunity to change the perception of the library. The old librarian is gone and it's a new day. For reasons such as these, advocating for school libraries is imperative.

Advocacy can take many forms. This chapter addresses some of the ways that we, as library professionals, can advocate for our field, our clientele (students and faculty), and ourselves.

RESEARCH AS ADVOCACY

Most school librarians have plenty on their plates. Oftentimes, reading professional journals and books, especially those focusing on research (how boring and/or impractical—what you really think you need is an activity to use with a particular grade or class!), is one of the last things many librarians want to do. Be aware, however, that research can be your friend; it can support your requests for more help, more funds, more time, and so on. Research can point out to us what has worked in the past and what has not. For example, "Studies conducted over the past two decades, both in Colorado and nationwide, show that students in schools with endorsed librarians score better on standardized achievement tests in reading, compared with students in schools without endorsed librarians" (Library Research Service 2013a, 1). The American Library Association echoes that sentiment in their research foundation paper *School Libraries Work!* (American Association of School Librarians 2008). Wow! This information alone is worth sharing with the district school board that believes cutting library staff will save money! With the focus in the 21st century on standards and test scores, data supporting such a statement can be priceless. And, the data is there—in the form of a number of statewide and federal studies on school libraries (Library Research Service 2013b). More research in this area is currently being funded by libraries and state professional organizations; one of the latest is led by Keith Curry Lance and focuses on South Carolina school libraries (Lance, n.d.). People who make funding and staffing decisions may not totally understand all the ins and outs of the library, but they usually understand and react to data that supports a position. So, one way that the school librarian can advocate for his or her library is through research data—numbers, statistics, and other information. Textbox 10.1 shows an example of a flyer that might be sent to school administration. This flyer uses research to promote the concept of more technology in school libraries.

Research can help you to argue for additional materials, extra hardware and software, and added access to information as provided by your particular school library. For example, the June 25, 2013, Pew study on younger Americans' library use, states that Americans, ages 16–29, are heavy technology users. Such data can be used to

**TEXTBOX 10.1
EXAMPLE: RESEARCH FLYER DATA**

**TECHNOLOGY IN SCHOOL LIBRARIES
MEANS HIGHER ACHIEVEMENT IN K–12:
READING, WRITING, AND TESTING**

"School librarians provide the blueprint for teaching students research skills, digital citizenship, safety online, and information communication skills" (American Association of School Librarians 2013, 3).

"Where networked computers link library media centers with classrooms, labs, and other instructional sites, students earn higher CSAP reading test scores" (Lance et al. 2000, 3).

"Higher Achievement Associated with Illinois School Libraries Being More Accessible Via Educational Technology" (Lance et al. 2005, xvi)

"SLMSs (school library media specialists) can and do have an impact on supporting and facilitating student learning via technology and in training classroom teachers in more effective use of such technologies used both in and out of school" (Small, Snyder, and Parker 2009, 21).

boost school library digital media availability, including e-books and e-book readers, Internet access, and more (Zickuhr, Rainie, and Purcell 2013). Indeed, as is stated in the research report *How Pennsylvania School Libraries Pay Off: Investments in Student Achievement and Academic Standards*, "there is overwhelming evidence that students are more likely to succeed academically where they have school library programs that are better staffed, better funded, better equipped, better stocked, and more accessible. Such library programs have the resources required to ensure that their schools provide the information-rich environments necessary to the academic success of their students" (Lance and Schwartz 2013, 161). Where can you find this research? Search online, read current professional journals, attend school library conferences, look for current research studies. The data is there—use it!

Now, let's move on to advocating for our libraries via social media, newsletters, presentations, flyers, library websites, and other promotional media.

PUBLICITY AS ADVOCACY

According to the *Library Advocate's Handbook* (American Library Association 2010b), there are many means of advocacy for your library. Included in this list are talking about your library, creating print and online publicity (brochures, pamphlets, newsletters, etc.), planning an event to showcase your library, and being an ambassador for the library (32–34). Publicizing the library, as an advocacy approach, is addressed next.

There are numerous types of publicity possible for your school library. Here are a few to consider:

- Library web pages
- Facebook or other social networking sites
- Brochures, flyers, pamphlets, newsletters (print or digital)
- Bookmarks advertising library materials and services
- Newspaper articles
- Television or radio ads
- Library events such as author visits, a "welcome-back-to-school breakfast," technology workshops, video game clubs, reading programs, teacher in-services, and so on (see more on library events in chapter 8, "Programming and Collaboration")
- Celebrations of library-related "holidays," such as School Library Month, National Library Week, Teen Read Week, Teen Tech Week, Banned Books Week, Banned Websites Awareness Day, Freedom of Information Day, National Poetry Month, Children's Book Week, World Book and Copyright Day
- Book trailer and other contests
- Virtual library tours

Many things can bring your patrons into the library—and keep them coming—including library services, programming, and lots of publicity! Referring back to the example of the new middle school librarian mentioned earlier in this chapter, all of these things would be a breath of fresh air to students and staff who had been alienated by the previous librarian. They help take advantage of an opportunity to show the library in a new light.

Textboxes 10.2 and 10.3 provide two examples of advocacy involving a summer reading program collaboration between the school library and the public library. Textbox 10.2 is a newspaper article; textbox 10.3 is a script for a radio spot.

TEXTBOX 10.2
SAMPLE NEWSPAPER ARTICLE

GO APE FOR READING
SUMMER READING PROGRAM SPONSORED BY
THE PUBLIC LIBRARY AND YOUR SCHOOL LIBRARY

By Maria B. Stone and Bethany A. Petersen

The summer reading program, Go Ape for Reading, for children in grades 3–8 and sponsored by The Public Library and Your School Library, starts June 2, 2014. Winners will earn a trip to the Ledge on the Skydeck of the Willis Tower in downtown Chicago, as well as other prizes. Registration materials may be picked up at The Public Library and Your School Library or by accessing http://sumread@tpl.org. For more information, contact Maria B. Stone, children's librarian, The Public Library at mstone@tpl.org, or Bethany A. Petersen, school librarian, Your School Library at bapetersen@ysl.edu.

TEXTBOX 10.3
SAMPLE RADIO SPOT SCRIPT

Announcer (Bill Smith): Today as part of our community outreach, we would like to feature the summer reading program, Go Ape for Reading, co-sponsored by The Public Library and Your School Library. I'd like to introduce Maria B. Stone, children's librarian at The Public Library, and Bethany A. Petersen, school librarian at Your School Library, to tell you about this exciting summer reading program for kids.

Stone: Thank you, Bill. Bethany and I have been busy working to create a great summer reading program for our local children in grades 3–8. This includes all students in the area going into or leaving these grades. Our theme this summer is Go Ape for Reading. We are really excited to offer this opportunity to our younger library patrons.

Petersen: The reading program starts on June 2 and ends August 15, 2014. Our grand prize is a trip to Chicago to stand out on the Ledge at the Willis Tower. Other prizes include two tickets to a local minor league baseball game, books, movie and music DVDs, an iTunes gift card, and boxes of candy from the Candy Shop in our community.

Stone: Registration materials can be picked up at The Public Library or Your School Library during summer school, or by accessing http://sumread@tpl.org.

Petersen: For more information, you may also contact us: Maria B. Stone, children's librarian, The Public Library at mstone@tpl.org or Bethany A. Petersen, school librarian, Your School Library at bapetersen@ysl.edu.

Stone and Petersen: Please join us for a great reading summer as we Go Ape for Reading!

Announcer: Thank you, Maria and Bethany. Remember, audience, to encourage your children to Go Ape for Reading this summer!

ADVOCACY IN THE SCHOOL

Again, let's look to our example in the introduction of the new middle school librarian who could not figure out why she had so few patrons in the library. (Sometimes we need to advocate *in* our schools as well as in the community at large.) So, how can the new librarian bring more people (students *and* teachers) into a library, where for years they have felt unwelcome? Beyond the uses of publicity mentioned in the previous sections, here are some ideas that may help (remember that chapter 8, "Programming and Collaboration," can also help with this issue):

- Find even one teacher with whom to collaborate. Once others see success, it will be easier to bring more teachers and classes into the library. One possibility here would be to get to know another new teacher and collaborate with him or her. This would "move the ball forward" and have the added benefit of developing a good professional relationship for both of you when you probably need it most.

- Join some school committees; when possible, inform the members how the library can help them.
- Ask the principal for a few minutes at each teachers' meeting. Talk about new resources, give a brief tutorial of a new technology, or offer to pool resources for a student research project.
- Invite faculty and staff in for a "treats and technology" hour some day after school or on a teacher's work day. (Bring food and they will come!)
- Introduce yourself to those you do not know (students and staff). Be friendly and approachable.
- Offer to display student-selected book favorites.
- Listen to what others have to say.
- Provide resources and help when asked, and if not asked, offer.
- Sponsor a book fair; that will bring in students.
- Become a lead advocate for library-related issues of interest to others in the school: intellectual freedom, privacy, copyright, the many types of literacy, information access equity (American Library Association 2010a).
- Start a collection of letters from local, state, or national dignitaries and others (famous people born in your state, for example) of interest to your students and faculty. Ask each respondent to send a letter telling your school what his or her favorite reading materials were when he or she was growing up. Frame the letters and hang them on the walls in the library. Every time a new letter comes in, publicize the fact in the school. People will come in to view the collection—and hopefully stay to use the library!
- Create your own list of ideas, using those above as a starting place.

Textboxes 10.4 and 10.5 are text messages that the school librarian might send to fellow faculty (textbox 10.4) and to school students (textbox 10.5), given the popularity of personal cell phones and texting in the 21st century. (It is possible that both groups would receive these texts before the school day began or after it ended, since certain schools do not allow cell phone use during the school day, particularly for students.)

Now let's move on to advocacy from your personal point of view.

TEXTBOX 10.4
SAMPLE TEXT MESSAGE TO FACULTY

U R invited 2 Your School Library 4 in-service. 2/7/14. 2–3PM. Learn 2 use our new Chromebooks 2 become Google Educators.

TEXTBOX 10.5
SAMPLE TEXT MESSAGE TO STUDENTS

U R invited 2 Your School Library 4 *Hunger Games* Day. Games, movies, stories, & food. Sat., May 17, 2014. 10A–4PM.

ADVOCATING FOR YOURSELF

Here is a story about advocacy from a retired school librarian.

> When I first became a school librarian, I was assigned three elementary schools. Each week, I spent a day and a half in each, with the last half day varying, given whichever school needed me most. It was time consuming traveling between schools; difficult to remember all the teachers' names, let alone the students; and the amount of work often over-whelming (I had no aide or assistant). Plus, in my district, the elementary school librarian was considered the classroom teacher's "free time;" consequently I would take each elementary class once per week, for a class period, when at a particular school. I quickly realized that I would be able do so much more, if I only were able to spend all my time in just one of the schools or if flexible scheduling were the norm. As a new librarian, I had not found my voice, however. I did not know or understand advocacy. (Personal reflection, anonymous)

At one time, each of us has been or will be the new school librarian. Our library (or libraries) may vary, we may have flexible scheduling (see chapter 7, "Services," for more on this subject), and we may have help in running our facility. We may, however, have other work issues that we would like changed. This is when advocacy can come into play. How can one advocate for oneself and still be a team player?

Each situation is different; however, here are some recommendations for letting people know who you are, what you do, and how you can work with them.

- Create a web page or bulletin board introducing yourself to your constituency. Inform them as to your education, skill sets, and interests. Let them know what you can do for them in terms of library resources, services, and programming.
- Remind individuals, if necessary, that you, too, are a teacher and have a classroom (the library). Do this in a pleasant, nonthreatening manner.
- Offer to help your faculty and students; demonstrate your enthusiasm for your job.
- Consider establishing a personal brand (Schneider 2012); that is, how can you make yourself recognizable (in a good way)? This may mean rearranging parts of the library to better fit the needs of the students (inform your clientele why this is so), wearing something other than "sensible shoes" (Bargmann 2008), establishing that you are an expert (blogger, programmer, grant writer, whatever) in addition to being the school librarian, and so on.
- Establish a library club, composed of interested students. Once a year hold a Library Day, where the members of the club each wear a hat representing one of

the jobs that a school librarian does (e.g., top hat for budget manager, fireman's hat for troubleshooter). The club members could wear the hats all day, along with a badge that says, "Ask me what I do in the library." Students and faculty would ask, and the student could respond with the school librarian responsibility represented by the hat he or she is wearing.

• Present research to support your position or needs to your administration.
• Demonstrate how that for which you are advocating supports the overall mission of the school and/or helps make the job of other faculty and staff easier.

If some of the preceding suggestions are discomforting, remind yourself that advocacy is one of those things where there are many choices. "We are blessed with an abundance of tremendous librarians in our profession, and quite a few of them lead from behind, through quiet example, low-key strategy, and sotto voce mentoring" (Schneider 2012, 37). There is more than one way to advocate for yourself; find the best fit for you.

Textboxes 10.6 and 10.7 provide two examples of personal advocacy: a bulletin board, introducing the new school librarian to the students and staff (textbox 10.6) and an email the librarian might send to his or her fellow faculty (textbox 10.7).

TEXTBOX 10.6
PERSONAL ADVOCACY BULLETIN BOARD

Introducing:
Miss Petersen,
Your New School Librarian!

Hometown
Boone, North Carolina

Education
BA (Education)
Appalachian State University
Boone, North Carolina
MSLS (Library Science)
University of Kentucky
Lexington, Kentucky

Hobbies
Reading
Horseback riding
Traveling
Cooking
Jewelry making

TEXTBOX 10.7
PERSONAL ADVOCACY EMAIL

From: Bethany A. Petersen <bpetersen@BES.NET>
To: teachers@BES.NET
Subject: What I can do for you!

Dear Teachers,

I would like to introduce myself to you. I am Bethany A. Petersen, your new school librarian. I look forward to working with you this school year and want to let you know some of the things that the library (and I as the librarian) can do for you. I have listed some items below in bullet points.

- Pull books for your course units
- Teach your students how to use online data bases
- Co-create a Weebly website with you
- Help you write a grant
- Run a book fair
- Research for materials to support a lesson you are teaching
- Provide space in the library workroom for your latest project
- Display your students' art work
- Book-talk to your students
- Work with individual students who need extra help with searching skills
- Read stories
- Teach all students in the school about Internet safety
- Participate on grade-level/curriculum committees
- Advise lip dub creators
- Fix simple computer problems
- Evaluate Internet sites
- Serve as the school copyright expert

If you need something that is not there, please feel free to contact me. If I can do it or get it for you, I will!

I look forward to working with you!

Bethany
School Librarian
Butler Elementary School

COMMUNITY ADVOCACY

Advocacy can mean reaching out to your community, whether to the public library or other community organizations and groups. This can be in the form of marketing (for example, see the earlier Publicity as Advocacy section) the benefits of your school library to the community at large (especially in an area where there may be no local public library available), or establishing collaboration areas with your public library.

Let's look first to the public library. Working with the public library can be a benefit to both school and public libraries. Such collaboration may encourage after-school use of the public library in the form of homework help, research, and access to technology. It can include a project where the school librarian works in tandem with the public library to ensure that the school students obtain library cards. It could mean a joint funding venture to bring in a guest author, a special exhibit featuring the history of the school and displayed in the public library, or the lending of books and other materials from the public library to support curricular needs in a poor school district. It might mean a cooperative project involving both the school and community—for example, a communal reading and book discussion (American Association of School Librarians 2014c). Joining forces with the public library can be a plus to both groups.

Textbox 10.8 is a sample brochure and textbox 10.9 provides four sample tweets that the public and school libraries could collaborate on, given the idea of the summer reading program mentioned earlier in this chapter.

TEXTBOX 10.8
PUBLIC/SCHOOL LIBRARY
COLLABORATION BROCHURE

GO APE FOR READING

Books about Apes
For All Ages
Available from The Public Library and Your School Library

THE PUBLIC LIBRARY

Goodall, Jane. *In the Shadow of Man.* (print)
Goodall, Jane. *My Life with the Chimpanzees.* (audio, e-book, and print)
Jackson, Dan. *Apes.* (e-book)
Jango-Cohen, Judith. *Gorillas.* (print)
Nichols, Michael with Elizabeth Carney. *Face to Face with Gorillas.* (e-book and print)
Roe-Pimm, Nancy. *The Heart of the Beast: Eight Great Gorilla Stories.* (print)
Thompson, Shawn. *The Intimate Ape: Orangutans and the Secret Life of a Vanishing Species.* (e-book and print)

YOUR SCHOOL LIBRARY

Davis, Jill. *Orangutans Are Ticklish: Fun Facts from an Animal Photographer.* (print)
Edwards, Roberta. *Who Is Jane Goodall?* Who Was . . . ? series. (print)
Goodall, Jane. *My Life with the Chimpanzees.* (print)
Jenkins, Martin. *Ape.* (print)
Milton, Joyce. *Gorillas: Gentle Giants of the Forest.* (e-book and print)
Pinkwater, Daniel. *Second-Grade Ape.* (e-book and print)

Moreover, there are other groups within the community, with whom forming collaboration with your school library may be beneficial. It could be there is a local animal organization that is willing to provide service dogs to sit and listen to poor readers, a woman's association able to provide food and prizes for a reading contest, a group of military veterans who will talk about their war experiences for a school project about the Vietnam conflict, a service guild that wishes to donate a new computer lab, or a local computer club with members who can sit one on one with students and teach them how to design and develop personal web pages. There is no need for the school library to exist in a vacuum; indeed, reach out to others, use community information and resources to benefit your students' learning!

**TEXTBOX 10.9
PUBLIC/SCHOOL LIBRARY
COLLABORATION TWEETS**

#SummerReading
Summer reading program 4 grades 3–8 starts June 3 @ The Public Library. Pick up information in Your School Library or The Public Library.

#CChicago
Earn trip to Willis Tower in Chicago if U win summer reading program at Your School Library & The Public Library. http://sumread@tpl.org

#ClimbingGorilla
Summer reading theme at Your School Library & The Public Library: Go Ape for Reading. http://sumread@tpl.org

#GorillaOnLedge
Win a chance to view Chicago from the Willis Tower Ledge! Join TPL&YSL Summer Reading! http://sumread@tpl.org

MORE ADVOCACY INFORMATION

In addition to the information already given, AASL provides a number of online toolkits that can be used to advocate for the school library (American Association of School Librarians 2014a). The School Library Program Health and Wellness Toolkit, for instance, "supports your proactive efforts to keep your library program healthy as you work to build the program and to prevent cuts" (American Association of School Librarians 2014b, 1). The School Library Crisis Toolkit is designed to help the school librarian whose position or program is in danger of being cut or reduced (American Association of School Librarians 2014a, 1). Another toolkit, the Parent Advocate Toolkit, is intended "to help school librarians build parent support for their programs" (American Association of School Librarians 2014d). The toolkit entitled Instructional Classification Toolkit, provides a variety of resources which support the school librarian classification as an educator (American Association of School Librarians 2014a). Lastly, the @ Your Library Toolkit for School Library Programs contains a plethora of advocacy resources, including graphics, marketing and promotional materials, grant information, informative publications, recruitment information (to recruit future school librarians), and relevant research (American Association of School Librarians 2014d).

As you advocate for your field, your program, and/or your employment, keep in mind that "school librarians need to be cautious when advocating for their own programs and jobs. When school librarians speak out for libraries or librarians, it can sound whiny and self-serving. However, to advocate for students and student learning is meaningful and far more likely to be effective and is a necessary piece of the advocacy puzzle" (American Association of School Librarians 2014b, 1).

KEY CONCEPTS FROM THIS CHAPTER

- Advocacy is important to school libraries.
- Advocacy can take many forms.
- Research is an important advocacy tool.
- One way to advocate for your school library is through publicity, online and print.
- Use advocacy to bring more users into the library.
- Advocate for yourself.
- Advocate to your community.
- Consult AASL's advocacy toolkits.
- Be a positive, assertive advocate.

Coming in chapter 11: "The 'Extra' Things."

DISCUSSION QUESTIONS

1. Argue for using library research as an advocacy tool.
2. What would you in include on a web page advertising your library?
3. Given the school library of your choice, how might you advocate for yourself?

ACTIVITIES

1. Create a one- to two-page advocacy plan on the positives of the school library collection and its programs and services for a school of your choice. Consider using school library research as part of your justification. Include the following:
   - Your choice of school
   - Library programs and activities
   - How you would communicate with your audience (students, teachers, administrators, public)
   - Anything else that you deem important to an advocacy plan
2. Over the past few years, many school library research studies have been developed and reported on by Keith Curry Lance and others. Is your state one of them? Investigate school library research studies for your state. What is there? How can you use this information to advocate for your library?
3. Create a web page or bulletin board introducing you, the school librarian, to your students and faculty. Be sure to mention your education; the fact that school librarians, too, can be teachers; and your reading and technology interests and skill sets.

REFERENCES

American Association of School Librarians. 2008. *Research Foundation Paper: School Libraries Work!* Chicago, Ill.: American Library Association.

———. 2013. "Strong School Libraries Build Strong Students." http://www.ala.org/aasl/sites/ala.org.aasl/files/content/aaslissues/advocacy/AASL_infographic.pdf.

———. 2014a. "School Library Crisis Toolkit." http://www.ala.org/aasl/advocacy/tools/toolkits/crisis.

———. 2014b. "School Library Program Health and Wellness Toolkit." http://www.ala.org/aasl/advocacy/tools/toolkithe or shealth-wellness.

———. 2014c. "Toolkits." http://www.ala.org/aasl/advocacy/tools/toolkits.

———. 2014d. "Welcome to the School Library Campaign." http://www.ala.org/advocacy/advleg/publicawareness/campaign@yourlibrary/prtools/schoollibrary/schoollibrary.

———. 2014e. "What Is Advocacy?" http://www.ala.org/aasl/advocacy/definitions.

American Library Association. 2010a. *ALA 2015.* Chicago, Ill.: American Library Association.

———. 2010b. *Library Advocate's Handbook.* Chicago, Ill.: American Library Association.

———. 2014c. "School Libraries." http://www.ala.org/news/mediapresscenter/americaslibraries/soal2012/school-libraries.

Bargmann, Monika. 2008. "Sensible Shoes." *LIBREAS: Library Ideas.* 13 (2): 1–10.

Gebeloff, Robert. 2011. "In Lean Times, Schools Squeeze Out Librarians." http://www.nytimes.com/2011/06/25/nyregion/schools-eliminating-librarians-as-budgets-shrink.html?pagewanted=all&_r=0.

Johnson, Doug. 2010. "State Staffing Requirements." http://dougj.pbworks.com/w/page/18142589/State-staffing-requirements.

Lance, Keith Curry. n.d. "School Library Impact Studies: The Impact of School Librarians and Library Programs on Academic Achievement of Students: The South Carolina Study." http://keithcurrylance.com/school-library-impact-studies/.

Lance, Keith Curry, Rodney, Marcia J., and Hamilton-Pennell, Christine. 2000. "How School Librarians Help Kids Achieve Standards: The Second Colorado Study." http://www.lrs.org/data-tools/school-libraries/impact-studies/.

———. 2005. *Powerful Libraries Make Powerful Learners: The Illinois Study.* Canton, Ill.: Illinois School Library Media Association.

Lance, Keith Curry and Schwarz, Bill. 2013. *How Pennsylvania School Libraries Pay Off: Investments in Student Achievement and Academic Standards.* PA School Library Project. http://paschoollibraryproject.org/research.

Library Research Service. 2013a. "School Libraries and Student Achievement." www.lrs.org

———. 2013b. "School Libraries Impact Studies." http://www.lrs.org/data-tools/school-libraries/impact-studies/.

Schneider, Karen G. 2012. "Personal Branding for Librarians: Distinguishing Yourself from the Professional Herd." *American Libraries* (November/December): 34–37.

Small, Ruth V., Snyder, Jaime, and Parker, Katie. 2009. "The Impact of New York's School Libraries on Student Achievement and Motivation: Phase I." http://eric.ed.gov/?id=EJ859484.

Zickuhr, Kathryn, Rainie, Lee, and Purcell, Kristen. 2013. "Younger Americans' Library Habits and Expectations." http://libraries.pewinternet.org/2013/06/25/younger-americans-library-services/.

11

The "Extra" Things

So far in this book, we have addressed many of the major concerns and issues facing today's school librarians. But wait—there are more, and these are important, too. For example, there are disasters, both natural and human made, such as hurricanes, tornados, fires, floods, earthquakes, vandals, and school shootings. Unfortunately, such disasters can happen in schools and as a part of the school, the school library can be affected by these things. Then there is the issue of time. What school librarian has enough time to get everything done he or she feels needs to be completed in a day, week, month, or even year? Lastly, how many school librarians actually take care of themselves—physically and mentally? Or does such attention to self end up on the "back burner" as something to do when everything else gets done? These are the subjects upon which we concentrate in this chapter.

DISASTERS IN THE SCHOOL LIBRARY

The school librarian has many responsibilities, and as such disasters, both those natural and those created by humans, may not always be a first consideration, in that one can hope they will never happen. In most school systems, however, there is some sort of disaster readiness already set up. With the variety of natural (examples: Hurricanes Katrina and Sandy) and human-created (examples: Columbine High School and Sandy Hook Elementary) disasters, school systems are not only preparing for possible traumatic events, but also practicing for what might occur with fire and tornado drills, fictional intruder alerts, and more. It is best to always be prepared, and we focus on that preparedness here.

Let's look first at some points that hold true, no matter the type of disaster.

- Safety of those in the library (library personnel, students, faculty, and any others) is of prime importance. It is vital to
  - remain calm,
  - get those in the library to a safe location,
  - contact the disaster command center specified by your school district, and
  - keep out of the way of any emergency workers.
- When disaster planning, aim for the worst-case scenario. Know who the school go-to person is in case of calamity and the easiest and quickest way to contact that person.
- Carry a cell phone or have other access to communication tools available in order to contact your school emergency contact, 911, and/or crisis personnel.
- Be ready. Since you cannot always determine what those in the library will do in an emergency, run practice drills. (Often districts or school principals will do this periodically.)
- Remember that all disaster plans are actually guidelines. You will need to act/react according to what is occurring.
- In the case of misinformation, correct it immediately.
- Consider that disasters can happen to anyone, anywhere. Try not to take what occurs personally.
- Make library collection care and salvaging a goal, once all people are safe.
- Establish a list of experienced collection care experts ahead of time.
- Bear in mind what in the collection is damaged/missing and prioritize those items of most importance.
- Be positive. Think over how this negative situation may mean, through recovery operations, a way to grow the collection and school library services. (Alire 2006; Alire 2000; Harvard Library 2013; Howard 2012; New York University Libraries, n.d.)

Natural

Every school library needs to consider its own disaster plan (if it has one) and that of the school district in the case of natural disasters and the library's physical facility and collection (both print and technology). Natural disasters—such as hurricanes, tornados, earthquakes, blizzards, high winds, and floods—can mean loss of electrical power; water damage to facilities, equipment, and materials; materials disappearing (wind, flooding, vandals); a damaged facility (possibly requiring future construction); and so on. Be mindful of the types of natural disasters common to your area and use that awareness to develop a set of guidelines to follow in case of these types of emergencies. In addition, FEMA (Federal Emergency Management Agency 2013) provides a plethora of general disaster information, which can be helpful in preparing emergency plans (see http://www.fema.gov/).

Fire

A fire can be a man-made or natural disaster. With a fire, there is always the possibility that things in the school library will be wholly or partially burned, melted, or otherwise damaged—oftentimes beyond repair. However, here are some pointers to consider when working with fire damage to the library collection, its computers and other equipment, and other materials that might have been in the library at the time of the fire:

- Do not enter the school library until the fire is out and emergency personnel have deemed it to be safe.
- Determine which material and what equipment is salvageable.
- Sooty items, if intense heat does not make them too brittle, may possibly be cleaned.
- Ozone generators can help rid the facility and collection of smoky odor. (How to Clean Stuff.net 2013)

Water

In addition to flooding as a natural occurrence (see earlier in this chapter), water damage can also occur as a result of broken water pipes, emergency crews focusing pressurized water from fire hoses onto materials in the hopes that they will not burn, and mold (usually a result of wet items or high humidity). Thus, here are a few tips for school library collection preservation when considering possible water and mold damage:

- Store collections somewhere other than basements.
- Print materials can expand up to 10% with water damage.
- Items soiled by dirt and other contaminants may need to be cleaned before drying occurs.
- Damp items can often be air dried.
- Mold can form in as little as 72 hours.
- Use of dehumidifiers helps stop the formation of mold.
- Freezing and then vacuum freeze-drying may save wet print materials from molding.
- Air-dry photographs stored in cases and photo albums.
- Separate single wet photographs; if not they will stick together.
- Single wet photographs should be rinsed with clean cold water and then either frozen or air-dried.
- Archival nonprint, such as videotapes, audiotapes, computer floppies, and more can often be kept wet for several days. Do not freeze. They may need to be shipped wet to an expert for possible restoration.

- Do remember that how to treat the wet or moldy item usually depends on its format. Therefore, always check with conservation experts (this includes websites as well as books and articles on preservation) as to how best to work with each piece. (Alire 2006; Alire 2000; Minter 2002; Northeast Document Conservation Center, n.d.; Walsh 1997)

And More . . .

How prepared are we to discover that the library was vandalized the night before? Are we, as school librarians, ready to respond to an armed intruder appearing in a library crowded with students? These are difficult questions to answer and beyond the purview of this book. However, your school should have policies and procedures in place for such emergencies and schedule drills periodically. As the school librarian, you can be aware of disaster measures by volunteering to be part of the committee developing such policies and procedures, reviewing all emergency criteria, and considering ways that the library can follow what has been created. You can also prepare yourself by being cognizant of emergency resources, talking over specific school library disaster issues with your principal, and establishing security that might be particular just to the library (for example, what library doors remained locked, except in emergencies, or how to keep track of who is in the library at any one time). Many schools have security personnel, lock their buildings (except for the main door), have procedures stating that all guests must check in at the main office first, have metal detectors, and have fencing, along with safety procedures including reporting suspicious individuals to the main office, checking to see if library and classroom doors have inside locks, and so on. Be mindful of what has been established for your school, and if an emergency arises, be as prepared as you can be.

TIME ISSUES

Probably all of us—school librarians or not—desire a more balanced work and personal life than we currently have. And, almost any educator one talks to will say that there is too much to do. How can the school librarian get all those things done that he or she feels are important to the library program, that the principal requires him or her to accomplish, that fellow teachers request, or that students need? Well, the answer is that it takes time! This section focuses on time management—a subject that most of us think we know but few understand well.

How can the school librarian manage his or her time well? In the ideal world, we would be able to balance our work and personal lives, achieve all our goals, and not stress out in the process. In reality, that can be a daunting task. So, what to do? The answer comes down to time management: taking the many tasks and responsibilities that we have and deciding what needs to be done well, what needs to just be done, and what we can skip without negatively affecting our lives. All this requires that we recognize what we are good at and what our habits and problem areas are. Do we panic if we cannot get something done? Are we timely workers or procrastinators? Given the preceding, what are some of the things that the school librarian can do to make sure that he or she gets the work done each day, week, month, or year?

One of the most important things to do is to create some sort of calendar, schedule, or time line. For example, given a daily agenda, one might put in those things you are required to do that day (such as teaching three classes, attending a teacher's meeting, and hall monitoring) and the times when they are to be done. Next, schedule some time for those activities that are done routinely throughout most work days (such as helping students find the library materials, shelving books, and working on the library website). Then consider some time for those extra things (that you have not planned on) to occur (for example, a teacher comes in and needs material on Abraham Lincoln right away). If there are deadlines to any of these undertakings, make sure they are also on the agenda. If at all possible, attempt to arrange your more difficult or strenuous activities for those peak performance times in your day. Remember to also schedule those nonwork/personal items that are necessary to that particular day. Lastly, plan a little time to do something for yourself, once the work day is done, such as exercise, play with your child, go to a nice restaurant, read a book, whatever is important to you and helps you relax. Make sure that you review your agenda during the day. Remind yourself that you are a librarian; librarians are supposed to be organized, so organize! Keeping a schedule and working to follow it is one way to help with your time management (Emmet 2000; Haliczer 2005; Mind Tools 2013). Figure 11.1 is an example of a daily work agenda for a high school librarian.

Monday, October 2, 2013	
Time	Activity
7:30 AM	Library Opens for Early Arrivals
8 AM	Meeting with Library Aide
8:15 AM	School Day Begins
8:30-9:15 AM	Teach Web Research Skills: Mrs. Walker's English Class
9:30-10:30 AM	Work on Pulling Books for Mr. Klaus's Class
10:30-11:30 AM	Study Hall Supervision
11:30-12 PM	Lunch (Also Use Time to Preview DVD Catalog)
12-1 PM	Mr. Samuel's Class in doing Astronomy Research
1:15-2 PM	Meeting with History Department
2-2:30 PM	Time to Work on DVD Ordering
2:30 PM	School Day Ends
2:30-4 PM	Library Open for After-School Study
2:45-4 PM	Library Club Meets (I am advisor)
4:15 PM	Leave School for Day

Figure 11.1.   High School Librarian Daily Work Agenda

Others things to take into account when time-managing:

- Set aside specific moments to read your email during the work day; constantly looking at it is a time-waster.
- Garbage cans are there for a reason—throw away those things that you do not need to or will not read.
- Acquire routines or practices that work for you and stick with them.
- Recall that unimportant things might not be worth doing.
- Reorganize yourself when your timetable becomes disorganized.
- Realize that there are some days when you will not get everything done.
- Prioritize those things you must do from those you want to do.
- Accept the fact that there are always going to be more things to do than time. (Emmet 2000; Haliczer 2005; Mind Tools 2013)

On a side note, if you are a library director with other librarians and technology people that you oversee and/or supervise, such as library aides, assistants, or a secretary, you may find yourself concerned with how others also use their time. Take the criteria discussed here and apply it to your subordinates. They, too, can benefit from time management.

Remember that some of us are the school librarians who like to leave at the end of our work day with our desks clear. (Very few actually achieve that goal, however!) Others of us have a daily list or scatter notes and projects across our desk and working areas with all those things that we feel or know should be done. Organize according to your strengths and stick with it!

TAKING CARE OF YOURSELF IN THE LIBRARY

Job-related stress, as described in the *Merriam-Webster Online Dictionary* (2013), is "a state resulting from a stress . . . one of bodily or mental tension resulting from factors that tend to alter an existent equilibrium" (1). Like in any other job, school librarians sometimes meet/work with problems or toxic individuals, thus causing us stress. Problems may vary with individuals. People who cause stress can be administrators, fellow teachers, other librarians, aides/assistants, or parents. In this part of the chapter we take a few minutes to address the issue of taking care of yourself in the library. Please note that this section is not designed to replicate a psychology text or handle any critical personnel issues. It is placed here to assist the school librarian in his or her everyday work environment.

Imagine that you are a brand-new K–8 librarian. It appears that some of the teachers in your school are "going behind your back" to your library assistant, who has been there for some time and with whom they are more comfortable. You feel that the teachers should be coming to you with materials and library instruction requests. How can you promote yourself as the "expert" while still maintaining a good relationship with your assistant? Like the scenarios in activity 3 at the end of this chapter, the preceding example is culled from the real-life experiences of a fellow school librarian. Following is information that may be helpful to you, if something like this happens where you work.

The World Health Organization (2013, 1) defines healthy employment as "one where the pressures on employees are appropriate in relation to their abilities and resources, to the amount of control they have over their work, and to the support they receive from people who matter to them." Some stressors for school librarians/ library information specialists may include the lowering of library budgets; pressure from administration and patrons to find new money sources for collection expansion; more work, due to loss of an aide; increased accountability due to standards the school and/or library is required to address; and so on. According to the Mayo Clinic (2013), one of the first things to do is to recognize how stress affects you. Do you overeat, become depressed, angry, or cry? Once you have reflected on how you react, it is time to learn to manage your problems and anxieties. Stress management techniques that may work for you include the following:

- Cut back on responsibilities. Although this is not always possible, perhaps there is an assistant or library volunteer who might be able to pick up some of the simple duties you have, such as shelving library materials or pulling books for classes. Delegate.
- Consider time (see discussion of time management earlier in this chapter). Feeling anxious for not getting something done on time can be a big stressor.
- Find someone else in a similar situation. Realizing that you are not alone in the problems you are experiencing is in itself stress reducing. Also reach out to friends and family. Although they may not understand what you are going through, their love and support can help you through the rough patches.
- Accept your limitations; prioritize. Recognize that you cannot do everything; thus, focus on the important issues.
- Do something that makes you happy and is relaxing. Whether it is a hobby, travel, cooking, or a massage, do something for you.
- Exercise. Use physical activity to work away the strain you are feeling.
- Sleep. "Lack of sufficient sleep affects your immune system and your judgment and makes you more likely to snap over minor irritations. Most people need seven to eight hours of sleep a day" (Mayo Clinic 2013, 2).
- Be positive. While this is easier to state than it is to do, the concept is good—try to keep a positive attitude and focus on solutions, not on what is wrong.
- Be calm and speak quietly. The louder and more emotional you are, the louder and more emotional others tend to be as well. Choose to be as professional as possible.
- Ask questions. Talk it out. If you do not understand what is happening or why, ask. Obtaining the answer will help you find the solution.
- Find win-win solutions. Is there such a solution through compromise? If so, go for it.

- Do not reproach yourself for the choices you make. Do the best that you can at the time that the problem is occurring.
- Use humor. Using nonthreatening humor can defuse many sticky situations.
- Do not let the toxic individual/bully take away your power. Just because someone says something negative to you does not mean it is true. Remind yourself of that—often.
- Walk away. If nothing is working, choose to leave the toxic situation or person. You are not helping yourself by remaining.
- Go to a professional. If nothing else helps, it is time to go to a supervisor; union representative, employee assistance program, or someone else who is skilled in helping through your particular crisis: doctor or counselor. (Bernstein, n.d.; Butler and Fiehn 2006; Maple 2005; Mayo Clinic 2013; Munde 2012)

Now let's go back to our dilemma of the new school librarian who does not know how to respond when the teachers in her school seem more comfortable going to her library assistant for requests than to her. How best might she handle this situation? While any number of the preceding suggestions might be used, the point on asking questions/talking it out (see list) would be a good starting place. Once the new librarian realizes what is going on (by talking to her assistant, administrator, and/or to faculty), she may be better able to recognize what she can do as the school librarian, as compared to what the assistant is able to do. By remaining calm and professional and accepting her limitations (after all, she is new and does not know the faculty as well as the library assistant does), the school librarian might also delegate some responsibilities to her assistant (perhaps the pulling of books and other material for faculty) while taking on others that are more likely to require her expertise (e.g., collaborating with a particular teacher on a research lesson for his class or selecting and evaluating websites to support a particular seventh grade curriculum). In this way, parameters can be set—in a reassuring, rather than an aggressive, manner. By seeking out other educators (such as the music or art teacher) who may similarly work with the whole school population, our new school librarian may also come to recognize that she is not alone. She might also receive coping mechanisms from her newly found friends and colleagues. At all times, it is helpful if our new librarian remains positive and nonthreatening to her assistant, and looks at the situation from a win-win perspective.

To each of you who are or wish to be in the school library profession: take care of yourself and enjoy your position; being a school librarian can be a wonderful and fulfilling experience.

KEY CONCEPTS FROM THIS CHAPTER

- Be prepared for natural disasters as well as those created by humans.
- In the case of a disaster, safety of those in the library is of primary importance to the school librarian.
- When disaster planning, aim for the worst-case scenario.

- Always have close access to a cell phone or another communication tool, in case of a catastrophe.
- Bear in mind what in the collection is damaged/missing and prioritize those items of most importance.
- Determine your strengths and weaknesses, when it comes to time management, and organize according to your strengths.
- Keep a calendar, schedule, daily agenda, or time line.
- If at all possible, divest yourself of time-wasters.
- Recognize that you need to take care of yourself before you can take care of all the aspects of the school library.
- School librarian stressors include
  - decreasing library budgets;
  - more work and less people to do it;
  - increased standards accountability.
- Practice stress management techniques, including
  - cutting back on responsibilities;
  - finding a friend;
  - accepting your limitations;
  - remaining positive;
  - staying calm;
  - not reproaching yourself;
  - using humor;
  - walking away.
- Look at stressful situations from a win-win perspective.

Coming in chapter 12: "Evaluating the School Library and the School Library of the Future."

DISCUSSION QUESTIONS

1. What kinds of disasters are you trained to handle in your school? How might disaster preparation differ from the school library to the classroom?
2. What do you want out of time management? What are your peak performance times and how can you use these to your advantage as you attack the work of the school library?
3. What ways can you take care of yourself, as a librarian, when faced with a belligerent student, teacher, administrator, library aide, or another individual?

ACTIVITIES

1. View "Guns in Our Schools" (C-Span Video Library 2013; http://www.c-spanvideo.org/program/311538-20#). Role-play how you might respond if you discovered an armed student in the library in the middle of a school day.

2. Choose a work day and create a sample daily agenda for yourself (you may use the one in this chapter as a template).
3. Choose one of the scenarios listed here (all are real-life experiences). Discuss how you would respond to your chosen scenario.

   a. Envisage that you are an elementary librarian. You are seeing every class once a week for a set period of time; that is, when the students are in the library, the classroom teacher has a planning period. You approach your principal with the idea of flexible library scheduling. His reply, "As far as I am concerned, you are a babysitter and free time up for my teachers. I will *not* support flexible scheduling." How do you respond? What can you do?

   b. You have just been hired as a middle school library information specialist. You find that there is an aide already in the library who has been there for a number of years, during which time she has had free rein over how it was run (there was no library professional before you were hired). Almost immediately a power struggle begins—you have your ideas; she has hers. You have gone to college to do this; she has on-the-job experience. How do you handle this situation?

   c. Imagine you are employed in a large high school as one of two library information specialists. You and your fellow professional are like oil and water. On top of that he has been there longer than you and considers himself the leader when it comes to decision making. How can you turn this situation into a smoothly operating team and still respect yourself?

REFERENCES

Alire, Camila, ed. 2000. *Library Disaster Planning and Recovery*. New York, N.Y.: Neal-Schuman.

——, ed. 2006. "Library Disaster Planning." Presentation at Northern Illinois University, DeKalb, Illinois.

Bernstein, Albert J. n.d. "Psychology That Works." http://www.albernstein.com/index.htm.

Butler, Rebecca P. and Fiehn, Barbara. 2006. "How to Take Care of Yourself Both In and Out of the Library." Presentation at the Illinois School Library Media Association, Decatur, Illinois.

C-Span Video Library. 2013. "Guns in Our Schools." http://www.c-spanvideo.org/program/311538-20#.

Emmet, Rita. 2000. *The Procrastinator's Handbook: Mastering the Art of Doing It Now*. New York, N.Y.: Walker & Company.

Federal Emergency Management Agency. 2013. Home page. http://www.fema.gov/.

Haliczer, Deborah. 2005. "Time Management." Presentation at Northern Illinois University, DeKalb, Illinois.

Harvard Library. 2013. "Emergency Preparedness Plan." http://library.harvard.edu/preservation/emergency-preparedness-plan.

How to Clean Stuff.net. 2013. "How to Clean Smoke Damage." http://www.howtocleanstuff.net/how-to-clean-smoke-damage/.

Howard, Jennifer. 2012. "What Katrina Can Teach Libraries about Sandy and Other Disasters." http://chronicle.com/blogs/wiredcampus/what-katrina-can-teach-libraries-about-sandy-and-other-disasters/40986.

Maple, Leslie T. 2005. "Sustaining the Verve: How Teachers Can Stay Energized in a Stressful Occupation." http://www.ascd.org/publications/classroom-leadership/jun2005/Sustaining-the-Verve.aspx.

Mayo Clinic. 2013. "Stress Management." http://www.mayoclinic.com/health/stress-management/SR00032/NSECTIONGROUP=2.

Merriam-Webster Online. 2013. "Stress." http://www.merriam-webster.com/dictionary/stress.

Mind Tools. 2013. "Time Management." http://www.mindtools.com/pages/main/newMN_HTE.htm.

Minter, Bill. 2002. "Water Damaged Books: Washing Intact and Air Drying—A Novel (?) Approach." *The Book and Paper Group Annual* 21: 105–109.

Munde, Gail. 2012. "Caring for Your Tribe." *Knowledge Quest* 40 (5): 22–26.

New York University Libraries. n.d. "Disaster Plan Workbook." http://library.nyu.edu/preservation/disaster/toc.htm.

Northeast Document Conservation Center. n.d. "Freezing and Drying Wet Books and Records." http://www.nedcc.org/free-resources/preservation-leaflets/3.-emergency-management/3.12-freezing-and-drying-wet-books-and-records.

Walsh, Betty. 1997. "Salvage Operations for Water Damaged Archival Collections: A Second Glance." http://cool.conservation-us.org/waac/wn/wn19/wn19-2/wn19-206.html.

World Health Organization. 2013. "Occupational Health: Stress at the Workplace." http://www.who.int/occupational_health/topics/stressatwp/en/.

12

Evaluation and the Future

Waiting on the web and residing in articles and books is a veritable treasure trove of evaluation criteria and rubrics for school libraries and librarians. In addition to those available in print and digital formats, a few librarians choose to generate their own—sometimes in partnership with their principal or fellow librarians and teachers. Why? Because we all want to know whether we are doing things right; and if the gauges we find do not quite fit our particular environment, then we fashion our own. After we have determined how we are doing, then we look to our next task, activity, program, technology, library—we look to the future. This chapter addresses school library evaluation and the future of our field.

EVALUATING THE SCHOOL LIBRARY
AS A SINGULAR ENTITY

What are we doing right? What are we doing wrong? What is just acceptable? How can we continuously improve what we are doing? In this section, we consider evaluation—of the various roles of the school library, the school librarian, and school library staff.

The school library program, in general, has many parts. Some of these pieces (resources, facilities, and library staff) are covered below separately, in terms of evaluating them. However, it is also possible to find or create a general form to evaluate the library program as a whole. For example, the guidelines in AASL's (American Association of School Librarians) *Empowering Learners: Guidelines for School Library Media Programs* (2009b) have been developed into a school library program assessment rubric. This rubric, which is found in *A Planning Guide for Empowering Learners* (2010), is divided into "four major school library program aspects: developing visions for learning, teaching for learning, building the learning environment, (and) empowering learning through leadership" (American Association of School Librarians 2010, 47). Within these four sections are fit, with slight rewording and the addition of goals, the AASL guidelines. For example, under the second aspect "Teaching for Learning" is found "Multiple Literacies" (American Association of School Librarians 2010, 50 and 52) with the following guideline listed: "The school library program provides instruction that addresses multiple literacies, including information literacy, media literacy, visual literacy, and technology literacy" (American Association of School Librarians 2010, 52). Within "Multiple Literacies" are "Learning Process" and "Legal, Ethical, and Social Responsibility." Three goals are listed for "Learning Process": the first is "comprehensive," the second is "in-progress," and the third is "basic." The ideal level for attainment is the comprehensive one: "The school librarian has current knowledge of technology tools supporting multiple literacies (information literacy, media literacy, visual literacy, and technology literacy) and guides students in applying them to the learning process" (American Association of School Librarians 2010, 52). Three goals, "articulated, informal, and incidental," are additionally listed for the "Legal, Ethical, and Social Responsibility" piece. Once again, the first one articulated is the ideal: "The school librarian implements a comprehensive plan to embed legal, ethical, and social responsibility concepts into the information-seeking process" (American Association of School Librarians 2010, 52). The school library program assessment rubric from *A Planning Guide for Empowering Learners* (2010) goes through each of AASL's guideline in a similar manner.

There are other general school library program evaluation rubrics as well. For instance, the "Rubric for Program Evaluation" found in Donham (2013) uses the divisions of "inquiry-based learning, reading, collection, technology, collaboration, access, climate, communication, [and] leadership" (320–325). Similarly to the AASL planning guide, within each of these divisions are related subdivisions with three sets of goals for each (an ideal, an acceptable, and a basic). Another rubric example (which also appears as if it could serve as a data collection tool), "Looking at the School Library: An Evaluation Tool," itemizes three pages of library activities under the six headings of "Access, Staffing, Collection, Programs, Facility, [and] Library Administration and Funding" (Rowland and Jeffus 2003, 1–3). Sample statements under "Programs" include the following:

- "School library offers a variety of programs to motivate reading and library use for all levels of the student population.
- Teachers, parents, students and community members are solicited and involved in the library.
- Library media teacher collaborates with classroom teachers to integrate information skills and use of technology into curriculum." (Rowland and Jeffus 2003, 2)

While there may be no need to create your own evaluation rubric or a data collection tool, in that there are others already available online and in books and periodicals, do read over them carefully. Make sure that you have permission or a license to use said rubrics (unless they are in the public domain). Also, make sure that your choice is current in terms of something that evolves quickly (such as technology or digital communications). In addition, if there are additions or deletions that you would like to make, be sure that you have permission to change your rubric selection to fit your needs.

What many rubrics do not do is to detail exactly how each piece of information will be collected. Thus, here are some suggestions for data collection tools, given a particular piece of information needed. (Please use these as models; they do not address all the information you may need or wish to gather.) For each tool listed, there is a possible subject on which data is needed, as well as an idea (in parentheses) for data collection.

- Circulation statistics (collect electronically via an automated system)
- Database use (collect electronically via your databases or through the vendor)
- In-library use of materials (ask patrons to place materials on a cart instead of back on the shelf; at the end of each day, count the number and types of materials used in-library)
- Staff development: librarian teaching classroom teachers how to use an iPad in the classroom (print questionnaire)
- Student use of library research tools (librarian observation)
- Student reading literacy (state-monitored testing)
- Student use of Google Apps (online survey through Google Forms)
- Library use before and after school (head count by library aide at a specific time before and after school)
- Library web page access (electronic counter imbedded into web page)
- Borrowing of library Chromebooks during the day (sign-up sheet that patrons initial when they are loaned the Chromebooks)
- Literature interests of students (face-to-face interviews)
- Student use of social media for educational purposes (Facebook questionnaire)

There are certainly other sorts of data collection that can occur; these are just some examples to get you started as you determine what you need to know and how best to find that answer.

Now, let's look at using collection analysis and curriculum mapping as evaluation tools.

Resources (Print, Nonprint, Analog and Digital, Hardware and Software)

A detailed discussion of print and nonprint, analog and digital, and hardware and software selection and evaluation can be found in chapter 3, "Policies and Procedures." In addition, collection analysis instruments exist, including commercial products that are part of cataloging and circulation systems. These tools help isolate strengths and weaknesses of a particular collection as well as provide quantitative data (Follett 2014; North Texas Regional Library System, n.d.). Such information is useful in identifying areas for improvement, including the addition of materials and the weeding of resources no longer important to the collection.

Curriculum mapping is another tool that can help in evaluating a school library. Curriculum mapping records subjects and units taught (or that educators anticipate will be taught) in a classroom, school, and/or district over a period of time—for example, a year—and the types of resources and assistance needed for each subject or unit. Once the curriculum has been mapped, the school librarian can use this information to support the addition of new resources or to identify areas of surplus materials (Illinois School Library Media Association 2010; Association for Supervision and Curriculum Development 2001).

Next, let's turn to facilities—without which we might not have resource storage, a place to teach, and so much more.

Facilities

A listing of items to evaluate, for a strong physical as well as virtual library space (see also chapter 5, "Facilities"), would include the following:

- Space requirements: how much room does the library have altogether; that is, seating, office, collection, technology, classroom, and so on, space
- Library collection and circulation: shelving for print and nonprint materials, including a professional collection; technology storage; circulation desk and peripherals (including an automated circulation system); security
- Administrative areas: library office, teacher workroom, storage
- Instructional spaces: library classroom and/or computer lab with teacher's workstation, reference area, leisure reading area, conference room(s), media production room (digital and possibly analog), area for dedicated library computers
- Environmental features: ADA (Americans with Disabilities Act) requirements, line of sight, lighting, window coverings, color scheme, carpeting, furniture, temperature controls, displays, electrical outlets, bulletin boards, signage, traffic flow, exits
- Spaces accessed virtually via the Internet and databases in order to provide digital learner resources.

Note: Some items (e.g., storage, classroom, and technology) appear on more than one list. (Illinois School Library Media Association 2010; Pennsylvania Department of Education, Office of Commonwealth Libraries 2011; Picciano 2011)

Figure 12.1 illustrates what a facilities evaluation rubric might look like. This particular rubric utilizes a yes/no model with room for comments after each criterion.

Personnel

In this section, we address how those who work in the school library might be evaluated. Because there can be a wide variance in school districts and their libraries across the nation, please remember that all of the following measures and benchmarks may change according to where they are applied.

FACILITIES EVALUATION			
Evaluation Criterion	Yes	No	Comments
1. Space provided meets the needs of the library.			
2. Library collection is adequate and age appropriate for clientele.			
3. Administrative areas are adequate to support the needs of library staff.			
4. Instructional spaces are adequate to support the mission of the library.			
5. Instructional spaces are comfortable, inviting, and well maintained.			
6. Furniture and support equipment is age appropriate for the clientele.			
7. Environmental features met the needs of the library.			
8. Environmental and safety features meet appropriate regulations.			
9. Spaces may be accessed virtually as required to meet clientele needs.			

Figure 12.1.   Facilities Evaluation

Librarians

The type of school library in which the librarian works (e.g., public or private; elementary, middle school, high school, or another combination; city, suburban, or rural; whether or not he or she has help: another librarian, technology specialist, aide, assistant, secretary; and more) may all influence his or her evaluation. In addition, many schools/school districts adopt evaluation tools based on national, state, and/or local standards and guidelines as well as models like the Danielson framework (American Association of School Librarians 2009a; Chicago Public Schools 2012; Department of Education State of Hawaii 2013; Little 2014; School Library Systems Association of New York State and New York Library Association, n.d.), which assigns rubrics with sections for domains, components, elements, and levels of performance for a wide range of school educators, including "school library media specialists" (The Danielson Group 2013; Offery, Oliver, and Immordino, et al., n.d.). (Note: Charlotte Danielson is "an internationally-recognized expert in the area of teacher effectiveness, specializing in evaluations of teaching practice that both ensure teacher quality as well as promote professional learning" [The Danielson Group 2013, 1].)

These evaluations often proceed with the librarian's principal or another supervisor (or perhaps the librarian) filling out the rubric, form, or criteria set being used; perhaps an in-library observation by said supervisor (or another administrator); and finally a face-to-face follow-up between the librarian and the administration where the results of said document and observation are discussed. The written evaluations normally contain statements, lists, or questions in a rubric (or another form) designed to measure the school librarian's ability to run the library program, teach and collaborate with other educators, promote literacy, model good ethics, and so much more. In many instances, said statements are rated according to categories—for example, "Distinguished . . . Proficient . . . Basic . . . Unsatisfactory" (American Association of School Librarians 2009a, 2).

Summarized next are samples of the numerous benchmarks/requirements for school librarians, available in rubrics and other assessment-style forms. This list is not comprehensive, but it is representative of what is available. For more information, please search the Internet and/or contact your school district for their forms. Because the benchmarks in each evaluation are listed by standards and guidelines, full or partial statements, examples, and more, the bulleted points represent particular evaluations; that is, format consistency will vary.

- "Demonstrating knowledge of current teaching strategies and practices in the field of library science" (Chicago Public Schools 2012, 1).
- "Demonstrating knowledge of students" (American Association of School Librarians 2009a, 2).
- "Establishing and maintaining library procedures" (Department of Education State of Hawaii 2013, 3).
- "The library media specialist abides by all school board policies and regulations" (Winchester Public Schools, n.d., 14).

- "School library media coordinators lead in their schools" ("Rubric for Evaluating North Carolina's School Library Media Coordinators," n.d., 2).
- "Advocates for, prepares, and oversees a library media program budget that reflects the priorities of the entire school community" (Illinois School Library Media Association 2010, 69).
- "School library media coordinators develop a library collection that supports 21st century teaching and learning" ("Rubric for Evaluating North Carolina's School Library Media Coordinators," n.d., 7).
- "Creating an environment of respect and rapport" (American Association of School Librarians 2009a, 5).
- "Establishing a culture of investigation and an appreciation of learning and literature" (Chicago Public Schools 2012, 4).
- "Encourages reading guidance, and maintains an awareness of student reading habits and interests" (Jackson Public School District, n.d., 14).
- "Collaborating with classroom teachers in the design of effective instructional units and lessons" (Chicago Public Schools 2012, 6).
- "Librarian collaborates to align instruction (and program goals) to NYS Common Core Learning Standards" (School Library Systems Association of New York State and New York Library Association, n.d.).
- "Librarian teaches information and literacy skills and the use of technology for learning" (School Library Systems Association of New York State and New York Library Association, n.d.).
- Develops a variety of formal and informal assessments to monitor student intellectual growth (Illinois School Library Media Association 2010, 68).
- "Demonstrates a positive relationship with students and maintains discipline" (Jackson Public School District, n.d., 15).
- "Assisting students and colleagues in the use of technology in the library/media center" (Department of Education State of Hawaii 2013, 4).
- "The library media specialist assists students and staff in the use and production of media" (Winchester Public Schools, n.d., 11).
- "Using questioning and research techniques" (American Association of School Librarians 2009a, 7).
- "Librarian provides equitable access information, literature, and resources and extends the access beyond the school day through technology" (School Library Systems Association of New York State and New York Library Association, n.d.).
- "Evaluates and selects materials and technologies that support the school's philosophy and curriculum" (Illinois School Library Media Association 2010, 68).
- "Maintains accurate records on utilization of materials, services, and facilities" (Jackson Public School District, n.d., 16).
- "The library media specialist serves on school and division-wide committees as a resource for and contribution to discussion of the library media center into curricular and other functions as appropriate" (Winchester Public Schools, n.d., 13).
- "Conducts in-service activities for teachers" (Jackson Public School District, n.d., 18).

- "The library media specialist uses community resources to extend learning opportunities" (Winchester Public Schools, n.d.).
- "School media coordinators function effectively in a complex, dynamic environment" ("Rubric for Evaluating North Carolina's School Library Media Coordinators," n.d., 15).
- "The school librarian and the public librarian communicate frequently about programs and resources" (Donham 2013, 325).
- "Reflecting on practice" (American Association of School Librarians 2009a, 9).
- "Growing and developing professionally" (Chicago Public Schools 2012, 10).

Figures 12.2a and 12.2b provide an example of a school librarian evaluation rubric. This rubric, like that of the facilities form in figure 12.1, uses a yes/no template with a column for comments.

Once the librarian has been evaluated, we look to the work of his or her staff.

Library Support Staff

School library paraprofessional/support staff (aides, assistants, secretaries, etc.) often performs much of the day-to-day operations of the school library (circulation, pulling materials for teachers, shelving books, and similar duties). In doing so, they are able to relieve the school librarian of such duties, thus allowing him/her more time for instruction, collaboration, and other library programming and services (Colorado State Library 2013). (See also chapter 6, "The School Librarian, Relationships and Personnel.") Thus, typical criteria for evaluating school library support staff may include assigning terminology, such as exemplary, target, acceptable, or unacceptable to the following (or similar) statements:

- Support staff assists school librarian.
- Support staff is responsible for library circulation activities.
- Support staff shelves books and other library materials.
- Support staff repairs books and other library materials.
- Support staff processes library materials.
- Support staff reads library shelves.
- Support staff pulls materials for teachers, upon request.
- Support staff assists with clerical needs as requested.
- Support staff helps with inventory.
- Support staff supervises student volunteers.
- Support staff aids patrons with noninstructional technology requests (Colorado State Library 2013; Idaho Department of Education 2004; Pennsylvania Department of Education, Office of Commonwealth Libraries 2011). See figure 12.3.

Because the duties of school library support staff can vary from school library to school library, depending on any number of facts (e.g., age of students; number of professional

LIBRARIAN EVALUATION			
Assessment Criterion	Yes	No	Comments
1. Demonstrates knowledge of current teaching strategies in the library field.			
2. Demonstrates knowledge of current practices in the library field.			
3. Demonstrates knowledge of students' needs in her/his specific school.			
4. Establishes and maintains library policies and procedures which align with school mission.			
5. Is knowledgeable of and abides by all school board policies and regulations.			
6. Develops and oversees a library program budget aligned with school mission.			
7. Develops a collection that supports 21st century teaching and learning.			
8. Selects materials and technologies that support the school's mission.			
9. Creates an environment of respect and rapport in the library.			
10. Establishes a culture of investigation, using questioning and research techniques.			
11. Fosters an appreciation of learning and literature.			
12. Maintains an awareness of student reading habits and interests.			
13. Collaborates with classroom teachers in instructional design.			
14. Aligns library instruction to common core standards.			
15. Teaches information literacy skills.			
16. Develops a positive relationship with students and maintains dicipline.			
17. Develops a positive relationship with colleagues.			
18. Assists students and colleagues in the use of technology.			
19. Provides equitable access to information and resources.			
20. Extends information access beyond the school day through use of technology.			
21. Effectively supervises library support staff to support the school mission.			

Figure 12.2a.   Librarian Evaluation

LIBRARIAN EVALUATION (cont)			
Assessment Criterion	Yes	No	Comments
22. Serves on appropriate committees to support the school/district mission.			
23. Conducts in-service activities as appropriate.			
24. Uses community resources to extend student learning opportunities.			
25.Communicates with the public librarian about utilizing common resources.			
26. Remains current in the field through seminars, workshops, conferences, etc.			

Figure 12.2b.   Librarian Evaluation (continued)

LIBRARY SUPPORT STAFF EVALUATION					
Assessment Criterion	E	T	A	U	Comments
1. Support staff complies with school/ district policies and procedures.					
2. Support staff assists librarian to promote the school mission/vision.					
3. Support staff coordinates library circulation activities.					
4. Support staff acurately shelves books and other library materials.					
5. Support staff repairs books and other library materials.					
6. Support staff processes library materials.					
7. Support staff reads library shelves as required.					
8. Support staff pulls materials for teachers upon request.					
9. Support staff assists with clerical needs as requested.					
10. Support staff assists with inventory.					
11. Support staff effectively supervises student volunteers.					
12. Support staff aids patrons with non-instructional technology requests.					
EVALUATION KEY:					
E = Exemplary T = Target					
A = Acceptable U = Unacceptable					

Figure 12.3. Library Support Staff Evaluation

librarians, other support staff, technology personnel, or others on staff; resources available in the library; whether materials are purchased or otherwise obtained/processed; availability of a computer lab with supervisor in the library; and so much more), evaluation criteria, too, may vary from school to school and district to district. Thus, the above criteria are examples; add, delete, or revise according to your own situation.

Volunteers

"Volunteers will be evaluated periodically to assess the positive growth of the volunteer program. Negative evaluations will result in the dismissal of a volunteer" (Waukegan Public Library, n.d., 3). The sentiment expressed by this statement is excellent and certainly one that school library administrators might borrow when looking to evaluate the school library volunteer program.

It is often possible to evaluate school library volunteers under much the same criteria as a paraprofessional or staff member, since in many cases they handle similar responsibilities; the main difference is that since volunteers are not paid, they may not be amiable to or might question the evaluation process. That said, here are some questions to ask when evaluating the library volunteer, whether an adult or a student:

- Does he or she act in a professional manner when working in the library?
- Is he or she polite to library patrons (students and faculty)?
- Is he or she interested in/excited about the work?
- Does he or she show up for work at the required time?
- Is he or she willing to learn new things?
- Does he or she finish requested work?
- Can he or she work independently?
- Will he or she ask questions when uncertain about a particular task?
- Does he or she communicate well with patrons and the volunteer supervisor? (Colorado State Library 2013; Idaho Department of Education 2004; Waukegan Public Library)

A rubric for evaluating school library volunteers might look like figure 12.4.

And More

Probably almost any part of the school library can and has been or will be measured by someone, somewhere, at some time. This includes many things not listed earlier, but for which there may be a need in your particular school library environment. For example, it could be that the budget needs to be revisited, the gift policy reevaluated, or the challenge form reassessed to see if it reflects new technologies. In some circumstances, it may be that you will need to create your own evaluation tool,

VOLUNTEER EVALUATION					
Assessment Criterion	E	T	A	U	Comments
1. Volunteer complies with school/ district policies and procedures.					
2. Volunteer assists librarian to promote the school mission/vision.					
3. Volunteer acts in a profesional manner when working in the library.					
4. Volunteer is polite to library patrons (students and faculty).					
5. Volunteer is excited about/enjoys library work.					
6. Volunteer is willing to learn new things.					
7. Volunteer comes to work on time.					
8. Volunteer is dependable.					
8. Volunteer finishes work accurately and in a timely manner.					
9. Volunteer can work independently as required.					
10. Volunteer asks questions when uncertain about a task.					
11. Volunteer communicates well with patrons and volunteer supervisor.					
EVALUATION KEY:					
E = Exemplary T = Target					
A = Acceptable U = Unacceptable					

Figure 12.4.   Volunteer Evaluation

rather than depend on one already generated by a professional organization, fellow educator, or another expert. If that is the case, there are many rubrics and similar evaluation criteria from which to model (see the Internet, professional periodicals, and books). "Go forth and prosper" (Shelley 2014).

THE SCHOOL LIBRARY OF THE FUTURE

What does the school library of the future look like? While that is really anybody's guess, there are some things that will probably take place. The biggest evolutionary theme will undoubtedly be in technology and related areas. Here are some "guesstimates" of our future:

- More, newer, evolving technology
- The "new" digital (whatever that is!)
- School libraries comprised mainly of e-books
- Growth in the learning commons concept
- Information *super*-overload
- Better student and parent access to the school library—from the home or other nonschool venues
- Electronic overdue notices via social media (there may be some already!)
- Advancement in library support to classrooms;
- Administration recognizing that the school library is *really* the heart of the school
- Virtual school libraries
- The holographic librarian
- Computer-generated reference services for basic K–12 research questions;
- More and better production studios in face-to-face (F2F) school libraries
- Wireless, wireless everywhere
- F2F libraries with chargers for new and evolving technology
- And so much more (Abarbanal et al. 2013; Johnson 2013; Lynch 2014)! What do you think?

EMBRACING CHANGE

Change can be difficult; we all have times we are "set in our ways." However, one thing we can all be sure of is that change will continue and it will occur at an ever-increasing rate. The school library of yesterday—the one with vertical files; hardware in the forms of record players, filmstrip strip projectors, and cassette tape players; and audiovisual media such as 16 mm films, vinyl records, and microfiche—is already gone in most places, excepting museums and archives. The librarian, who reads picture books to children in a circle or who directs students in print research of materials for a project, still exists, but he or she now also pulls up stories and information online, through databases and the Internet. As school librarians, we are in a world that is always changing. We cannot hide our heads in the sand, but must be willing to learn new things and try new technologies. Welcome to a new and ever-changing world, one with information and access points in multiple formats!

KEY CONCEPTS FROM THIS CHAPTER

- School librarians want to know if they are doing things right.
- An excellent general school library evaluation rubric can be found in *A Planning Guide for Empowering Learners* (American Association of School Librarians 2010).
- School library evaluations can be based on standards and guidelines.
- All evaluation rubrics are not necessarily data collection tools.
- There are many tools available for collecting data, including surveys, question-naires, interviews, and observations.
- Collection analysis and collection mapping are two tools for evaluating library resources.
- Library facilities today are both physical and virtual.
- Many schools/school districts adopt evaluation tools based on national, state, and/or local standards and guidelines as well as models like the Danielson framework.
- The type of library the school librarian works in may influence his or her evaluation.
- Evaluations of school librarians are based on many things, including his or her ability to run the library program, teach and collaborate with other educators, promote literacy, and model the ethical use of materials.
- School library paraprofessional/support staff (aides, assistants, secretaries, etc.) often performs much of the day-to-day operations of the school library.
- School library volunteers can often be evaluated under much the same criteria as a paraprofessional or staff member, since in many cases the two groups handle similar responsibilities.
- Probably almost any part of the school library can and has been or will be mea-sured by someone, somewhere, at some time.
- The biggest evolutionary theme for school libraries of the future will undoubt-edly be in technology and related areas.
- Change can be difficult.
- School librarians must be prepared to learn new things and work with new technologies and resources.

Coming in appendix A: "Annotated Bibliography of Selected Library Policies and Procedures Manuals."

Coming in appendix B: "Annotated Bibliography of Selected School Library Professional Organization Websites."

Coming in appendix C: "Annotated Bibliography of Selected National and State School Library Standards and Guidelines."

Coming in appendix D: "Annotated Bibliography of Selected School Library Instruction and Collaboration Tools."

Coming in appendix E: Annotated Directory of Selected Grant Resources for School Libraries.

DISCUSSION QUESTIONS

1. Why are there so *very* many rubrics, models, and frameworks available for the evaluation of school librarians?
2. Should volunteers be evaluated? If so, using what criteria?
3. Describe your ideal school library of the future. How do you see it appearing and functioning? Who would be the personnel? What would the facility look like? How would resources change? How will technology evolve? What would be the needs of students and faculty?
4. How can we prepare *today* for the trends of *tomorrow*?

ACTIVITIES

1. Surf the web for school library evaluation tools. Prepare an annotated bibliography of three tools that you believe are exemplary.
2. Pick and choose from the countless school librarian evaluation rubrics found on the web, or in professional journals and books. Create your own school librarian evaluation tool, using criteria from those selected.
3. Develop a conference proposal for a presentation on your perceptions of the school library of the future. Include a set of talking points. Select a national, state, or local organization to which you might send the proposal. (Hint: Many organizations have proposal suggestions and/or forms. Check with the organization of your choice and follow the directions as you prepare your proposal.)

REFERENCES

American Association of School Librarians. 2009a. "AASL's L4L Sample School Librarian Performance and Evaluation System." http://aasl.ala.org/essentiallinks/index.php?title=Performance_Evaluation_of_School_Librarians.

———. 2009b. *Empowering Learners: Guidelines for School Library Media Programs.* Chicago, Ill.: American Library Association.

———. 2010. *A Planning Guide for Empowering Learners: With School Library Program Assessment Rubric.* Chicago, Ill.: American Library Association.

Abarbanal, Elisabeth, Davis, Sarah, Hand, Dorcas, and Wittmer, Matthew. 2013. "The New School Library: The Human Connection to Digital Resources and Academic Success." http://www.nais.org/Magazines-Newsletters/ISMagazine/Pages/The-New-School-Library.aspx.

Association for Supervision and Curriculum Development. 2001. "Overview of Curriculum Mapping." http://faculty.njcu.edu/mmaye/EDLDPLAN/cm_overview.pdf.

Chicago Public Schools. 2012. "2012 CPS Framework for Teacher-Librarians." http://islma.pbworks.com/w/file/fetch/60325154/CPS%20Framework%20for%20Teacher-librarians-FINAL.pdf.

Colorado State Library. 2013. "Colorado's Highly Effective School Library Programs: An Evaluative Rubric for 21st-Century Colorado School Librarians and Their Library Programs." http://www.cde.state.co.us/sites/default/files/Revised%20HESL%20evidence%20outcomes.pdf.

The Danielson Group. 2013. "The Framework." http://danielsongroup.org/framework/.

Department of Education State of Hawaii. 2013. "Hawaii Adapted Framework for Teaching School Library/Media Specialist Rubric." http://eesteacher.weebly.com/uploads/1/4/0/3/14039000/wp_hawaii_adapted_framework_librarian_2013-10-08.pdf.

Donham, Jean. 2013. *Enhancing Teaching and Learning: A Leadership Guide for School Librarians.* 3rd ed. Chicago, Ill.: Neal-Schuman.

Follett. 2014. "TITLEWAVE, TitleWise, TitleMAP, TitleCheck." http://www.flr.follett.com/intro/titleservices.html

Idaho Department of Education. 2004. "Idaho SLIM: School Librarian's Information Manual." http://www.sde.idaho.gov/site/school_libraries/.

Illinois School Library Media Association. 2010. *Linking for Learning: The Illinois School Library Media Program Guidelines.* 3rd ed. Canton, Ill.: Illinois School Library Media Association.

Jackson Public School District. n.d. "Library Media Specialist Performance Evaluation." http://www.jackson.k12.ms.us/departments/human_resources/publications/librarian_eval.pdf.

Johnson, Doug. 2013. "Power Up!/The New School Library." http://www.ascd.org/publications/educational-leadership/oct13/vol71/num02/The-New-School-Library.aspx

Little, David, 2014. "Using the Danielson Framework to Collect Evidence of Your Invaluable Role." *ISLMA News* 26 (3): 3.

Lynch, Matthew. 2014. "Libraries of the Future: Where Trends Are Taking K–12K–12 Public School Libraries." http://www.huffingtonpost.com/matthew-lynch-edd/libraries-of-the-future-w_b_4738085.html.

North Texas Regional Library System. n.d. "Evaluating Your Collection: Best Practices for North Texas Libraries." http://ntrls.org/ConsultantReports/NTRLS_EvaluatingYourCollection.pdf.

Offery, Wendy, April Oliver, and Michele Immordino, et al. n.d. "LMS Library Media Center: Danielson Sample Artifacts for Evidence in the Library Media Center. https://sites.google.com/a/ltps.info/lms-library-media-center/teachers/danielson-sample-evidence-library-media.

Pennsylvania Department of Education, Office of Commonwealth Libraries. 2011. "Guidelines for Pennsylvania School Library Programs." http://www.webjunction.org/content/dam/WebJunction/Documents/pennsylvania/378_PDE_Guide_Sch_Lib_FINAL_1_.pdf.

Picciano, Anthony G. 2011. *Educational Leadership and Planning for Technology.* 5th ed. Boston, Mass.: Pearson.

Rowland, Martha, and Barbara Jeffus. 2003. "Looking at the School Library: An Evaluation Tool." http://www.docs-archive.com/view/444c34a3e7d5f5bbd214b0b1d03d2c21/Looking-at-the-School-Library-An-Evaluation-Tool.pdf.

"Rubric for Evaluating North Carolina's School Library Media Coordinators." n.d. http://www.ncpublicschools.org/docs/dtl/standards/professional/rubric-evaluating.pdf.

School Library Systems Association of New York State and New York Library Association. n.d. "NYS School Library Program Evaluation Rubric." http://usny.nysed.gov/rttt/teachers-leaders/practicerubrics/Docs/nyla-rubric.pdf.

Shelley, Mary Wollstonecraft. 2014. "Mary Wollstonecraft Shelley Quote Citation." http://www.brainyquote.com/citation/quotes/quotes/m/marywollst184676.html?ct=Mary+Wollstonecraft+Shelley.

Waukegan Public Library. n.d. "Volunteer Handbook." http://www.waukeganpl.org/sites/default/files/pr/Volunteer%20Handbook.docx.

Winchester Public Schools. n.d. "Library Media Specialist Evaluation." https://www.wps.k12.va.us/tchrstaf/forms/eval_lms.doc.

Appendix A: Annotated Bibliography of Selected Library Policies and Procedures Manuals

There are a plethora of school library policies and procedures manuals, along with the various related pieces, on the web. Consequently, those included in this appendix are representative examples. Please note that some of the following topics contain material also found in other subject areas; for example, a school library policy and procedures manual can contain school library goals and objectives, sample copyright policies, intellectual freedom policies, and procedures. For more information and material in all sections, search further on the Internet.

Please see the numbers after each of the following subjects for an item representing that area.

Collection Development Policy and Procedures: 15, 16
Copyright Policy and Procedures: 10, 11, 20
Goals and Objectives: 1
Intellectual Freedom Policy and Procedures: 9, 22
Maintenance Policy and Procedures: 12, 21
Mission Statements: 6, 14
Selection and Evaluation Policy and Procedures: 7, 17, 18, 19
Technology Plans: 2, 3, 4, 5, 8, 13

1. Ann Arbor Public Schools. n.d. "Goals and Objectives of Our Program." http://www.aaps
.k12.mi.us/ins.libmedia/goals_and_objectives_of_our_program. The goals and objectives
for this city's public school libraries are divided into three distinct areas: mission statement,
student access, and collaboration (Ann Arbor Public Schools, n.d., 1).
2. Arcadia School District. 2012. "Information (Library Media) and Technology Plan." http://
www.arcadia.k12.wi.us/District/documents/Technology%20Plan%202009-2012.pdf. This
technology plan, from the public school district of Arcadia, Wisconsin, also contains a

variety of appendixes related to school libraries, including selection, reconsideration, inter-library loan, and copyright policies, as well as Internet safety materials.

3. Atlantic City School District. 2013. "Atlantic City Schools Educational Technology Plan 2010–2013." http://www.acboe.org/www/ACBOE/site/hosting/Technology/010110_AtlanticCity_P.pdf. From Atlantic City, New Jersey, this lengthy document demonstrates many of the main divisions found in a school technology plan, taking into account stakeholders, needs assessment, goals and objectives, implementation, funding, professional development, and evaluation.

4. Bullock County Board of Education. 2008. "Library Media Center: Policy and Procedure Manual." http://alex.state.al.us/librarymedia/BCS_LMC_Policies__Procedures_Manual.pdf. In Bullock County, Alabama, K–12 librarians adhere to the following policy and procedures when working with technology: "The LMS (Library Media Specialist) plans and coordinates the acquisition, circulation, repair, and discarding of equipment. . . . Equipment that is discarded must be removed from the fixed asset equipment inventory at the central office. . . . Equipment may only be checked-out by faculty, and students only with written permission from his/her teacher" (Bullock County Board of Education 2008, 10).

5. Harnett County Board of Education. 2013. "Harnett County Schools Strategic Technology Plan 2009–2013." http://harnett.nc.schoolwebpages.com/education/page/download.php?fileinfo=RGlzdHJpY3RfVGVjaG5vbG9neV9QbGFuXzA5XzEzLnBkZjo6Oi93d3c3L3NjaG9vbHMvbmMvaGFybV0dC9pbWFnZXMvZG9jbWdyLzE3ODNmaWxlOTI4MS5wZGY=&sectiondetailid=49067. This technology plan from North Carolina states in part, "The real benefit of technology in a safe and orderly educational environment, however, is in the resources it brings into the classroom and school library media center" (Harnett County Board of Education 2013, 5).

6. Hinsdale South High School District 86 Library Media Center. n.d. "Vision and Mission: Mission Statement of the District 86 Library Media Departments." http://south.hinsdale86.org/lib_sharepoint/Documents/VisionMission.htm. There are five main points to this vision/mission statement: teaching; collaborating; providing leadership, instruction, and expertise; providing access; and promoting life-long learning (Hinsdale South High School District 86 Library Media Center, n.d., 1).

7. Indian Prairie Community Unit School District 204. 2006. "Library Media Center Policy and Procedure Manual." http://clow.ipsd.org/documents/lmc_manual_revisions/LMC_Procedure_Manual.pdf. Included in this selection and evaluation information is the following statement addressing who is responsible for library materials: "Although the Board of Education is legally responsible for the instructional materials used in the district, the ongoing process of selecting materials for the LMC is primarily the responsibility of the library media center director assigned to each building. Since collections reflect the complexion and needs of each individual building's population and the specific curriculum that is adopted, the LMC Director involves many people—the principal, teachers, students, and parents—in the process of choosing materials" (Indian Prairie Community Unit School District 204, 2006, 28).

8. Jamestown School Department. 2013. "Technology Plan." http://www.jamestownri.com/school/Tech%20Plan%20web.pdf. Most school technology plans include some sort of acceptable use policy (AUP). These can vary exponentially, from school to school and district to district. The Jamestown, Rhode Island, school department has two AUPs, one for technology and the other for the Internet.

9. Kansas Association of School Librarians. 1999. "Intellectual Freedom Manual for Kansas." http://www.ifmanual.org/. States, as well as schools/districts and national groups, may create and maintain their own sets of policies and procedures for intellectual freedom issues, as is demonstrated by the Kansas Association of School Librarians.

10. Kent School District. 2010. "Copyright and Plagiarism Resources." http://www1.kent .k12.wa.us/ksd/it/inst_tech/StudentParentResources/copyright_plagiarism.html. The following is an introduction to a school copyright and plagiarism web page: "With the convenience of technology allowing individuals to transfer, copy, and digitize learning materials faster and easier than ever, understanding copyright law becomes even more important. We have an obligation to practice integrity and trustworthiness. All of us should honor the law when it comes to fair use and copyright and in so doing protect ourselves from legal liability" (Kent School District 2010, 1).

11. The Lawrenceville School. n.d. "Copyright Policy." http://www.lawrenceville.org/academ ics/bunn-library/copyright-policy/index.aspx. Private schools, too, maintain copyright policies, procedures, and guidelines, as is demonstrated by the Lawrence School in Lawrenceville, New Jersey.

12. Livonia Elementary Library. 2014. "Lost Books, Damaged Books, and Books Chewed by Puppies." http://bookwings.wikispaces.com/. Policies Maintenance of materials is for all media, print or nonprint, books or technology. Here is a procedure for print materials: "Lost or badly damaged books must be replaced. Library staff will send you a bill. Checks should be made payable to 'Livonia Central School District.' If you wish, you are welcome to simply buy a copy of the book for the library" (Livonia Elementary Library 2014, 1).

13. Maryland State Board of Education. 2012. "The Maryland Educational Technology Plan for the New Millennium: Anytime, Anywhere Technology to Improve Teaching and Learning." http://www.marylandpublicschools.org/NR/rdonlyres/9242FEDD-09F7-4BB0-8F1F-AE6FAE562EA8/13485/TechPlanFinalfromPrinter73007.pdf. States, too, develop technology plans, as is demonstrated by this one from Maryland, which speaks to the fact that "technology is all around us and rapidly changing" (Maryland State Board of Education 2012, 3).

14. New Canaan High School Library. 2014. "New Canaan High School Library Mission Statement." http://www.newcanaan.k12.ct.us/education/components/scrapbook/default .php?sectiondetailid=32925&. Part of this school library mission statement focuses on the following—"to help each student excel and achieve maximum potential by creating a 21st Century learning environment, fostering a love of reading, and promoting the effective use of information and communications technology" (New Canaan High School Library 2014, 1).

15. "New York City Collection Development Policy." 2006. http://schools.nyc.gov/NR/ rdonlyres/2D2B8535-3691-4207-9740-051CC5AF7549/20858/313NewYorkCityCollectio nDevelopmentPolicy.pdf. This collection development policy, from the *New York City School Library System Handbook*, covers mission and needs, access to resources and services in the school library media program, goals for collection development, materials selection, weeding, materials' challenges, and more ("New York City Collection Development Policy" 2006, 1–9).

16. Pine View High School Library. 2010. "Collection Development Policy." http://www.pine view.org/uploads/3/8/6/3/3863562/pvhs_library_collection_policy_updated_oct-2010. pdf. The Gifts section of this policy states in part, "The Pine View High School Library welcomes gift materials. These materials shall be subject to the same criteria as those obtained through the regular selection process" (Pine View High School Library 2010, 5).

17. Rocky Hill School. 2013. "Rocky Hill School Library: Program, Policy, and Procedure Manual." http://www.olis.ri.gov/network/standards/samples/erh_comb.pdf. The selection policy takes into account how diversity within the collection will be safeguarded: "The LTI (Library and Technology Integrator) will be responsible for selection policy under the advisement of the library committee, faculty, and students which will ensure the diversity of the collection" (Rocky Hill School 2013, 10).

18. Simsbury Public Schools. 2008. "Materials Selection Policy." http://www.simsbury.k12 .ct.us/page.cfm?p=2554. From Simsbury, Connecticut: "The Library/Media Center collaborates with classroom teachers in selecting and using materials that are an integral part of the curriculum. The materials are selected for interest, vocabulary, maturity and ability levels for students within the school" (Simsbury Public Schools 2008, 1).

19. University Laboratory High School Library. 2013. "Collection Development." http:// www.library.illinois.edu/uni/policies/collectiondevelopment.html. Part of the selection criteria for this high school library is as follows: "Materials shall be appropriate for the subject area and for the age, emotional development, ability level, learning styles, and social development of University Laboratory High School students" (University Laboratory High School Library 2013, 1).

20. Visalia Unified School District. 2010. "Copyright Guidelines." http://visalia.k12.ca.us/ library/policies/copyright.htm. The Visalia, California, school district has a nice web presence of copyright guidelines dos and don'ts for their faculty and staff. Please note that this web page has a Creative Commons license.

21. Walt Whitman Middle School, Library Media Center. 2013. "Policies and Procedures." http://www.fcps.edu/WhitmanMS/docs/2013%20Library%20Policies%20and%20Procedures%20Manual=Final.pdf. The subsequent procedure demonstrates how damaged technology is to be followed in a particular middle school, "Teachers should report broken equipment to the librarians as soon as possible. A work order will be entered requesting repair from Field Services" (Walt Whitman Middle School, Library Media Center 2013, 10).

22. Wausau School District. n.d. "Part 2: Procedures for Reconsideration of Materials." http:// www.wausauschools.org/cms/One.aspx?portalId=808927&pageId=4700181. Part 2 of this document covers "Procedures for Reconsideration of Materials," including a "Statement of Policy," a "Request for Informal Reconsideration," a "Request for Formal Reconsideration," "The Reconsideration Committee," "Resolution," the "Library Bill of Rights," and a "Request Form for Reconsideration of Library Materials" (see appendix B) (Wausau School District, n.d., 5–11).

Appendix B: Annotated Bibliography of Selected School Library Professional Organization Websites

There are a multitude of school library international, national, regional, state, and local professional organization websites, along with various related pieces, on the World Wide Web. Consequently, those included in this appendix are representative examples (excepting that a professional organization for each state is listed).

Please note that some of the following topics may contain material also found in other subject areas; for example, professional organizations usually have a publication and a listserv, blog, or other communication tool(s). For more information and material in all sections, search further on the Internet.

See the numbers after each of the following subjects for an item representing that area.

> Professional Organizations: 3, 4, 5, 9, 10, 11, 13, 14, 15, 17, 19, 20, 21, 22, 23, 25, 26, 27, 29, 30, 31, 32, 33, 35, 36, 37, 38, 39, 45, 46, 47, 49, 50, 51, 52, 53, 54, 55, 56, 57, 59, 60, 61, 62, 63, 66, 67, 68, 69, 70, 72, 73, 77, 78, 80, 81, 83, 85, 86, 87, 88, 89
> Professional Journals: 2, 6, 7, 8, 16, 24, 28, 34, 40, 41, 48, 71, 74, 76, 84
> Professional Internet Collaboration Tools: 1, 12, 18, 42, 43, 44, 58, 64, 65, 75, 79, 82

In addition to the illustrative professional school library online communications listed in this appendix, general social networking tools such as Twitter, Pinterest, Google+, and Facebook are also often used by school librarians to support their professional needs, interests, and so on.

1. AISLE—Association of Indiana School Library Educators. n.d. "About AISLE." http://lists.in.gov/mailman/listinfo/aisle. "This list is for members of the Association for Indiana

School Library Educators, an association of the Indiana Library Federation. It is a forum for discussion and information sharing among all members" (AISLE, n.d., 1).

2. Alabama School Library Association. n.d. "The Alabama School Librarian." https://www.smore.com/3163m-the-alabama-school-librarian?ref=email. "The Alabama School Librarian is a combined association newsletter and peer-reviewed (refereed) journal published by the Alabama School Library Association (ASLA). It is devoted solely to the field of school libraries and technology as related to school libraries" (Alabama School Library Association, n.d., 1).

3. Alabama School Library Association. 2014. "Who We Are." http://www.alasla.org/?PN=AboutUs. "ASLA (Alabama School Library Association) is a professional organization dedicated to the improvement of instruction through the utilization of media and technology. It provides a forum for school library media specialists, administrators, curriculum specialists, teachers, library media educators, graduate students, professional association leaders, and retired library media professionals, to promote excellence in education in Alabama through effective school library media programs" (Alabama School Library Association 2014, 1).

4. Alaska Association of School Librarians. 2014. Home page. http://akasl.org/. "The Alaska Association of School Librarians strives to keep Alaska's school library communities connected and informed about local library events, trends, and legislation" (Alaska Association of School Librarians 2014, 1).

5. American Association of School Librarians. 2014a. "About AASL." http://www.ala.org/aasl/about. AASL is a division of the American Library Association and the premier national organization for school librarians in the United States.

6. American Association of School Librarians. 2014b. *Knowledge Quest.* http://www.ala.org/aasl/kq. "*Knowledge Quest* is devoted to offering substantive information to assist building-level school librarians, supervisors, library educators, and other decision makers concerned with the development of school library programs and services" (American Association of School Librarians 2014b, 1). *Knowledge Quest* is the journal of the American Association of School Librarians.

7. American Association of School Librarians. 2014c. "*School Library Research* (SLR)." http://www.ala.org/aasl/slr. This journal "is the scholarly refereed research journal of the American Association of School Librarians" (American Association of School Librarians 2014c, 1).

8. American Libraries. 2015. "About American Libraries." http://americanlibrariesmagazine.org/about-american-libraries/. "*American Libraries,* the voice of the profession and the flagship magazine of the American Library Association, is published 6 times yearly, with occasional digital supplements." (American Libraries 2015, 1)

9. American Library Association. 2014. "About ALA." http://www.ala.org/aboutala/. "The American Library Association (ALA) is the oldest and largest library association in the world, providing association information, news, events, and advocacy resources for members, librarians, and library users" (American Library Association 2014, 1). It is also the "umbrella" organization for the American Association of School Librarians (AASL) as well as several other national library organizations and for most state library/school library groups.

10. Arizona Library Association. 2008. "Teacher-Librarian Division." http://www.azla.org/?7. "The mission of TLD is to promote literacy and academic achievement through student engagement, curriculum support, and collaboration through the school library and throughout the school community" (Arizona Library Association 2008, 1).

11. Arkansas Library Association. 2013. "Arkansas Association of School Librarians." http://arlib.org/organization/aasl/index.php. The Arkansas Association of School Librarians (ArASL) is a division of the Arkansas Library Association.

12. ARKLIB-L. n.d. http://mail.arlib.org/mailman/listinfo/arklib-l_arlib.org. ARKLIB-L is a listserv "for people interested in library issues in the state of Arkansas" (ARKLIB-L, n.d., 1).

13. Association for Educational Communications and Technology. 2014. What Is AECT?" http://aect.site-ym.com/?page=about_landing. "The Association for Educational Communications and Technology (AECT) is a professional association of thousands of educators and others whose activities are directed toward improving instruction through technology" (Association for Educational Communications and Technology 2014, 1). One of its divisions is the Division of School Media and Technology, which "provides leadership in educational communications and technology by linking professionals holding a common interest in the use of educational technology and its application to the learning process in the K–12 school environment" (Association for Educational Communications and Technology 2014, 1; http://aect.site-ym.com/group/school_media_tech) .

14. Association for Information Media and Equipment. 2014. Home page. http://www.aime.org/. "The Association for Informational Media and Equipment is a non-profit membership organization offering copyright information and support to teachers, librarians, media center directors, producers and distributors of informational film, video, interactive technologies, computer software and equipment. AIME serves as your organization's copyright resource" (Association for Information Media and Equipment 2014, 1).

15. Association for Library Service to Children. 2014. "Membership in ALSC." http://www.ala.org/alsc/membership. This division of the American Library Association focuses on "the way that libraries serve children around the country, from creative programming and best practices to continuing education and professional connections" (Association for Library Service to Children 2014, 1).

16. *Booklist Online*. 2014. "Frequently Asked Questions (FAQ): *Booklist* and *Booklist Online*: What Is *Booklist*?" http://www.booklistonline.com/faq. Published by the American Library Association, *Booklist* has both print and online components, as well as a website, database, webinars, and more. It "is a book-review magazine . . . widely viewed as offering the most reliable reviews to help libraries decide what to buy and to help library patrons and students decide what to read, view, or listen to" (*Booklist Online* 2014, 1).

17. California School Library Association. 2013. "About: CSLA Mission." http://csla.net/csla-mission/csla-mission-692/. The mission statement for this group is as follows: "CSLA advocates for excellence in school library programs, develops leaders in the school library field, and collaborates with other educational leaders to ensure that all California students are effective, responsible users and creators of ideas and information" (California School Library Association 2013, 1).

18. California School Library Association. 2014. *CSLA Blog*. http://cslablog.blogspot.com/. The *CSLA Blog* provides "news and updates" from their association (California School Library Association 2014, 1).

19. Canadian Library Association. 2011. "Canadian Association for School Libraries." http://www.cla.ca/AM/Template.cfm?Section=CASL2. The Canadian Association for School Libraries "provide(s) a national forum for promoting school library programs through advocacy, continuing education, and leadership" (Canadian Library Association 2011, 1).

20. Colorado Association of Libraries. 2013. "Colorado Association of School Libraries." http://www.cal-webs.org/?page=CASL. This group focuses on professional growth and standards as well as advocates and acknowledges school library programs and leadership (Colorado Association of Libraries 2013, 1).

21. CT Association of School Librarians. 2014. "About CASL." http://www.ctcasl.com/about.html. "CASL, the Connecticut Association of School Librarians, is the professional

association of Connecticut school library media specialists" (CT Association of School Librarians 2014, 1).

22. Delaware Association of School Librarians. 2015. "About Delaware Association of School Librarians." https://www.facebook.com/pages/Delaware-Association-of-School-Librarians/150136835034391?sk=info&tab=page_info. The mission of this organization is "to advocate for a full-time, professionally certified school librarian in every school in the state of Delaware." (Delaware Association of School Librarians 2015, 1)

23. District of Columbia Library Association. n.d. "DCLA Handbook: Bylaws: Object." http://www.dcla.org/Bylaws. The intent of the DCLA "is to promote and support libraries and information centers and to provide for professional development, continuing education, and collegial exchange among librarians and information specialists in Washington, D. C. and vicinity" (District of Columbia Library Association, n.d., 1).

24. Florida Association for Media in Education. 2014a. *Florida Media Quarterly*. http://www.floridamedia.org/?page=FMQ_Current_Issue. *Florida Media Quarterly* is "the official publication of the Florida Association for Media in Education" (Florida Association for Media in Education 2014a, 1).

25. Florida Association for Media in Education. 2014b. "Our Mission . . . Our Vision." http://www.floridamedia.org/. "FAME advocates for every student in Florida to be involved in and have open access to a quality school library media program administered by a highly competent, certified library media specialist" (Florida Association for Media in Education 2014b, 1).

26. Georgia Library Media Association. n.d. "*Advocating Excellence. Facilitating Change. Developing Leaders.*" http://www.glma-inc.org/. "GLMA is the largest professional organization serving school library media professionals in Georgia" (Georgia Library Media Association, 1).

27. Hawaii Association of School Librarians. n.d. "Who We Are." https://sites.google.com/site/haslsite/. "HASL is a statewide organization composed primarily of librarians from public schools, private schools, academic libraries, and special libraries" (Hawaii Association of School Librarians, 1).

28. Horn Book. 2014. "*Horn Book Magazine.*" http://www.hbook.com/horn-book-magazine-2/#_. *Horn Book Magazine* is a premier source of reviews of children's and young adult's materials. It has been in operation since 1924.

29. Idaho Library Association. 2013. "Membership." http://www.idaholibraries.org/membership/. "The Idaho Library Association . . . are academic, public, and school librarians. . . . Our interests are . . . literacy, intellectual freedom, and library service for all Idaho citizens" (Idaho Library Association 2013, 1).

30. Illinois School Library Media Association. 2013. "ISLMA Mission and Goals." http://www.islma.org/about_islma.htm. "To promote life-long learning by the students of Illinois, ISLMA will provide leadership and support for the development, promotion, and improvement of the school library media profession and programs in Illinois" (Illinois School Library Media Association 2013, 1).

31. Indiana Library Federation. 2013. "AISLE." http://www.ilfonline.org/?AISLE. AISLE is under the umbrella of the Indiana Library Federation; it exists "to promote school library media centers in Indiana and foster the professional growth of its members" (Indiana Library Federation 2013, 1).

32. Intellectual Freedom Round Table. 2014. "Membership Benefits: What Is the IFRT and Who May Join?" http://www.ala.org/ifrt/Membership/membershipbenefits. "The Intellectual Freedom Round Table (IFRT) is a forum for discussion of intellectual freedom

issues for libraries and librarians, and a channel of communication on intellectual freedom matters" (Intellectual Freedom Round Table 2014, 1). It is a round table committee of the American Library Association.

33. International Association of School Libraries. 2014. "School Libraries Online." http://www.iasl-online.org/. IASL's membership encompasses school librarians from across the globe.

34. International Association of School Librarianship. n.d. *School Libraries Worldwide.* http://www.iasl-online.org/pubs/slw/. "*School Libraries Worldwide* is the official professional and research journal of the International Association of School Librarianship" and it "publishes current research and scholarship on any aspect of school librarianship" (International Association of School Librarianship, n.d., 1).

35. International Society for Technology in Education. 2014. "About ISTE." https://www.iste.org/about. "ISTE serves more than 100,000 education stakeholders throughout the world" (International Society for Technology in Education 2014, 1). These stakeholders include school librarians.

36. Iowa Association of School Librarians. 2014. "About IASL." http://www.iasl-ia.org/p/about-iasl.html. "The Iowa Association of School Librarians advocates for strong school library programs in all Iowa schools and provides leadership, education and support for its members" (Iowa Association of School Librarians 2014, 1).

37. ITEM—Information and Technology Educators of Minnesota. 2014. "Mission." http://mnitem.org/mission. "Information and Technology Educators of Minnesota provides leadership and service by promoting professional growth, facilitating collaboration among its members, establishing standards, and advocating for 21st century learners" (ITEM 2014, 1).

38. Kansas Association of School Librarians. 2014. "About." https://www.facebook.com/KansasAssociationOfSchoolLibrarians/info. "The Kansas Association of School Librarians is a nonprofit, educational organization that promotes the interests of school libraries in the state of Kansas, encourages professional growth of library media specialists, and develops cooperation among all types of libraries and educational organizations to enhance library service" (Kansas Association of School Librarians 2014, 1).

39. Kentucky Association of School Librarians. n.d. "KASL." http://www.kysma.org/KASL/Welcome.html. "KASL is the professional organization of all Kentucky School Librarians" (Kentucky Association of School Librarians, 1).

40. Libraries Unlimited. 2014. *School Library Monthly.* http://www.schoollibrarymonthly.com/. "SLM content supports K–12 school librarians as they plan instruction collaboratively with teachers" (Libraries Unlimited 2014, 1).

41. *Library Media Connection.* n.d. "About LMC." http://www.librarymediaconnection.com/about_lmc/. "*Library Media Connection* delivers the insight, answers and encouragement school librarians need to transform their libraries into thriving hubs for 21st century learning and teaching. From practical inspiration from today's most innovative practitioners to unbiased, insightful peer reviews that support smart collection development, LMC covers technology, tackles the tough issues of budgeting, staffing, and more . . . and along the way serves as a catalyst for connecting librarians who share a passion for learning and literacy" (Library Media Connection, n.d., 1).

42. Library Reads. 2014. Home page. http://libraryreads.org/. Library Reads is similar to LibraryThing and other online book/social networks. It focuses on the monthly top ten books "that librarians across the country love" (Library Reads 2014, 1).

43. LibraryThing. n.d. Home page. https://www.librarything.com/. LibraryThing is an example of an online book group/social network, where a member can catalog the books he or she currently owns or is reading, discuss what they are reading with other individuals of similar tastes, and so on. Comparable such social networking/reading groups, which are used by all sorts of individuals including librarians, include Shelfari, Goodreads, and Anobii.

44. LM_NET Home. n.d. Home page. http://lmnet.wordpress.com/. "LM_NET is the original discussion group open to school library media specialists worldwide, and to people involved with the school library media field. LM_NET provides an excellent way to network with other school library professionals, connect to new ideas in school library practice, seek advice, and ask library related questions" (LM_NET Home, n.d., 1). LM_NET is what is commonly called a listserv.

45. Louisiana Library Association. 2014. "LASL (Louisiana Association of School Librarians)." http://llaonline.org/sig/lasl.php. LASL "provides leadership for the school library media specialist and stimulates personal and professional growth; sponsors continuing education activities and workshops; promotes communication among school library media specialists and encourages participation in LLA" (Louisiana Library Association 2014, 1).

46. Maine Association of School Libraries. 2012. "About Us." http://www.maslibraries .org/page-1366522. "MASL's 'Big Audacious Goal' is that all school community members understand, value and support effective school library programs" (Maine Association of School Libraries 2012, 1).

47. Maryland Association of School Librarians. 2014. "Purpose of the Maryland Association of School Librarians." http://maslmd.org/about-masl/purpose/. MASL encourages "the improvement of teaching and learning in Maryland by bringing together individuals who are engaged in the field of school library media and information studies" (Maryland Association of School Librarians 2014, 1).

48. Maryland Library Association. n.d. "About the Crab." http://www.mdlib.org/content .asp?contentid=151. "The CRAB is the official online newsletter for the Maryland Library Association, and is available to all MLA members." (Maryland Library Association, 1)

49. Massachusetts School Library Association. 2014. "Strategic Plan: Vision and Mission Statements: Mission." http://maschoolibraries.org/content/view/12/67/. "MSLA promotes school librarian leadership and school library programs that provide resources, instruction, and opportunities for collaboration that maximize student learning" (Massachusetts School Library Association 2014, 1).

50. Michigan Association for Media in Education. 2014. Home page. http://www.mimame .org/. MAME is "The statewide association for school library media specialists" (Michigan Association for Media in Education 2014, 1).

51. Mississippi Library Association. n.d. "School Librarians: The Need Has Never Been Greater for MLA to *Support* Our School Librarians." http://www.misslib.org/page-1818448. "MLA's mission is to provide professional leadership for the development, promotion, and improvement of library and information services and the profession of librarianship in order to enhance learning and ensure access to information for all" (Mississippi Library Association, n.d. 1).

52. Missouri Association of School Librarians. n.d. "About MASL." http://www.maslonline .org/?page=AboutMASL. MASL is "the premier professional organization for library media specialists who work in Missouri schools" (Missouri Association of School Librarians, n.d., 1).

53. Montana Library Association. 2014. "School Library Division." http://mtlib.org/ Governance/SLD/default.asp. The statewide organization for school librarians in Montana is the School Library Division of the Montana Library Association.

54. Nebraska School Librarians Association. n.d. "About NSLA: Purpose." http://www
.neschoollibrarians.org/about-nsla.html. "The purpose of the Nebraska School Librarians
Association is to advocate for school library programs, provide professional development
opportunities for school librarians, and develop leaders in the school library field" (Nebraska School Librarians Association, n.d., 1).

55. Nevada Library Association. 2014. "Nevada School and Children Librarians' Section
(NSCLS)." http://www.nevadalibraries.org/handbook/nscls.html. "The Nevada Associa-
tion of School Librarians was created as a section in 1958 by the NLA executive board.
. . . In 1987 . . . the Nevada Association of School Librarians and the Children's Library
Association agreed to join together to strengthen their voice in NLA" (Nevada Library As-
sociation 2014, 1).

56. New England School Library Association. n.d. "About Us." http://nesla.us/. "The mission
of the New England School Library Association (NESLA) is to educate and to foster communication and collaboration among the members of the school library associations within
the six New England States as well as other regional and national educational organizations
that benefit student learning" (New England School Library Association, n.d., 1).

57. New Hampshire School Library Media Association. n.d. Home page. http://nhslma
.org/. "NHSLMA is a professional organization representing school library media professionals and paraprofessionals" (New Hampshire School Library Media Association, n.d., 1).

58. New Hampshire School Library Media Association. n.d. "Listserv." http://nhslma.org/
page-1712518. NHSLMA provides protocol to ensure that its members have a positive
experience when communicating on their listserv.

59. New Jersey Association of School Librarians. 2014. "About the New Jersey Association of
School Librarians: Our Mission." http://www.njasl.org/about_us. "The New Jersey Association of School Librarians (NJASL) advocates high standards for librarianship and library
media programs in the public, private and parochial schools, in the State of New Jersey, to
ensure that students and staff become effective users of information" (New Jersey Association of School Librarians 2014, 1).

60. New Mexico Library Association. 2014. "Advocacy for School Libraries." http://nmla.org/
committees-sigs/school-libraries/. Advocacy for School Libraries is a special interest group
within the New Mexico Library Association.

61. New York Library Association. 2014. "NYLA/SSL: Section of School Librarians."
http://www.nyla.org/max/4DCGI/cms/review.html?Action=CMS_Document&DocID=
136&MenuKey=ssl. Membership in the NTLA/SSL connects school librarians across the
state.

62. North Carolina School Library Media Association. n.d. Home page. http://www.ncslma
.org/. The goal of the NCSLMA is to "is to provide school library media personnel with
support, opportunities for growth, and professional connections; to provide information
on state and national trends and issues, and to serve as an advocate for school library media
programs" (North Carolina School Library Media Association, n.d., 1).

63. North Dakota Library Association. 2013. "Membership." http://ndla.info/membership.
php. School librarians in North Dakota can network with their peers by joining the School
Library and Youth Services Section of the North Dakota Library Association.

64. North Dakota Library Association. n.d. "Welcome to the *SLAYS Blog!*" http://ndla.info/
slaysblog/. "Welcome to the *SLAYS* (School Library and Youth Services) blog. *SLAYS* . . .
brings together the School libraries and Youth Services librarians from across the state to
share ideas, give feedback and improve our patron's experiences in our libraries" (North
Dakota Library Association, 1).

65. Ohio Educational Library Media Association. 2014a. "OELMA Listserv." http://www
.oelma.org/about-oelma/blog-wiki-listserv. "A listserv is a 'virtual' community connecting
those with like interests, providing a casual, electronic discussion forum. Working somewhat like a distribution list, any message posted to OELMA-L is automatically mailed to
each participant's e-mailbox" (Ohio Educational Library Media Association 2014a, 1).

66. Ohio Educational Library Media Association. 2014b. "What Is OELMA?" http://www
.oelma.org/. "The Ohio Educational Library Media Association is Ohio's preeminent professional association for highly effective school librarians and libraries" (Ohio Educational
Library Media Association 2014b, 1).

67. Oklahoma Library Association. n.d. "Oklahoma School Librarians Division: Purpose."
http://www.oklibs.org/?page=OKSL. "The purpose of the Oklahoma School Librarians
Division (OKSL) is to bring together school librarians for a concerted effort to improve
school library programs in the state of Oklahoma" (Oklahoma Library Association, n.d., 1).

68. Oregon Library Association. n.d. "Oregon Association of School Libraries." http://www
.olaweb.org/oasl-home. "Our mission is to provide progressive leadership to ensure that
Oregon students and educators are effective users of ideas and information, and to pursue
excellence in school library media programs" (Oregon Library Association, n.d., 1).

69. Pennsylvania School Librarians Association. 2014. "About PSLA: Mission and Vision: The
PSLA's Mission." http://www.psla.org/about-psla/mission-and-vision/. "The mission of the
Pennsylvania School Librarians Association is to enable every student to effectively pursue
information and develop ideas as they construct and share knowledge through independent
and class-based explorations in excellent school library programs" (Pennsylvania School
Librarians Association 2014, 1).

70. School Librarians of Rhode Island. n.d. "About Us." http://www.slri.info/about-us. "The
School Librarians of Rhode Island (SLRI) is a professional organization representing school
library media professionals and support staff working for school library media, computer,
and instructional technology programs in Rhode Island" (School Librarians of Rhode
Island, n.d., 1).

71. *School Library Journal.* 2014. "About Us." http://www.slj.com/about-us/ "*School Library
Journal* aspires to be an accelerator for innovation in schools and public libraries that serve
the information, literacy, and technology needs of 21st century children and young adults.
SLJ produces resources, services, and reviews that make library and education professionals
savvier, and communities stronger" (*School Library Journal* 2014, 1).

72. South Carolina Association of School Librarians. n.d. "About Us." http://www.scasl
.net/. "The South Carolina Association of School Librarians advocates professional excellence, facilitates collaboration, and develops leadership to ensure that school library media
programs are integral to teaching and learning in every South Carolina School" (South
Carolina Association of School Librarians, 1).

73. South Dakota Library Association. n.d. Home page. http://www.sdlibraryassociation.org/.
"The South Dakota Library Association (SDLA) is a statewide organization representing
libraries, library employees, library trustees, and library supporters. SDLA provides leadership and educational opportunities, and supports its members in meeting the challenges of
providing quality library service to all South Dakotans" (South Dakota Library Association,
n.d., 1). This includes to K–12 school children.

74. Springer Link. n.d. "*TechTrends*: Description." http://link.springer.com/journal/11528.
"*TechTrends* is a leading journal for professionals in the educational communication and
technology field. It provides a vehicle that fosters the exchange of important and current
information among professional practitioners" (Springer Link, n.d., 1).

75. Teacher Certification Degrees. 2014. "Top 50 School Library Blogs." http://www.teacher-certificationdegrees.com/top-blogs/school-library/. Here is a listing of the top school library blogs, based on their popularity on social media sites and the number of other websites that link to them. On these blogs, "school librarians . . . share their ideas, experiences, and advice with the school library community" (Teacher Certification Degrees 2014, 1).

76. *Teacher Librarian.* 2014. "Submissions." http://www.teacherlibrarian.com/submissions/. "*Teacher Librarian* [formerly *Emergency Librarian*], founded in 1973, is a bimonthly journal dedicated to identifying and responding to the exciting challenges encountered by school library professionals" (*Teacher Librarian* 2014, 1).

77. Tennessee Association of School Librarians. n.d. Home page. http://www.tasltn.org/. The Tennessee Association of School Librarians (TASL) website encourages the reader to see, "the role of school librarians as an integral element on the K–12 education spectrum . . . as purveyors of information and technology resources" and "as collaborative school leaders" (Tennessee Association of School Librarians, n.d., 1).

78. Texas Association of School Librarians. 2014. "Join Your School Librarian Professional Organization!" http://www.txla.org/groups/tasl. The Texas Association of School Librarians asserts its purpose as "to promote library services and librarianship in school libraries in Texas and to cooperate in the promotion of general and joint enterprises with the Texas Library Association" (Texas Association of School Librarians 2014, 1).

79. *The Unquiet Librarian* (blog). n.d. "About Me." http://theunquietlibrarian.wordpress.com/about/. This is an example of a school librarian's personal blog.

80. Utah Educational Library Media Association. 2014. "UELMA Constitution." http://www.uelma.org/Constitution.html. "The mission of the Utah Educational Library Media Association is to provide professional support, leadership and enrichment for school library media educators, associates and programs" (Utah Educational Library Media Association 2014, 1).

81. Vermont School Library Association. n.d. "About Us." https://sites.google.com/site/vermontschoollibraries/about-us. "The Vermont School Library Association . . . is the professional association of Vermont School Librarians" (Vermont School Library Association, n.d., 1).

82. Virginia Association of School Librarians. 2014a. "Listserv." http://www.vaasl.org/membership/#tab0e92035d. "A benefit to our members, our listserve provides a forum for professional communication and new members are subscribed automatically." (Virginia Association of School Librarians 2014a, 1)

83. Virginia Association of School Librarians. 2014b. "Mission and Vision: Mission Statement." http://www.vaasl.org/about-vaasl/vision/. The Virginia Association of School Librarians wishes to be recognized as the "voice for excellence in Virginia's school libraries through the promotion of literacy, information access and evaluation, love of literature, effective use of technology, collaboration in the teaching/learning process, intellectual freedom, professional growth, instructional leadership and lifelong learning" (Virginia Association of School Librarians 2014, 1).

84. *VOYA.* 2014. "About." http://www.voyamagazine.com/about/. "*Voice of Youth Advocates*, or (*VOYA*), magazine is the leading library journal dedicated to the needs of young adult librarians, the advocacy of young adults, and the promotion of young adult literature and reading" (*VOYA* 2014, 1).

85. Washington Library Media Association. n.d. "About WLMA." http://www.wla.org/wlma-home. WLMA is the statewide professional organization for Washington teacher-librarians and school libraries.

86. West Virginia Library Association. 2014. Home page. http://www.wvla.org/. "The West Virginia Library Association (WVLA) was established in 1914 to promote library service

and librarianship in West Virginia" (West Virginia Library Association 2014, 1). This includes school libraries and librarians.

87. Wisconsin Educational Media and Technology Association. 2014. "Members Home." http://www.wemta.org/members/. "The Wisconsin Educational Media and Technology Association (WEMTA) is an independent professional association serving school library media and instructional technology professionals. Our organization is committed to providing leadership and professional growth opportunities to promote quality learning and information access to meet the needs of our educational community" (Wisconsin Educational Media and Technology Association 2014, 1).

88. Wyoming Library Association. n.d. "SLIG: Wyoming School Librarians." http://www .wyla.org/school-library-interest-group. The purpose of this special interest group is to "network, encourage and disseminate information helpful to the school library media community in Wyoming" (Wyoming Library Association, n.d., 1).

89. Young Adult Library Services Association. 2014. "About YALSA: Our Mission." http:// www.ala.org/yalsa/aboutyalsa. "The Young Adult Library Services Association (YALSA) is a national association of librarians, library workers and advocates whose mission is to expand and strengthen library services for teens, aged 12–18" (Young Adult Library Services Association 2014, 1). YALSA is a division of the American Library Association.

Appendix C: Annotated Bibliography of Selected National and State School Library Standards and Guidelines

This appendix is a representative sampling of national and state school library learning and educator standards, guidelines, and related websites from various state departments of education, state professional associations, as well as federal government and national professional organizations. For more information and material in either section, search further on the Internet.

See the numbers after each of the following subjects for an item representing that area.

National: 3, 6, 18, 32, 45, 53
State: 1, 2, 4, 5, 7, 8, 9, 10, 11, 12, 13, 14, 15, 16, 17, 19, 20, 21, 22, 23, 24, 25, 26, 27, 28, 29, 30, 31, 33, 34, 35, 36, 37, 38, 39, 40, 41, 42, 43, 44, 46, 47, 48, 49, 50, 51, 52, 54, 55, 56, 57, 58

1. Alabama Department of Education. 2008. "Alabama's School Library Media Handbook for the 21st Century Learner." http://alex.state.al.us/librarymedia/Library%20Media%20Handbook.pdf. "*Alabama Department of Education: Alabama's School Library Media Handbook for the 21st Century Learner* is designed to be used collaboratively by the learning community to guarantee that students improve in academics through 21st Century learning standards" (Alabama Department of Education 2008, iii).
2. Alaska Standards. 2006. "Standards: Content and Performance Standards for Alaska Students." http://education.alaska.gov/akstandards/. (Click on "Alaska Standards: Content and Performance Standards for Alaska" link found on this page.) The Library/Information Literacy Standards for the state of Alaska are located on pages 35 and 36 of this fourth edition.
3. American Association of School Librarians. n.d. "Standards for the 21st-Century Learner." http://www.ala.org/aasl/sites/ala.org.aasl/files/content/guidelinesandstandards/learning-standards/AASL_LearningStandards.pdf. This is the premier set of standards for school libraries and librarians in the United States.

4. Arizona Department of Education. 2014. "K–12 Academic Standards." http://www.azed .gov/standards-practices/. These standards encompass many areas and are not specific to school libraries. Conversely, the state of Arizona also has an educational technology standard at http://www.azed.gov/standards-practices/2009-technology-standard/.

5. Arkansas Department of Education. 2013. "Library Media." http://www.arkansased.org/ divisions/learning-services/curriculum-and-instruction/frameworks/curriculum_categories/ library-media. This document is divided up into three main strands, information literacy, social responsibility, and personal growth. Each of these strands is then divided further and assigned content area standards and proficiency goals for students in all grade levels.

6. Bellingham Public Schools. n.d. "Standards for Library Media Programs." http://belling hamschools.org/sites/default/files/departments/libmedtech/Supervisors/srbstandards.htm. This is actually part of a larger web presence for the Bellingham (Washington) Public Schools. That said, this particular site contains a plethora of links and short summaries for a number of national and state standards for school library programs.

7. Board of Education State of West Virginia. 2006. "Library Media Content Standards and Objectives for West Virginia Schools." https://wvde.state.wv.us/policies/p2520.17.doc. "This policy defines the content standards (or instructional goals) and objectives for the program of study required by Policy 2510 in library media" (Board of Education State of West Virginia 2006, 1).

8. California State Board of Education. 2010. "Model School Library Standards for California Public Schools: Kindergarten through Grade Twelve." http://www.cde.ca.gov/be/st/ss/ documents/librarystandards.pdf. "The *Model School Library Standards for California Public Schools, Kindergarten Through Grade Twelve* sets a groundbreaking vision for strong school library programs in California, including identification of the skills and knowledge essential for students to be *information literate*" (California State Board of Education 2010, v).

9. Colorado Department of Education. 2014. "Colorado School Libraries." http://www.cde .state.co.us/cdelib/librarydevelopment/schoollibraries/index#instruction. This website houses a number of links of importance to Colorado school libraries, among them several sets of standards, guidelines, benchmarks, and competencies for school librarians.

10. Connecticut State Department of Education. 2006. "Information and Technology Literacy Framework: PreK–12." http://www.sde.ct.gov/sde/lib/sde/pdf/Curriculum/itf.pdf. "The new Connecticut Information and Technology Literacy Framework flows from, and is aligned with . . . national goals, standards and principles for student learning" (Connecticut State Department of Education 2006, 3).

11. education.com. 2015. "State of Delaware Academic Content Standards." http://www .education.com/reference/article/Ref_State_Delaware/. While not specific to school libraries, Delaware content area standards "and grade-level expectations are available for English, Family and Consumer Sciences, Health, Mathematics, Physical Education, Science, Social Studies, World Language, and Visual and performing arts for all grades." (education.com. 2015, 1)

12. Florida Department of Education. 2013. "Library Media Services." http://www.fldoe.org/ BII/Library_Media/reads.asp. This website provides sets of goals for school librarians to achieve in terms of reading/literature for their students (and activities to reach these goals). In addition, American Association of School Librarian standards and Florida Standards for English Language Arts are presented in a pdf format.

13. Georgia Department of Education. 2014. "Introduction to Information Literacy." http:// www.gadoe.org/Curriculum-Instruction-and-Assessment/Curriculum-and-Instruction/

Pages/Introduction-to-Information-Literacy.aspx. Georgia's "Introduction to Information Literacy" web page discusses, in part, "five themes that are constant throughout the library/ media experiences of K–12 students (Georgia Department of Education 2014, 1) and relates these to Information Literacy Standards.

14. Hawaii State Department of Education. n.d. "Hawaii Common Core Standards." http:// www.hawaiipublicschools.org/TeachingAndLearning/StudentLearning/CommonCore StateStandards/Pages/home.aspx. "Hawaii Common Core Standards are a call to take another leap forward in our efforts toward ensuring that all of our students graduate from high school college-, career- and community-ready. . . . Teachers are working collaboratively with principals and leadership to design educational tools and practices that best deliver on these standards" (Hawaii State Department of Education, n.d., 1).

15. Idaho State Department of Education. n.d. "Information and Communication Technology Standards." http://www.sde.idaho.gov/site/content_standards/infoCommTechStandards.htm. Sets of standards for grades K–12, 3–5, 6–8, and 9–12 are provided in pdf format. Also included are goals and objectives for each standard. The standards address research and communication, especially focusing on digital formats.

16. Illinois School Library Media Association. 2012. "I-SAIL 2011." http://www.islma.org/ ISAIL.htm. "The purpose of the Illinois Standards Aligned Instruction for Libraries (I-SAIL) document is to empower, educate, and encourage school library information specialists to plan strategically with other teachers to incorporate information literacy skills in lessons and thereby provide college and career readiness for students" (Illinois School Library Media Association 2012, 1).

17. Indiana Department of Education. 2010. "Indiana Content Standards for Educators: School Librarian." http://www.doe.in.gov/sites/default/files/licensing/school-librarian.pdf. "The Indiana Educator Standards for School Librarian describe the knowledge and skills that school librarians need to help students achieve the learning outcomes defined by the American Association of School Librarians (AASL) Standards for the 21st-Century Learner" (Indiana Department of Education 2010, 1).

18. International Society for Technology in Education. 2014. "ISTE Standards." http://www .iste.org/standards. Included in this document are standards for students, teachers, administrators, and others. School libraries, while not specifically identified, may be, because of their relationship to technology and instruction, strongly influenced by these standards.

19. Iowa Department of Education. 2015. "School Library" Program Guidelines." https:// www.educateiowa.gov/pk-12/learner-supports/school-library#Program_Guidelines. "The Library Program Guidelines have been designed to assist districts in planning for library programs to meet the new state requirements, and to go beyond the basic requirement to create programs that positively impact student learning and achievement." (Iowa Department of Education 2015, 1)

20. Kansas State Department of Education. 2015. "Library, Media and Technology." http:// www.ksde.org/Agency/DivisionofLearningServices/CareerStandardsandAssessmentServices/ ContentAreaF-L/Library,MediaandTechnology.aspx. Click on first pdf link under "Standards and Fact Sheets" for the Kansas Model Standards for Library Media and Technology—K–12.

21. Kentucky Department of Education. 2013. "Beyond Proficiency @ Your Library." http:// education.ky.gov/curriculum/libmed/Pages/Beyond%20Proficiency%20@%20your%20 library.aspx. "This set of guidelines from the Kentucky Department of Education aligns with national library standards and provides a framework for the effective management of a quality school library media program" (Kentucky Department of Education 2013, 1).

22. Louisiana State Department of Education. 2004. "Guidelines for Library Media Programs in Louisiana Schools." http://www.louisianaschools.net/lde/uploads/15303.pdf. Two sets of guidelines are offered in this text: "library media program guidelines "and "student information literacy guidelines" (Louisiana State Department of Education 2004, 9).

23. Maine Association of School Libraries. 2012. "MASL's School Library Handbook." http://www.maslibraries.org/page-1406262. As of the date of this website, MASL's standards and guidelines for their school libraries were under development. Additionally, under the Maine Department of Education, "Maine Learning Results" (2007), http://www.maine.gov/education/standards.htm are listed content area standards; however, none are specific to school libraries.

24. Maryland State Board of Education. 2000. "Standards for School Library Media Programs in Maryland." http://marylandpublicschools.org/NR/rdonlyres/092A7763-3A8E-47D6-B57D-32FBDC668D0A/13091/SLMStandards1.pdf. "Standards for School Library Media Programs in Maryland" "outlines standards to ensure that every student receives information literacy skills instruction integrated into every discipline, supporting learning outcomes in every subject" (Maryland State Board of Education 2000, ii).

25. Massachusetts School Library Media Association. 2003. "Massachusetts School Library Media Program Standards for 21st Century Learning." http://maschoolibraries.org/dm documents/standardsrev.pdf. "The *Massachusetts School Library Media Program Standards for 21st Century Learning* . . . is a synthesis of current educational research, education reform initiatives, knowledge of leaders in the field, educational testing goals, national information literacy standards for student learning, national guidelines for school library media programs, and teaching and school accreditation standards. It provides a clear blueprint for educational administrators and library teachers to use to build a program that has a significant and measurable impact on student achievement" (Massachusetts School Library Media Association 2003, 1).

26. Michigan Department of Education. 2013. "School Library 21 [SL 21]." http://www.michigan.gov/documents/mde/lm_SL21_313134_7.pdf. "This tool is for measuring the quality of School Library programs within individual school buildings in Michigan" (Michigan Department of Education 2013, 1).

27. Minimum Requirements for the Approval of Public Schools: Chapter 0520–1-3. 2008. "0520–1-3-.07: Library Information Center, Requirement F." http://www.tasltn.org/assets/docs/tnstatereq_slmc.pdf. This piece of Tennessee law contains minimum standards for school libraries in that state.

28. "Minnesota Standards for Effective School Library Media Programs." n.d. http://api.ning .com/files/Ox7y5uBCFs4I1yrWT5ulzI35xYrRNA-0iICbTPhd1EnL873qANxXwj9tEO4 fpD5jwopJr6yhHcxkHkZca6*n6euIAVQ0kyQb/standardselements.pdf. Each standard is supported by research; comparisons and parallels to national, regional, and state standards; as well as listing minimum, standard, and exemplary levels for each standard.

29. Mississippi Department of Education. 2012. "School Library Media Guide." http://www .mde.k12.ms.us/curriculum-and-instruction/library-media. "The *Mississippi School Library Media Guide* has been created to assist library media specialists to better serve students and staff, and to ensure that no child in the state of Mississippi will be left behind" (Mississippi Department of Education 2012, 1). It includes goals and objectives, guidelines, and other criteria in order for school libraries and librarians to support the students of Mississippi in their learning.

30. Missouri Association of School Librarians. 2011. "2011 Draft Standards for Missouri School Librarians." http://www.maslonline.org/?page=DraftStandards2011. "The Missouri

Standards for School Librarians delineate performance expectations for professional 21st century school librarians in Missouri" (Missouri Association of School Librarians 2011, 1).
31. Montana Office of Public Instruction. 2008. "Montana Standards for Information Literacy/Library Media." http://opi.mt.gov/PDF/Standards/09IL_LMContentStandards.pdf. Listed in this pdf are the rationale and benchmarks/performance descriptors for each of the Montana information literacy/library media standards.
32. National Board for Professional Teaching Standards. 2012. "Library Media Standards. Second Edition." http://www.nbpts.org/sites/default/files/documents/certificates/NB-Standards/nbpts-certificate-ecya-lm-standards_09.23.13.pdf. "The National Board for Professional Teaching Standards has more than two decades of experience in developing high and rigorous standards for what accomplished teachers should know and be able to do" (National Board for Professional Teaching Standards 2012, 5).
33. Nebraska Department of Education. n.d. "Welcome to the Academic Standards Website." http://www.education.ne.gov/AcademicStandards/index.html. This website contains links to the most current academic standards for Nebraska K–12 schools. There are no definitive school library standards on the site.
34. New Hampshire School Library Media Association. n.d. "Standards for the 21st Century Learner." http://nhslma.org/page-1712796. Recorded on this site are URLs for the AASL Standards for 21st-Century Learners, Common Core Standards and resources, a draft of the New Hampshire certification standards, and other materials of interest to New Hampshire school librarians.
35. New Jersey Association of School Librarians. 2005. "School Library Media Program: Catalyst for Efficient Implementation of Core Curriculum Content Standards K–12." http://www.paterson.k12.nj.us/schools/ps08/curriculum/Library/Core%20Curriculum%20Content%20Standards/Catalyst%20for%20Efficient%20Implementation%20of%20CCCS%20(NJASL).pdf Included in this document is a matrix of the New Jersey Core Curriculum Content Standards and AASL Information Literacy Standards.
36. New Jersey Association of School Librarians. 2010. "NJASL Standards Comparison Chart: Grade 6–8." njschoollibraries.pbworks.com/f/NJStandardsComparison6–8.pdf. "The chart on these pages is intended to show the alignment among those standards of particular relevance to New Jersey School Library Media programs for grades 6–8. These standards include: *The Common Core State Standards for English Language Arts & Literacy in History/Social Studies, Science and Technical Subjects . . . AASL Standards for the 21st-Century Learner . . . Partnership for 21st Century Skills . . .* [and] *National Educational Technology Standards for Students"* (New Jersey Association of School Librarians 2010, 1).
37. New Mexico Task Force for School Libraries. 2004. "Standards for New Mexico School Libraries." http://nmla.org/docs/NM_Task_Force_for_School_Library_Standards_RevMar04.pdf. "The purpose of this document is to outline standards for New Mexico school library media programs" (New Mexico Task Force for School Libraries 2004, 2).
38. New York City School Library System. n.d. "Empire State Information Fluency Continuum: Benchmark Skills for Grades K–12 Assessments/Common Core Alignment." http://schools.nyc.gov/NR/rdonlyres/1A931D4E-1620-4672-ABEF-460A273D0D5F/0/EmpireStateIFC.pdf. "The inquiry skills and strategies articulated in the Empire State Information Fluency Continuum (IFC) are aligned with the CCLS (Common Core Learning Standards) and provide opportunities for librarians and teachers to engage in systematic collaborative planning as they incorporate the teaching of inquiry into the implementation of the CCLS through classroom instruction and project based learning" (New York City School Library System, n.d., 3).

39. "North Carolina School Library Media Coordinators Standards." n.d. http://it.ncwiseowl. org/UserFiles/Servers/Server_4500932/File/North%20Carolina%20School%20Library%20Media%20Coordinators%20Standards%202012.pdf. The five school library media coordinator standards for the state of North Carolina are presented and discussed.

40. North Dakota Department of Public Instruction. 2012. "North Dakota Library and Technology Content Standards: Grades K–12." http://www.dpi.state.nd.us/standard/tech-stds.pdf. In the forward to this document is stated, "While our state's content standards represent an official, statewide reference point for content and achievement, local school districts are encouraged to use the State's content standards as guides in the development of local, customized curriculum in the core content areas" (North Dakota Department of Public Instruction 2012, iii).

41. Office of Commonwealth Libraries. 2011. "Guidelines for Pennsylvania School Library Programs." http://www.webjunction.org/content/dam/WebJunction/Documents/pennsylvania/378_PDE_Guide_Sch_Lib_FINAL_1_.pdf. Based on such research and recommendations, the Pennsylvania Guidelines provide quantitative inputs appropriate to Pennsylvania schools and complement the national school library guidelines entitled *Empowering Learners* published by the American Association of School Librarians (Office of Commonwealth Libraries 2011, 5).

42. Ohio Department of Education. n.d. "Library Guidelines." http://education.ohio.gov/Topics/Ohio-s-New-Learning-Standards/Library-Guidelines. "The Library Guidelines represent a standards-based education (SBE) approach to school library programs." (Ohio Department of Education, 1)

43. Oklahoma State Department of Education. 2013. "Standards for Accreditation of Oklahoma Schools: 2012–2013: Standard VII: The Media Program." http://ok.gov/sde/sites/ok.gov.sde/files/Standard_VII-2013.pdf. The media program standard for Oklahoma school libraries is stated and discussed in detail.

44. Oregon Association of School Libraries. n.d. "Oregon School Library Standards." https://sites.google.com/site/oregonschoollibrarystandards/. Oregon's school library standards are covered, along with indicators and alignments to major organizations.

45. Partnership for 21st Century Skills. n.d. "Information, Media and Technology Skills." http://www.p21.org/about-us/p21-framework/61. Including information literacy, media literacy, and communications and technology literacy, this represents a national framework for student learning in the 21st century.

46. Rhode Island Department of Education. 2000. "Rhode Island State Standards for Information Literacy." http://www.ri.net/RIEMA/infolit.html#state. Six state standards for information literacy are enumerated.

47. South Carolina Department of Education. 2012. "Achieving Exemplary Libraries: Program Standards for South Carolina's School Libraries." http://ed.sc.gov/agency/programs-services/36/documents/Achieving_Exemplary_Libraries.pdf. "This document will guide administrators and school librarians in the process of evaluating their school's Library Program and provide a framework for support and improvement of each district's library programs" (South Carolina Department of Education 2012, 3).

48. South Dakota State Library. 2010. "School Library Content Standards." http://www.library.sd.gov/SDSL/publications/DOC/RPT-SDSLSchoolLibContentStandards.pdf. The standards are designed to be age-appropriate guides for successful student learning in the 21st century, learning that is differentiated, collaborative, and integrated across all content areas (South Dakota State Library. 2010, 2).

49. State of Nevada Department of Education. 2012. "Assessments and Standards." http:// www.doe.nv.gov/Standards_Assessments/. This is a general web page with links to various standards for Nevada schools. The Computer and Technology Standards, as well as other content area standards, could be applied in school libraries.

50. State of New Jersey, Department of Education. 2010. "New Jersey Core Curriculum Content Standards." http://www.state.nj.us/education/cccs/. "The New Jersey Core Curriculum Content Standards . . . are not curriculum. . . . Rather, the standards describe what students should know and be able to do upon completion of a thirteen-year public school education. The standards are also designed to help teachers prepare our students to be college- and career-ready." (State of New Jersey, Department of Education 2010, 1)

51. State of Washington, Office of Superintendent of Public Instruction. n.d. "School Library Media Programs and Teacher Librarians: Standards, Tech Proficiencies & School Accreditation." http://www.k12.wa.us/SchoolLibrary/Standards.aspx. This site presents a plethora of information on standards and proficiencies for school libraries and librarians.

52. Texas State Library and Archives Commission. 2014. "School Library Programs: Standards and Guidelines for Texas." https://www.tsl.texas.gov/ld/schoollibs/index.html. Links to a wide variety of standards and guidelines for Texas school libraries are included on this website.

53. Thinking about the Common Core Standards. n.d. "Common Core Standards and the School Library Media Center." http://thecommoncore.wordpress.com/common-core-and-the-school-library-media-center/. This site addresses "the crosswalks of where the CCS intersects, supplements and/or builds on AASL's Standards for the 21st Century Learner" (Thinking about the Common Core Standards, n.d., 1).

54. Utah State Office of Education. 2014. "Utah Standards for Library Media: Secondary (Grades 6–12)." www.schools.utah.gov/CURR/library/Core/Standards.aspx. The Utah state standards for school libraries "reflect those of the American Association for School Librarians (AASL) *Standards for the 21st-Century Learner*" (Utah State Office of Education 2014, 3).

55. Vermont School Library Association. 2013. "Revisions to School Quality Standards/ Education Quality Standards." https://s3.amazonaws.com/WebVault/SLJ/SchoolQualityStandards2000.pdf. Best practices for Vermont school libraries, along with directive comments, are suggested for each of the School Quality Standards.

56. Virginia Department of Education. 2012. "Library and Media Services: Regulations and Requirements: Standards of Quality." http://www.pen.k12.va.us/instruction/library/index .shtml. These standards do include libraries and librarians; however, they are general also to classroom teachers, administrators, and other school staffers.

57. Wisconsin Department of Public Instruction. 1998. "Wisconsin's Model Academic Standards for Information and Technology Literacy." http://standards.dpi.wi.gov/files/standards/ pdf/infotech.pdf. Wisconsin's Model Academic Standards for Information and Technology Literacy identify and define the knowledge and skills essential for all Wisconsin students to access, evaluate, and use information and technology. These standards connect and interrelate current perspectives in information literacy, media literacy, and technology literacy into a unified conceptual framework (Wisconsin Department of Public Instruction 1998, 1).

58. Wyoming Department of Education. 2014. "Content and Performance Standards." http:// edu.wyoming.gov/educators/standards/. While not school library specific, these standards "provide a common understanding among educators as to what students should learn at particular grades" (Wyoming Department of Education 2014, 1).

Appendix D: Annotated Bibliography of Selected School Library Instruction and Collaboration Tools

Like the materials in other appendixes, there are a plethora of school library instructional and collaboration tools, along with various related pieces, available on the web. Consequently, those included in this appendix are representative examples. Please note that some of the following topics may contain material also found in other subject areas; for example, tools used for library instruction may also be found in various collaboration areas. In addition, some of these materials are specifically for school libraries and librarians' use; others may be extended to the school and community as a whole. For more information and material in all sections, search further on the Internet.

Please see the numbers after each of the following subjects for an item representing that area.

Library Instruction Tools/Examples: 4, 10, 11, 12, 13, 14, 15, 17, 18, 19, 23, 30, 31, 38, 39, 42, 43, 44
Collaboration Tools/Examples
    Administration: 21, 22, 41
    Extended Team: 1, 8, 16, 20, 25, 33, 34, 36
    Students: 2, 9, 26, 27, 40
    Teachers: 3, 5, 6, 7, 24, 28, 29, 32, 35, 37

1. American Association of School Administrators. 2014a. "5 Ways to Build a Culture of Collaboration with Staff, Teachers and Parents." http://www.aasa.org/content.aspx?id=12512. This article selects five points that a school administrator might follow in order to create and maintain a "culture of collaboration" in the school between the different shareholders (American Association of School Administrators 2014, 1).

2. American Association of School Librarians. 2014b. "Best Websites for Teaching and Learning 2013." http://www.ala.org/aasl/standards-guidelines/best-websites/2013#media. These websites, which are listed with corresponding standards from Standards for the 21st-Century Learner, "foster the qualities of innovation, creativity, active participation, and collaboration . . . are free, Web-based sites that are user friendly and encourage a community of learners to explore and discover" (American Association of School Librarians 2014b, 1).

3. Deal, Ashley. 2009. "A Teaching with Technology White Paper: Collaboration Tools." http://www.cmu.edu/teaching/technology/whitepapers/CollaborationTools_Jan09.pdf. This informative white paper features a number of online collaboration tools, located at the end of the paper. Additionally, it offers "a working model of the collaborative process and outlines basic approaches to assessing project-based group work" (Deal 2009, 1).

4. Denton Division of Technology and Information Systems. n.d. "DISD Library Services." http://www.dentonisd.org/Page/1071. Examples of elementary, middle school, and high school library lesson plans are provided on this site, along with a variety of other resources for the school librarians of Denton, Texas. Materials on this site are also helpful for other school librarians, who may see samples of things that they could also do with their students.

5. Dyer, Kathy. 2014. "33 Digital Tools for Advancing Formative Assessment in the Classroom." http://www.nwea.org/blog/2014/33-digital-tools-advancing-formative-assessment-classroom/. Dyer shares "33 digital tools . . . that are free or inexpensive and help teachers implement formative assessment in their classrooms" (Dyer 2014, 1).

6. EdTechTeacher. 2014. "Tech Tools by Subject and Skills." http://edtechteacher.org/tools/. Free online teacher resources are available on this site. School librarians would be able to use the tools here in collaborative efforts with their fellow teachers.

7. Education Week: Teacher PD Sourcebook. 2011. "Writing Re-Launched: Teaching with Digital Tools." http://www.edweek.org/tsb/articles/2011/04/04/02digital.h04.html. The focus of this web article is on using digital tools for collaborative writing in K–12 education.

8. Edutopia. 2011a. "Five Steps to Better School/Community Collaboration." http://www.edutopia.org/blog/school-community-collaboration-brendan-okeefe. This article provides five steps and a discussion of each one to enhance the collaboration of schools with the communities that surround/are near them.

9. Edutopia. 2011b. "Web Tools Blog Series: Tools to Help Students Collaborate." http://www.edutopia.org/blog/classroom-collaboration-tools-eric-brunsell. This particular blog emphasizes using web tools to nurture student cooperation/teamwork with others.

10. Fink, Lisa Storm. 2014. "Lesson Plan: A Case for Reading—Examining Challenged and Banned Books: Instructional Plan." http://www.readwritethink.org/classroom-resources/lesson-plans/case-reading-examining-challenged-410.html?tab=4#tabs. A series of four related 50-minute lesson plans, which can be adapted for grades 3–10, are covered here. Objectives, activities, and assessments (including a rubric) for studying challenged and banned books are also included.

11. Google. n.d. "Search Education: Lesson Plans." http://www.google.com/insidesearch/searcheducation/lessons.html. Offered by Google is a "series of lessons to assist you in teaching skills related to the Google search engine. These lessons are intended for students at a range of grade levels and technological expertise." (Google. n.d. "Search Education: Lesson Overview." http://www.google.com/insidesearch/searcheducation/lesson-overview.html .)

12. Greller, Julie. 2008–2014a. "*A Media Specialist's Guide to the Internet*: Grades K–5." http://mediaspecialistsguide.blogspot.com/p/elementary-school-teachers.html. School library media specialist and blogger, Julie Greller offers a wide variety of elementary library instructional and collaborative resources that she has collected from all over the Internet.

13. Greller, Julie. 2008–2014b. "*A Media Specialist's Guide to the Internet*: Grades 6–8." http:// mediaspecialistsguide.blogspot.com/p/middle-school.html. School library media specialist and blogger, Julie Greller offers a wide variety of middle school library instructional and collaborative resources that she has collected from all over the Internet.

14. Greller, Julie. 2008–2014c. "*A Media Specialist's Guide to the Internet*: Grades 9–12." http://mediaspecialistsguide.blogspot.com/p/high-school.html. School library media specialist and blogger, Julie Greller offers a wide variety of high school library instructional and collaborative resources that she has collected from all over the Internet.

15. Hanover County Public Schools. n.d. "Lesson Plans to Complement the Hanover County Library Media Curriculum." http://hcps2.hanover.k12.va.us/instruction/media/Lesson PlanBook.htm. As the title states, the lesson plans on this website are offered for the use of school librarians in Hanover County, Virginia. However, since they are freely available on the web, it is possible to peruse these for ideas and suggestions, grades K–8, in your school library.

16. Illinois Holocaust Museum and Education Center. 2014. "Mission." http://www.ilholo caustmuseum.org/pages/about/mission/. "The Museum is dedicated to preserving the legacy of the Holocaust by honoring the memories of those who were lost and by teaching universal lessons that combat hatred, prejudice and indifference. The Museum fulfills its mission through the exhibition, preservation and interpretation of its collections and through education programs and initiatives that foster the promotion of human rights and the elimination of genocide" (Illinois Holocaust Museum and Education Center 2014, 1).

17. "Information Literacy and Technology Lesson Guides." n.d. http://techtraining.dpsk12 .org/ilttechlessons/iltlessonguides.html. On this website are access points to an extensive number of technology-related and library lessons for grades K–5.

18. International Reading Association. 2014. "ReadWriteThink: Classroom Resources: Lesson Plans." http://www.readwritethink.org/classroom-resources/lesson-plans/. The International Reading Association presents an overabundance of classroom lesson plans for many age and grade levels, K–12. A lot of these may also work for school librarians as they teach library skills and/or collaborate with the classroom teachers.

19. Loudoun County Public Schools. 2014. "Lesson Plans for Elementary Students: Lessons by Loudoun Librarians for Loudoun Librarians." http://www.lcps.org/site/Default. aspx?PageID=728. The title says it all: elementary school library lessons from the librarians who teach them; subjects range from "Parts of a Book" to "Historical Fiction" to "Online Resources" (Loudoun County Public Schools 2014, 1).

20. McCrea, Bridget. 2013a. "7 Free Apps for Keeping Parents and Teachers Connected." http://thejournal.com/articles/2013/06/11/7-free-apps-for-keeping-parents-and-teachers-connected.aspx. Bridget McCrea selects and describes seven applications that parents, teachers, students, and others may use to augment the collaborative process.

21. McCrea, Bridget. 2013b. "8 Free Collaboration Tools for Educators." http://campustechnol-ogy.com/articles/2013/06/05/8-free-collaboration-tools-for-educators.aspx. McCrea explains the uses of the following free online tools: Flowboard, Google Drive, Google + Hangouts, Join Me, OpenClass, Citrix Podio, ResearchGate, and SocialFolders.me.

22. Michigan Online Resources for Educators. 2014. "Join the MORE Community." http:// www.edweb.net/more. "The purpose of this community is to provide a way for educators to connect and collaborate on teaching . . . , creating lesson plans, and sharing information on how they use resources from MORE or anything else related to improving classroom instruction" (Michigan Online Resources for Educators 2014, 1).

23. Modesto City Schools. 2010. "K–6 Library Media Lessons." https://mcsold1.monet.k12 .ca.us/Academics/MCSPages/LibraryMediaLessons.aspx. From the Modesto, California, schools, these lessons list standards, objectives, activities, vocabulary, assessments, and resources.

24. Murray, Janet. 2008. "Applying Big6TM Skills, AASL Standards and ISTE NETS to Internet Research." http://janetsinfo.com/big6info.htm. The Big6TM Skills are correlated to both AASL standards and NETS (National Educational Technology Standards) along with basic and advanced activities to teach the associated information literacy skills.

25. National Network of Partnership Schools. 2014. Home page. http://www.csos.jhu.edu/ p2000/index.htm. "NNPS invites schools, districts, states, and organizations to join together and use research-based approaches to organize and sustain excellent programs of family and community involvement that will increase student success in school" (National Network of Partnership Schools 2014, 1).

26. National Underground Railroad Freedom Center. 2014. "For Educators." http://freedom center.org/educators. "We use the lessons of the Underground Railroad with K–12 curriculum to create lively and engaging docent-led tours that will bring learning to life outside of the classroom. Our exhibits and diverse programs help students gain greater connections between the history of institutionalized slavery in America and global modern-day abolition. And if you can't make a visit. . . . We offer historical interpreters, traveling trunks and digital backpack activities for your classroom" (National Underground Railroad Freedom Center 2014, 1).

27. Open Education Database. 2014. "101 Web 2.0 Teaching Tools." http://oedb.org/ ilibrarian/101-web-20-teaching-tools/. The authors of this web article state that "online tools and resources have made it easier for teachers to instruct students, and for students to collaborate with those teachers and with other students and parents. These 'Web 2.0' teaching tools aren't magical, but they may seem to defy definition at times since they save time, help you to stay organized, and often take up little space on a computer" (Open Education Database 2014, 1). Many of these tools are free.

28. Pappas, Christopher. 2014. "The 5 Best Free Collaboration Tools for Teachers." http:// elearningindustry.com/the-5-best-free-collaboration-tools-for-teachers. Pappas covers information about and how to use Google Drive, Podio, TitanPad, Show Document, and thinkbinder.

29. Raths, David. 2013. "Teachers List the Very Best Apps for Turning Your iPad into a Collaborative Device." http://thejournal.com/articles/2013/05/08/10-apps-for-turning-the-ipad-into-a-collaborative-device.aspx. The title says it all—1:1 iPads in the classroom as collaborative tools.

30. Resources for School Librarians. 2014a. "A Directory of Lesson Plan Sites for Computer and Internet Use Instruction." http://www.sldirectory.com/libsf/resf/techplans.html#top. Focusing on lesson plans covering computers and digital media, this directory delivers links, safe sites, and instruction covering social media, Internet searching and safety, copyright activities, digital citizenship materials, instructional videos, website evaluation, and much more for students. This site is especially useful for technology teachers and school librarians.

31. Resources for School Librarians. 2014b. "A Directory of Lesson Plan Sites for Information Skills Instruction." http://www.sldirectory.com/libsf/resf/libplans.html#top. Maintained by a retired school librarian, this site provides a wide variety of K–12 library lesson plans from various organizations across the United States. Among the subject areas covered are "General Collections of Lesson Plans," "Yearly Curriculum for the library," "Introduction

to Library Use," "The Dewey Decimal System and the Catalog," "Reference Books and Web Sites," "Worksheets and Online Tools," "Library Research Methods and Reports," and "Miscellaneous and Holiday Lessons" (Resources for School Librarians 2014, 1).

32. Resources for School Librarians. 2014c. "A Directory of Lesson Plan Sites for Teaching Literature in the Library and the Classroom." http://www.sldirectory.com/libsf/resf/bookplans.html#top. Still another collection of K–12 instructional materials for school librarians and teachers to use with students, this site emphasizes literature: genres; book talks; availability in formats, both print and nonprint, digital and analog; as well as literature lessons for a variety of holidays.

33. Richmond Public Schools. n.d. "The RPS Office of School-Community Partnerships." http://web.richmond.k12.va.us/Departments/SchoolCommunityPartnerships.aspx. The Richmond, Virginia, Public Schools maintain this site, which supports school-community collaboration.

34. Rutgers. 2009. "Strategies for Effective Collaboration with Parents, Schools and Community Members." http://sdfsc.rutgers.edu/file/Workshop%20Handouts/CH%20Effective%20Collaboration%2009.pdf. This PDF provides the reader with information under the following chapter titles: "What Do We Mean by Effective Collaboration?" "Overcoming Barriers to Collaboration," "A Committee of the Whole . . . ," "Models for Change: Tips and Tools," and "How Do You Know It's Working?" (Rutgers 2009, 3–4).

35. Scholastic. 2014. "Lesson Plans." http://www.scholastic.com/teachers/lesson-plans/free-lesson-plans. "Thousands of free lesson plans, unit plans, discussion guides, and extension activities" (Scholastic 2014, 1) pre-K through grade 12; many can be used by school librarians and teachers in collaborative instruction.

36. School Mental Health Project. n.d. "School-Community Partnerships: A Guide." http://smhp.psych.ucla.edu/qf/Commout_tt/School-Com2–8.pdf. This abbreviated version of a longer document provides information as to why school-community partnerships exist, defines what such alliances are, offers distinguishing characteristics between and among various partnerships, and supplies principles by which such affiliations may subscribe.

37. Teacher Reboot Camp. 2014. "Fostering Meaningful Peer Collaboration with Digital Tools." http://shellyterrell.com/2014/01/15/feedback/. The author states that she is, "using Google tools and apps to foster meaningful collaboration and peer feedback. Teachers can use the same process to engage students in meaningful collaboration, research, and writing" (Teacher Reboot Camp 2014, 1).

38. The Teachers Corner. 2014. "Librarians." http://www.theteacherscorner.net/librarians/. The Teachers Corner is a free international website of lesson plans, bulletin board ideas, collaboration projects, thematic units and more, shared by practicing teachers, librarians, and professional organizations. The "Librarians" page includes instructional units, songs, lists of award winning books, and other resources for use by the school librarian.

39. TeachersFirst. 2014. "TeachersFirst." http://www.teachersfirst.com/index.cfm. "TeachersFirst is a rich collection of lessons, units, and web resources designed to save teachers time by delivering just what they need in a practical, user-friendly, and ad-free format" (TeachersFirst 2014, 1). This site supports school library instruction when searched using search terms such as *information literacy* or *research*.

40. TeachThought. 2014. "Digital Project-Based Learning: 7 Tools for Student Collaboration." http://www.teachthought.com/technology/digital-project-based-learning-7-tools-student-collaboration/. "Digital Project-Based Learning: 7 Tools for Student Collaboration" discusses choosing tools for the facilitation of collaboration/communication between "small groups of students and teachers" (TeachThought 2014, 1).

41. *THE Journal*. 2012. "7 Habits of Highly Effective Tech-leading Principals." http://
thejournal.com/Articles/2012/06/07/7-habits-of-highly-effective-tech-leading-principals
.aspx?Page=2 and http://thejournal.com/Articles/2012/06/07/7-habits-of-highly-effective-
tech-leading-principals.aspx?Page=3. Pages 2 and 3 three of this web article cover how the
school administrator might foster collaboration between students, teachers, and school
administrators.

42. UNC School of Education. n.d. "Learn NC: K–12 Teaching and Learning from the UNC
School of Education: Curriculum Standards: Information and Technology Skills." http://
www.learnnc.org/?standards=Information_and_Technology_Skills—Grades_9-12. Lesson
plans for the use of school librarians, technology specialists, and others who teach in the
areas of information and technology, for students from kindergarten through 12th grade.

43. U.S. Department of Commerce, National Telecommunications and Information Administration. n.d. "DigitalLiteracy.Gov: Lesson Plans and Curriculum." http://www.digitallit-
eracy.gov/resources-by-term/81. This site, from the federal government, provides a variety
of databases, tutorials, curricula, presentations, and so on, from across the United States.
Many of these are for use by school librarians as they work with students, K–12.

44. Utah Education Network. n.d. "Utah Curriculum Resources: USOE Library Media—
Home Page." http://www.uen.org/Lessonplan/LPview.cgi?core=9. "These materials have
been produced by and for the teachers of the State of Utah" (Utah Education Network, 1).
The Library Media home page includes examples of lessons that a school librarian might
use with students ranging from grade 3 through senior high.

Appendix E: Annotated Bibliography of Selected Grant Resources for School Libraries

For more information and material on grants for school libraries, search further on the Internet; here is a representative sample of what is available.

1. American Association of School Librarians. 2014a. "Beyond Words: The Dollar General School Library Relief Fund." http://www.ala.org/aasl/awards/beyond-words. "Dollar General, in collaboration with the American Library Association (ALA), the American Association of School Librarians (AASL) and the National Education Association (NEA), is sponsoring a school library disaster relief fund for public school libraries in the states served by Dollar General. The fund will provide grants to public schools whose school library program has been affected by a disaster. Grants are to replace or supplement books, media and/or library equipment in the school library setting" (American Association of School Librarians 2014, 1).
2. American Association of School Librarians. 2014b. "Innovative Reading Grant." http://www.ala.org/aasl/awards/innovative. This grant "supports the planning and implementation of a unique and innovative program for children which motivates and encourages reading, especially with struggling readers" (American Association of School Librarians 2014b, 1).
3. Galeschools.com. 2014. "The Gale/Library Media Connection TEAMS Award." http://www.ohioschoolleaders.org/grant/galelibrary-media-connection-teams-award. "The Gale/Library Media Connection TEAMS Award recognizes and encourages the critical collaboration between the teacher and media specialist to promote learning and increase student achievement. The awards are given every two years" (Galeschools.com 2014, 1).
4. Grant Wrangler. n.d. "Featured Grants for Teachers: About Grant Wrangler." http://www.grantwrangler.com/. "Grant Wrangler is a free grant listing service. . . . We list grants for teachers, school grants, and money for arts, history, mathematics, science, technology, literacy, and more. We also help education foundations, community foundations, corporate foundations, and other grant-giving organizations more effectively promote their grants and awards to teachers and schools." (Grant Wrangler, 1)

5. The Heart of America Foundation. 2014. "What is READesign Library Makeover ?" http://www.librarymakeover.org/READesign.htm. "The READesign Library Makeover program engages volunteers, especially local youth, as well as corporate team members and other members of the community, in service and community involvement through library beautification and improvement activities, book distributions and one-on-one reading activities with children. The project provides tangible results in the form of a revitalized library, as well as the intangible results of engaging people in caring, compassionate community service to children in need." (The Heart of America Foundation 2014, 1)

6. Illinois State Library. n.d. "School District Library Grant Program." http://www.cyber driveillinois.com/departments/library/grants/schoolpercapgrant.html. This program, "the first of its kind in the nation, is designed to help provide more library books and materials for the students of public schools in Illinois. The state legislature has authorized up to a $.75 per pupil expenditure for qualifying schools" (Illinois State Library, n.d. ,1).

7. ISLMA/LBSS Endowment Fund. n.d. "Read for Information Grant Application." http://www.lbssfund.org/Read4InfoGrantApp.html. This grant was "created to show the importance of "literary nonfiction" in the new Common Core Standards . . . . As priorities change in building our collections, this means we'll need to buy more informational texts." This grant is from the Illinois State Library Media Association (ISLMA/LBSS Endowment Fund, n.d., 1).

8. The Laura Bush Foundation for America's Libraries. 2014. "The Laura Bush Foundation for America's Libraries Awards More Than $1,000,000 in Grants to School Libraries." http://www.laurabushfoundation.com/. "The mission of the Laura Bush Foundation for America's Libraries is to support the education of our nation's children by providing funds to update, extend and diversify the book and print collections of America's school libraries" (The Laura Bush Foundation for America's Libraries 2014, 1).

9. Library Works. 2015. "Grants & Funding." http://www.libraryworks.com/lw_grants/grants_0310.aspx#!grants%E2%80%94funding/cshn. This site lists current grants available to libraries and education.

10. The Libri Foundation. 2014. Home page. http://www.librifoundation.org/#MENU. "The Libri Foundation is a nationwide nonprofit organization which donates new, quality, hardcover children's books to small, rural public libraries in the United States through its BOOKS FOR CHILDREN program" ("The Libri Foundation 2014, 1).

11. The Lisa Libraries. n.d. "Books: Adventures for the Mind." http://www.lisalibraries.org/frames.html. "The Lisa Libraries donates new children's books and small libraries to organizations that work with kids in poor and under-served areas" (The Lisa Libraries, n.d., 1).

12. The Lois Lenski Covey Foundation. n.d. Home page. http://loislenskicovey.org/. "The Foundation's most important activity is its Library Grant Program, which awards grants to lending libraries serving at-risk children" (The Lois Lenski Covey Foundation, n.d., 1)

13. The NEA Foundation. 2012. "Grants to Educators." http://www.neafoundation.org/pages/grants-to-educators/. Aimed toward educators and students, school librarians, as well as other teachers, may apply. "Over the last 10 years, we have awarded more than $7.1 million to fund nearly 4,500 grants to public school educators to enhance teaching and learning" (The NEA Foundation 2012, 1).

14. RGK Foundation. n.d. "Grant Program." http://www.rgkfoundation.org/public/guidelines. "RGK Foundation awards grants in the broad areas of Education, Community, and Health/Medicine. The Foundation's primary interests within Education include programs that focus on formal K–12 education (particularly mathematics, science and reading),

teacher development, literacy, and higher education" (RGK Foundation, n.d., 1). There-fore, school libraries might apply in the areas of reading and literacy.

15. Snapdragon Book Foundation. 2009. Home page. http://snapdragonbookfoundation.org/. "Founded by a former school librarian, this foundation exists to put books in the hands of kids" (Snapdragon Book Foundation 2009, 1).

16. U.S. Department of Education. 2014. "Programs: Improving Literacy through School Libraries." http://www2.ed.gov/programs/lsl/index.html. "This program helps LEAs [local education agencies] improve reading achievement by providing students with increased ac-cess to up-to-date school library materials; well-equipped, technologically advanced school library media centers; and professionally certified school library media specialists" (U.S. Department of Education 2014, 1).

AWARDS AND OTHER POSSIBLE FUNDING SOURCES FOR SCHOOL LIBRARIES

1. American Association of School Librarians. 2014a. "Collaborative School Library Award." http://www.ala.org/aasl/awards/collaborative. "The Collaborative School Library Award recognizes and encourages collaboration and partnerships between school librarians and teachers in meeting goals outlined in *Empowering Learners: Guidelines for School Library Programs* through joint planning of a program, unit or event in support of the curriculum and using school library resources" (American Association of School Librarians 2014, 1).

2. American Association of School Librarians. 2014b. "National School Library Program of the Year Award." http://www.ala.org/aasl/awards/nslpy. "The award recognizes exemplary school library programs that are fully integrated into the school's curriculum" (American Association of School Librarians 2014b, 1).

3. American Association of School Librarians. 2014c. "Roald Dahl's Miss Honey Social Justice Award." http://www.ala.org/aasl/awards/social-justice. "The award is to acknowledge teach-ing by school librarians and the use of school library resources to convey a child's sense of justice as exemplified by many of the characters in the works of Roald Dahl" (American Association of School Librarians 2014c, 1).

4. American Library Association. 2014. "Sara Jaffarian School Library Program Award for Exemplary Humanities Programming." http://www.ala.org/programming/jaffarianaward. "The purpose of the Sara Jaffarian School Library Program Award is to recognize, promote, and support excellence in humanities programming in elementary and middle school librar-ies that serve children K–8" (American Library Association 2014, 1).

5. Art Resources Transfer. n.d. "Distribution to Underserved Communities Library Program: Our Mission." http://www.ducprogram.org/index.php. "The Distribution to Underserved Communities Library Program (DUC) distributes books on contemporary art and culture free of charge to rural and inner-city libraries, schools and alternative reading centers na-tionwide" (Art Resources Transfer, n.d., 1).

6. Barnes & Noble Booksellers. 2012. "Sponsorships and Charitable Donations." http://www .barnesandnobleinc.com/our_company/sponsorship/Sponsorship_main.html. "Barnes & Noble considers local and national support requests from nonprofit organizations that focus on literacy, the arts or education (pre-K–12)" (Barnes & Noble Booksellers 2012, 1). A school library could apply.

7. DonorsChoose.org. 2014. "How It Works." http://www.donorschoose.org/help/help.html
. "DonorsChoose.org is an online charity that makes it easy for anyone to help students in
need. Public school teachers from every corner of America post classroom project requests
on our site, and you can give any amount to the project that most inspires you. When a
project reaches its funding goal, we ship the materials to the school. You'll get photos of the
project taking place, a letter from the teacher, and insight into how every dollar was spent"
(DonorsChoose.org 2014, 1). School librarians, as well as teachers, are using this charity.
Donations to DonorsChoose.org are tax deductible.

Index

About the Author

Rebecca P. Butler, PhD, is a Distinguished Teaching Professor in the Department of Educational Technology, Research, and Assessment at Northern Illinois University (NIU), DeKalb, Illinois. At NIU, she teaches master's and doctoral students in library information specialist and instructional technology courses. Previous to NIU, she taught in the Department of Curriculum and Instruction at East Tennessee State University (ETSU), Johnson City, Tennessee. At both NIU and ETSU, she has developed and taught courses in the administration of school libraries.

Dr. Butler holds a BA in Library Science from the University of Northern Iowa, an MSLS (Library Science) from the University of Kentucky, and a PhD in Educational Technology from the University of Wisconsin–Madison.

During her professional career, she has worked in a number of library-related positions: school librarian, public and private (U.S. and Venezuela); public librarian (Illinois); special/historical librarian (Ohio); medical librarian (Illinois); and library educator/university professor (Tennessee and Illinois).

She is a published author of books on copyright law for educators, including *Copyright for Academic Librarians and Professionals* (2014), *Copyright for Teachers and Librarians in the 21st Century* (2011), and *Smart Copyright Compliance for Schools: A How-to-Do-It Manual* (2009). In addition, Dr. Butler (Dr. B. to her students) has also written numerous articles and columns, over the past 25 years, on school library and educational technology issues for both library and instructional technology professional journals. This is her first textbook for school library administration.

Lightning Source UK Ltd.
Milton Keynes UK
UKHW010359230519

343189UK00001B/137/P